READY-TO-EAT
10-MINUTE
DESSERTS

Quick, simple & delicious recipes
for all occasions

Anna Helm Baxter

Photography by Lauren Volvo

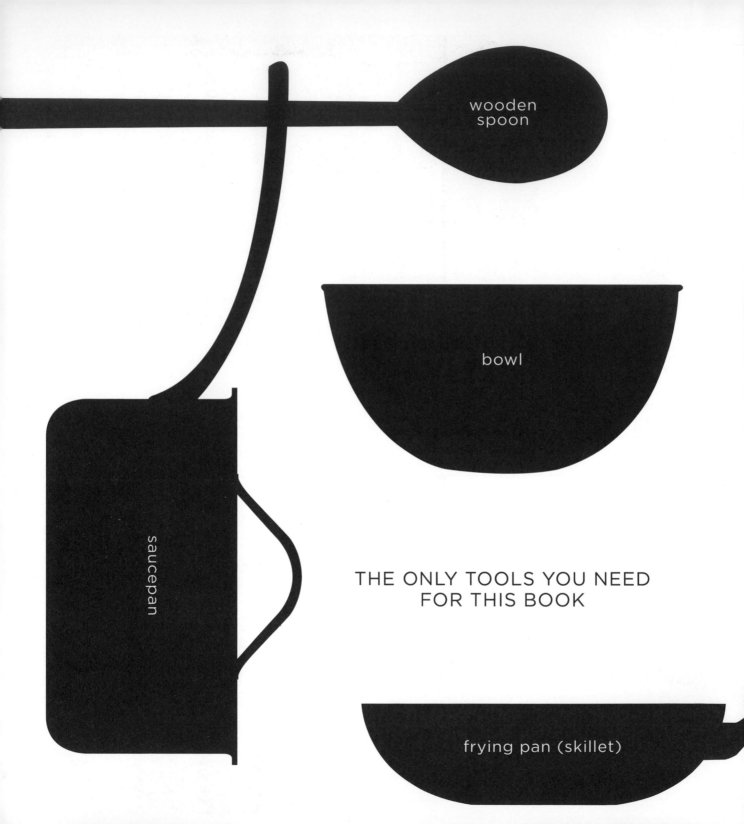

wooden spoon

bowl

saucepan

THE ONLY TOOLS YOU NEED
FOR THIS BOOK

frying pan (skillet)

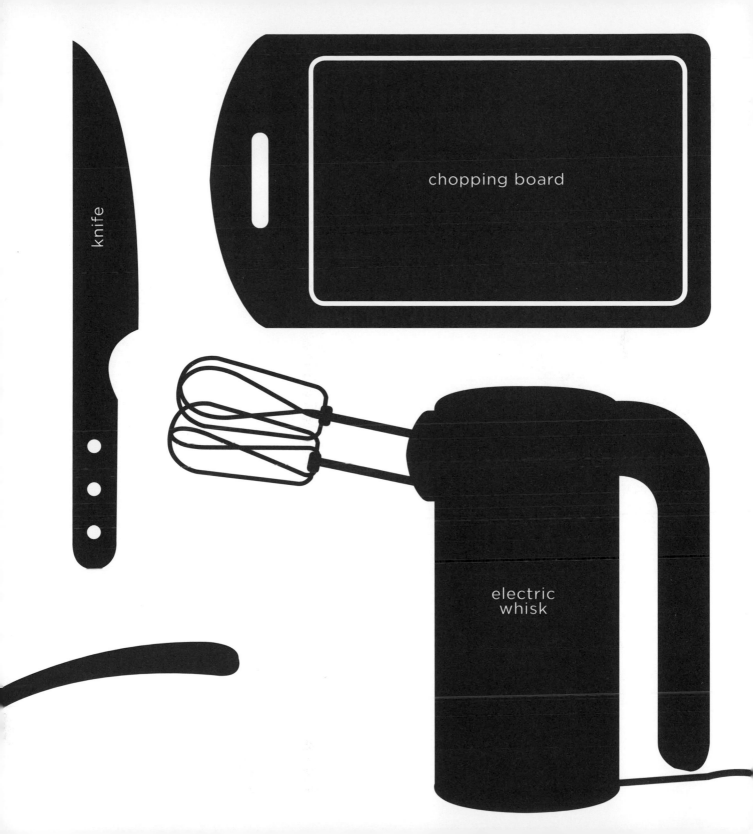

knife

chopping board

electric
whisk

CONTENTS

10-MINUTE DESSERTS

Calling all those with a sweet tooth! Making desserts and sweets doesn't have to be difficult and time consuming. Fanciful and fun desserts can be made with only 10 minutes notice, even by novice chefs in the most basic of kitchens.

Set your timer! Most recipes in this book can be completed from start to finish in under 10 minutes – some even quicker once you have made the recipe a couple of times. The rest require chilling or some time in the oven and will take a pinch of forward planning, but the hands-on time remains the same.

The key to speed is having a well-stocked storecupboard and chilled staples to hand – good-quality biscuits (cookies), cream, ice cream, chocolate, fruits and yoghurt. Just because you are using shop-bought ice cream doesn't mean that you can't pass a dessert off as homemade – simply dress it up with some unusual toppings, grill (broil) some fruit, make a quick fudge sauce or sandwich it

6

between two biscuits (cookies). Pages 8–9 walk you through how to make an ice cream dessert from start to finish, with no fancy machinery required; and pages 14–15 give plenty of ideas for time-saving ingredients that will provide a small boost on the way to success.

The second trick is to read the recipes and familiarise yourself with the steps before you start cooking. Some recipes should not be started until all the ingredients are weighed and measured, whereas others allow for time to weigh and measure as you cook. Take note of this as you read the recipes and you'll be in and out of the kitchen in 10 minutes.

Warning: you could find yourself with lots of hungry diners, lining up for second helpings.

Happy cooking!

HOW TO MAKE AN ICE CREAM DESSERT

Making ice cream is easy! Contrary to popular belief, it doesn't require lots of time, expensive equipment or hard labour. The base starts with only two ingredients and from there you can customise your own flavours and how you serve it, whether that be simply or expensive.

1.

GET STARTED
Using an electric whisk, whisk a 397 g (14 oz) tin of sweetened condensed milk with 600 ml (20 fl oz/2½ cups) well-chilled double (heavy) cream.

2.

FLAVOUR YOUR BASE
A little citrus zest, spice or extract can be all that's needed to flavour ice cream. Start with 1 teaspoon (you can add more if necessary after step 3). Try orange, lemon or lime zest, ground cinnamon, cardamom or mixed spice and pure extracts such as vanilla, peppermint, almond or coffee.

3.

GET WHISKING!
Continue whisking the flavoured cream and condensed milk until soft billowing peaks form. At this point, taste to see if it needs any more base flavours.

4.

CHUNKS & CHEWS
This is where the fun happens, so go crazy and get creative! Add chopped chunks of nougat, chocolate, caramels, nuts, biscuits (cookies), frozen fruits or pretzels.

5.

ADD A RIPPLE
Spoon the mixture into a 900 g (2 lb) loaf tin (pan) or airtight container. Now use a blunt knife to swirl sauces such as caramel, chocolate, raspberry coulis, softened sorbet or jams (jellies) into the creamy base.

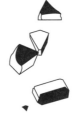

6.

CHILL OUT
Sit back and relax while the ice cream freezes. If using a loaf tin, cover with cling film (plastic wrap) after 1 hour.

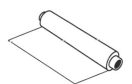

7.

SERVE IT UP
Sandwich between biscuits (cookies) or British scones, scoop on top of toasted sponge cake, French toast or in a cone. Add to a glass with cubes of chocolate brownies for a sundae or scoop on top of grilled (broiled) fruits. The options are endless.

8.

GET SAUCY
Drizzle over caramel, chocolate, strawberry or raspberry coulis. Make an ice cream float by pouring fizzy drinks over scoops of ice cream.

9.

TOP IT OFF
Dip ice cream sandwiches in chocolate and then coat with chopped nuts, honeycomb bars or sprinkles. Top sundaes with granola, toasted coconut, chopped nuts or whipped cream.

TIPS TO MAKE DESSERTS SPECTACULAR

Buying good-quality chocolate makes a big difference to the flavour and outcome of chocolate-based desserts. Choose something high in cocoa solids and cocoa butter, with a smooth glossy texture. I highly recommend Valrhona chocolate, which is GMO-free, Fairtrade and has unique flavour profiles. To maximise shelf life, store chocolate in a cool, dark place at a consistent temperature.

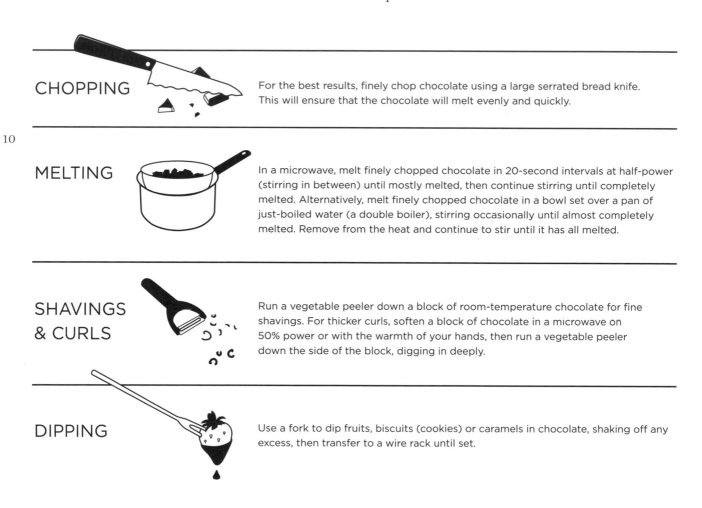

CHOPPING

For the best results, finely chop chocolate using a large serrated bread knife. This will ensure that the chocolate will melt evenly and quickly.

MELTING

In a microwave, melt finely chopped chocolate in 20-second intervals at half-power (stirring in between) until mostly melted, then continue stirring until completely melted. Alternatively, melt finely chopped chocolate in a bowl set over a pan of just-boiled water (a double boiler), stirring occasionally until almost completely melted. Remove from the heat and continue to stir until it has all melted.

SHAVINGS & CURLS

Run a vegetable peeler down a block of room-temperature chocolate for fine shavings. For thicker curls, soften a block of chocolate in a microwave on 50% power or with the warmth of your hands, then run a vegetable peeler down the side of the block, digging in deeply.

DIPPING

Use a fork to dip fruits, biscuits (cookies) or caramels in chocolate, shaking off any excess, then transfer to a wire rack until set.

USEFUL EQUIPMENT

It's a good idea to have some additional kitchen tools to help speed up prepping and finishing recipes. Think of them as quick shortcuts or a much needed extra set of hands. If only they could do the washing up too!

This is great for adding a chef's flare to a simple dessert.   **KITCHEN BLOWTORCH**

Use a loaf tin (pan) for freezing ice creams, semifreddos and biscuit (cookie) cakes.   **LOAF TIN (PAN)**

A tart ring is much more affordable than a tart tin (pan) and is also easy to use.   **TART RING**

Use this for honeycomb, brittle and anywhere else you would need greaseproof paper.   **REUSABLE BAKING MAT**

This will speed up making whipped cream.   **ELECTRIC HAND MIXER**

Use a liquidiser or blender for granitas, milkshakes and instant sorbets.   **LIQUIDISER**

SIMPLE SYRUPS

Simple syrups are a great way to add sweetness, spice, unique flavours and moistness to desserts. Customise your syrups by using the ideas on the opposite page. They will keep for 3–6 months in airtight containers in the refrigerator – perfect for when surprise guests show up!

You can make thicker syrups in order to sweeten and flavour whipped cream by using the ratio 3 parts sugar to 1 part water. Add 1–2 tablespoons chilled syrup to 250 ml (8½ fl oz/1 cup) cream and whip to medium peaks, before tasting and adding more syrup if necessary.

12

SIMPLE SYRUP

makes 150 ml (5 fl oz/⅔ cup)

110 g (4 oz/½ cup plus 1 tablespoon) granulated sugar
125 ml (4 fl oz/½ cup) water

method

In a small saucepan, bring the sugar and water to the boil. Simmer gently until the sugar dissolves, then remove from the heat, add any flavour boosters and cool. Once cool, strain.

GREAT ADDITIONS

These flavour suggestions are a great way to boost your simple syrups. Peel zests with vegetable peelers and use whole spices to avoid cloudiness.

GINGER

LEMON PEEL &
MINT LEAVES

STAR ANISE

HONEY

LIME PEEL
& CARDAMOM

ORANGE PEEL

LEMONGRASS

CINNAMON
STICK

COFFEE BEANS

LIQUOR
RUM, PIMM'S, GRAND
MARNIER, SCHNAPPS

ROSEMARY
SPRIGS

TIME-SAVING INGREDIENTS

STORE-BOUGHT
SPONGE CAKE

AMARETTI

14

FROZEN FRUIT

VANILLA ICE CREAM

STORE-BOUGHT BROWNIES

PETIT BEURRE
BUTTER BISCUITS (COOKIES)

CRÈME FRAÎCHE

Store-bought ingredients are a great way to cut a few corners and give yourself a little head start on your way to making desserts in 10 minutes. Keep your storecupboard stocked with these items and you will be halfway to sweet success.

CRÈPES

MERINGUES

NUTELLA®
CHOCOLATE SPREAD

15

CARAMELS

VANILLA PASTE

WAFFLE
BISCUITS
(COOKIES)

DULCE DE LECHE

MADELEINES

SAUCES

Sometimes all it takes is a simple homemade sauce to elevate an otherwise basic dessert. All of these sauces can be made ahead of time and kept in the refrigerator in airtight containers for up to five days. Fruit sauces can be frozen for up to three months.

SALTED CARAMEL SAUCE

Time: 10 minutes

18

makes 325 ml (11 fl oz/1⅓ cups)

200 g (7 oz/1 cup) granulated sugar
90 g (3¼ oz/⅓ cup plus 1 tablespoon) unsalted butter, at room temperature
120 ml (4 fl oz/½ cup) double (heavy) cream, warmed
1 teaspoon coarse sea salt

Gluten-free

method

Heat a large deep frying pan (skillet) over a high heat until very hot. Sprinkle over the sugar in an even layer and shake the pan vigorously as the sugar melts and turns deep amber around the edges. Remove from the heat and stir in the butter until it melts. Add the cream (it will bubble up), stirring. Stir in salt and immediately transfer to an airtight jar.

CHOCOLATE GANACHE

Time: 10 minutes

makes 450 ml (15 fl oz/scant 2 cups)

250 g (9 oz) good-quality dark chocolate, finely chopped
225 ml (8 fl oz/scant 1 cup) double (heavy) cream

Gluten-free

method

Place the chocolate in a heatproof bowl. Heat the cream in a small saucepan until hot and bubbles are forming around the edges of the pan. Pour the hot cream over the chocolate, stirring for 1 minute. Leave for 5 minutes, then stir until completely smooth.

FUDGE SAUCE

Time: 10 minutes

makes 225 ml (8 fl oz/scant 1 cup)

100 ml (3½ fl oz/⅓ cup plus 1 tablespoon) double (heavy) cream
75 g (2½ oz/scant ¼ cup) golden syrup
2 tablespoons dark brown sugar
2½ tablespoons unsweetened cocoa powder
90 g (3¼ oz) good-quality dark chocolate, finely chopped
2 teaspoons unsalted butter

method

Bring the cream, syrup, sugar, cocoa powder and half the chocolate to the boil in a small saucepan, then gently simmer for 5 minutes. Remove from the heat and add the remaining chocolate and butter, stirring until smooth.

BLUEBERRY SAUCE

Time: 10 minutes

makes 300 ml (10 fl oz/1¼ cups)

250 g (9 oz) blueberries
1 tablespoon lemon juice
50 ml (2 fl oz/3½ tablespoons) water
50 g (2 oz/¼ cup) granulated sugar

Dairy-free

method

Bring the blueberries, lemon juice, water and sugar to the boil in a medium saucepan.
Reduce the heat and simmer until slightly thickened, about 5 minutes.

BLACK CHERRY SAUCE

Time: 10 minutes

makes 200 ml (7 fl oz/generous ¾ cup)

340 g (12 oz/scant 2 cups) pitted black (sweet) cherries (fresh or frozen; thawed if frozen), halved
50 g (2 oz/¼ cup) granulated sugar
1 tablespoon water

Gluten-free

method

Combine the cherries, sugar and water in a large saucepan. Bring to the boil, then simmer, stirring frequently, until the cherries break down and the liquid turns into a thick syrup.

RASPBERRY COULIS

Time: 10 minutes

makes 175 ml (6 fl oz/¾ cup)

250 g (9 oz) raspberries
2 tablespoons icing (confectioner's) sugar
1 tablespoon lemon juice

Dairy-free

method

Cook the berries, sugar and lemon juice in a medium frying pan (skillet), until the berries start to break down. Purée until smooth, then pass through a fine sieve to remove pips.

VANILLA CUSTARD

Time: 10 minutes

makes 500 ml (17 fl oz/2 cups)

400 ml (13 fl oz/1⅓ cups) whole milk
100 ml (3½ fl oz/⅓ cup plus 1 tablespoon) double (heavy) cream
3 large egg yolks
2½ tablespoons cornflour (cornstarch)
55 g (2 oz/⅓ cup) golden caster (superfine) sugar
1 teaspoon vanilla bean paste

method

Heat the milk and cream in a medium, heavy saucepan over a medium heat until hot, but not boiling. Whisk the yolks, cornflour, sugar and vanilla in a bow, until thick and creamy. Gradually add the hot milk, whisking constantly. Return to the pan and cook, stirring, over a medium heat until thickened. Add more cream, if liked.

SPICED RUM SAUCE

Time: 10 minutes

makes 150 ml (5 fl oz/⅔ cups)

100 g (3½ oz/½ cup) light brown sugar
30 g (1 oz/2 tablespoons) unsalted butter
60 ml (2 fl oz/¼ cup) double (heavy) cream
1 tablespoon spiced rum
pinch of ground cinnamon

32

method

Heat the sugar and butter in a large frying pan (skillet) over a medium heat, until the sugar melts. Add the cream, rum and cinnamon and simmer gently for 1 minute.

Gluten-free

FRUIT

Fruits serve as a great starting point for many desserts. Not only are they sweet and juicy but their vibrant colours will bring beauty and fun to the plate. Get creative and think beyond simple fruit salads – in this chapter you will find recipes for frozen, grilled (broiled), sautéed and marinated fruits.

BERRIES WITH WHITE CHOCOLATE SAUCE

Time: 10 minutes

serves 4

125 ml (4 fl oz/½ cup) double (heavy) cream
140 g (4½ oz) white chocolate, chopped, or white chocolate buttons or chips
450 g (1 lb) mixed frozen berries (blackberries, blueberries, raspberries, redcurrants, small strawberries)
4 amaretti biscuits (cookies), crumbled

method

Heat the cream and chocolate in a small saucepan over a medium-low heat, until the chocolate melts. Scatter the frozen berries over a platter, drizzle with chocolate sauce and sprinkle with the crumbled biscuits.

ETON MESS

Time: 10 minutes

serves 4

450 g (1 lb) strawberries, hulled and quartered
1 tablespoon caster (superfine) sugar
400 ml (13 fl oz/1⅓ cups) double (heavy) cream
110 g (3¾ oz) meringues (about 12), lightly crushed

method

Toss the strawberries with the sugar and set aside. Whip the cream in a large bowl until soft peaks form. Fold in the meringues and most of the strawberries with their juices. Spoon into dishes and top with the remaining strawberries.

BLACKBERRY FOOL

Time: 10 minutes

serves 2

200 g (7 oz) blackberries
2 tablespoons lemon juice
40 g (1½ oz/3¼ tablespoons) golden caster (superfine) sugar
200 ml (7 fl oz/generous ¾ cup) double (heavy) cream

Egg-free

method

Mash the berries with the lemon juice and half the sugar. Whip the cream with the remaining sugar until medium-stiff peaks form. Fold in the blackberries. Divide among glasses to serve.

CREAMY FROZEN RASPBERRY MOUSSE

Time: 5 minutes

42

serves 4

500 g (1 lb 2 oz/2¼ cups) thick quark, fromage blanc or fromage frais
35 g (1¼ oz/¼ cup) icing (confectioner's) sugar
2 teaspoons lime juice
225 g (8 oz) frozen raspberries
20 g roasted unsalted almonds, roughly chopped

Gluten-free

method

Mix together the quark, icing sugar and lime juice. Fold the frozen raspberries through until they streak pink. Divide among bowls and sprinkle with almonds.

ROASTED PEARS WITH CRUMBLE TOPPING

Time: 10 minutes + Baking: 35 minutes

44

serves 4–8

35 g (1¼ oz/2½ tablespoons) unsalted butter, at room temperature
75 g (2½ oz/½ cup plus 1 tablespoon) plain (all-purpose) flour
35 g (1¼ oz/scant 3 tablespoons) light brown sugar
pinch of fine sea salt
4 ripe pears, halved and cored
50 g (2 oz) fresh cranberries

Nut-free

method

Preheat oven to 190°C (375°F/Gas 5). Rub the butter and flour together to form crumbs. Add the sugar and salt, squeezing together to create clumps. Place the pears, skin side down, in a baking dish and scatter over the cranberries. Add 4 tablespoons water to the base of the dish, then top the pears with crumble. Bake for 30–35 minutes, until tender.

RUM-SPICED WATERMELON

Time: 10 minutes
Chilling: 45 minutes

Gluten-free

serves 4

1 small seedless watermelon (about 1.5 kg/3¼ lb),
   quartered and cut into thick wedges
1 quantity Simple Syrup (see page 12) made with
   3½ tablespoons spiced rum
2 limes, cut into wedges

method

Arrange the watermelon in a single layer on
a rimmed platter and pour over the syrup.
Chill for at least 45 minutes, or overnight.
Remove from the syrup and serve
on a platter with lime wedges.

46

HONEYDEW WITH BASIL, MINT & SEA SALT

Time: 5 minutes

*Refined
sugar-free*

serves 4

1 ripe honeydew melon, skinned, deseeded
   and cut into large pieces
large handful of basil and mint leaves
¼ teaspoon coarse sea salt flakes

method

Place the melon on a platter and scatter
with basil and mint. Sprinkle with sea salt.

CITRUS WITH CARDAMOM & LIME SYRUP

Time: 10 minutes

Gluten-free

serves 4

4 citrus fruits, such as grapefruit, naval oranges, blood oranges
2 tablespoons chilled Simple Syrup (see page 12), made with lime peel and cardamom
zest of 1 lime

method

Slice skin and pith away from citrus fruit and slice into rounds. Drizzle with syrup and sprinkle with lime zest to serve.

47

GRAPEFRUIT & CUCUMBER GRANITA

Time: 10 minutes
Freezing: 4 hours

Dairy-free

serves 4

1 large pink grapefruit, pith removed and flesh segmented
300 g (10½ oz) seedless cucumber, peeled and cut into 5 cm (2 in) pieces
1 tablespoon fresh lime juice
3½ tablespoons quantity Simple Syrup (see page 12), made with fresh mint

method

Blend all the ingredients together in a liquidiser then transfer to a 900 g (2 lb) loaf tin (pan) and freeze until firm. Scrape with a fork and serve in glasses.

RHUBARB & VANILLA WITH YOGHURT

Time: 10 minutes

serves 2–4

¼ teaspoon vanilla paste
1 teaspoon orange zest
100 ml (3½ fl oz/⅓ cup plus 1 tablespoon) fresh orange juice
350 g (12 oz) rhubarb, trimmed and cut into 1 cm (½ in) pieces
50 g (2 oz/generous ¼ cup) caster (superfine) sugar
400 g (14 oz/scant 2 cups) plain yoghurt

method

Place vanilla, orange zest, juice, rhubarb and sugar in a saucepan and gently simmer
until the rhubarb is tender. Swirl through yoghurt to serve.

AÇAÍ BERRY SMOOTHIE BOWL

Time: 10 minutes

50

serves 2

1 banana
200 g (7 oz/scant 1 cup)
   frozen açaí berry purée
50 g (2 oz)
   frozen raspberries
100 g (3½ oz/scant ½ cup)
   plain yoghurt
1 tablespoon cacao nibs
2 tablespoons granola
2 tablespoons dessicated (dried shredded) coconut

Egg-free

method

Purée the banana, açaí purée, raspberries and yoghurt in a blender, adding up to 75 ml (2½ fl oz/⅓ cup) cold water if necessary. Divide among bowls and top with cacao nibs, granola and dessicated coconut, to serve.

INSTANT MANGO SORBET

Time: 5 minutes

52

serves 4

450 g (1 lb/1½ cups) frozen mango chunks
175–200 ml (6–7 fl oz/¾–generous ¾ cup) orange juice

method

In a powerful liquidiser, purée the frozen mango and 175 ml (6 fl oz/¾ cup) orange juice
(adding more, if necessary) until smooth. Serve immediately or freeze until ready to use.

PASSION FRUIT SEMIFREDDO

Time: 10 minutes + Freezing: 4 hours

54

serves 4–8

150 ml (5 fl oz/⅔ cup) double (heavy) cream
75 g (2½ oz/generous ⅓ cup) caster (superfine) sugar
200 g (7 oz/scant 1 cup) crème fraîche
1 large passion fruit

method

Whip the cream and sugar until soft peaks form. In another bowl, whisk the crème fraîche until soft peaks form. Gently fold in the whipped cream. Fold in half the passion fruit, then transfer to a 450 g (1 lb) loaf tin lined with cling film (plastic wrap). Cover and freeze until firm. To serve, invert, remove cling film and top with the remaining passion fruit.

FROZEN LIME PIE

Time: 10 minutes + Freezing: 4 hours

serves 4–8

100 g (3½ oz) Speculoos
    biscuits (cookies), crushed
    into fine crumbs
50 g (2 oz/3½ tablespoons)
    unsalted butter, melted
100 g (3½ oz/scant ½ cup) cream cheese
200 g (7 oz/generous ¾ cup) sweetened condensed milk
125 ml (4 fl oz/½ cup) evaporated milk
60 ml (2 fl oz/¼ cup) lime juice (2–3 limes)
2 teaspoons lime zest

method

Combine the biscuit (cookie) crumbs and butter, then press into a 15 cm (6 in) ring mould on a lined baking tray. Beat the cream cheese until smooth, then gradually add both milks, beating until smooth. Stir in lime juice and zest, then spread into the mould and freeze until set. Remove mould to serve.

BLACK CHERRY KNICKERBOCKER

Time: 10 minutes

serves 4

4 brownies (about 4 cm/1½ in square), cut into cubes
8 tablespoons pomegranate seeds (½ large pomegranate)
½ quantity Black Cherry Sauce (see page 26)
500 ml (16 fl oz/1 pint) tub vanilla ice cream
100 ml (3½ fl oz/⅓ cup plus 1 tablespoon) double (heavy) cream, whipped

Soy-free

method

Layer 250 ml (8½ fl oz/½ cup) serving glasses or jars with brownies, pomegranate seeds, sauce and ice cream. Top with whipped cream.

PINEAPPLE WITH SPICED RUM SAUCE

Time: 10 minutes

60

serves 4

1 small pineapple, peeled and sliced into thick rounds
4 scoops vanilla ice cream
1 quantity Spiced Rum Sauce (see page 32)

method

Heat a grill pan over a high heat or a grill (broiler) to high. Cook the pineapple rounds until lightly charred, 1–2 minutes per side. Transfer to plates, and top with ice cream and sauce.

GRILLED PEACH MELBA

Time: 10 minutes

62

serves 4

250 g (9 oz) raspberries
2 tablespoons golden caster (superfine) sugar
1 tablespoon lemon juice
4 peaches, halved and stoned
4 scoops vanilla ice cream

method

Toss together the raspberries, sugar and lemon juice. Heat a grill pan over a high heat and cook the peaches, cut-side down, for about 1–2 minutes until lightly charred. Turn and cook on the other side for 1 minute, then transfer to serving dishes. Top with ice cream and spoon over the macerated raspberries.

CARAMELISED PEACHES WITH COCONUT

Time: 10 minutes

64

serves 4

30 g (1 oz/2 tablespoons) unsalted butter
3 tablespoons granulated sugar
4 peaches, stoned and cut into wedges
1 x 400 ml (13 fl oz) tin coconut milk, chilled overnight upside down
4 shortbread biscuits (cookies), lightly crushed

method

Melt the butter and sugar in a frying pan (skillet) until the sugar dissolves. Add the peaches and cook, shaking the pan occasionally, until the peaches start to caramelise. Remove from the heat. Open the tin of coconut milk, discard the water and whisk the thick coconut cream to medium-stiff peaks. Serve with peaches and shortbread crumbs.

PEAR, GOAT'S CHEESE & PISTACHIO TARTLETS

Time: 5 minutes

serves 4

100 g (3½ oz/¾ cup) soft rindless goat's cheese, at room temperature
2 tablespoons icing (confectioner's) sugar
8 digestive biscuits (graham crackers) or 16 petit-buerre butter biscuits (cookies)
2 small pears, cored and thinly sliced into half moons
4 tablespoons pure maple syrup
1 tablespoon shelled pistachios, very finely chopped

method

Mash together the goat's cheese and icing sugar, then spread
over the biscuits. Top with pear slices, drizzle with maple syrup and sprinkle
with the chopped pistachios.

ALMOND & FIG TART

Time: 10 minutes + Baking: 25 minutes

68

serves 6–8

50 g (2 oz/½ cup) ground almonds
50 g (2 oz/3½ tablespoons) unsalted butter, at room temperature
50 g (2 oz/¼ cup) icing (confectioner's) sugar
1 large egg plus 1 large egg yolk
175 g (6 oz) pre-rolled puff pastry round (about 30 cm/12 in diameter)
200 g (7 oz) fresh figs, sliced

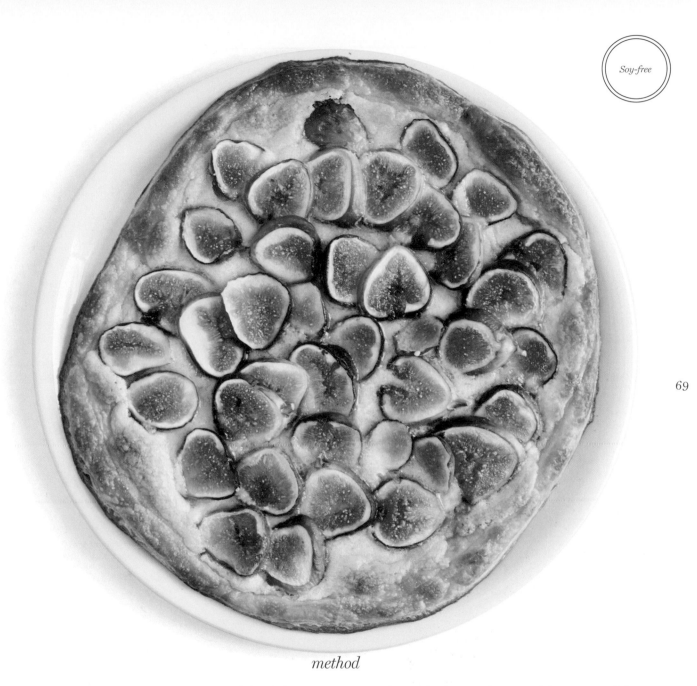

method

Preheat the oven to 190°C (375°F/Gas 5). Line a large baking sheet with a reusable baking mat. Whizz the almonds, butter, icing sugar and egg yolk in a food processor until a smooth paste forms. Unroll the puff pastry onto the baking sheet. Score a 2.5 cm (1 in) border around the pastry. Spread the almond paste within the border, then top with the sliced figs. Lightly beat the whole egg and use to brush the border. Bake for 20–25 minutes, until the pastry is puffed and golden brown.

CHOCOLATE BANANA POPS

Time: 5 minutes

70

serves 4

175 g (6 oz/1 cup) milk chocolate buttons
40 g (1½ oz/⅓ cup) unsalted roasted peanuts, chopped
4 small peeled and frozen bananas, skewered with ice lolly sticks

Gluten-free

method

Melt the chocolate in a tall, wide-mouthed, heatproof 750 ml (25 fl oz/1½ pint) jar. Dip the frozen bananas into the melted chocolate to coat two-thirds of the way. Quickly tap off any excess and immediately sprinkle with the chopped nuts. Transfer to a tray lined with greaseproof paper and either serve or return to the freezer.

PEAR & BLACKBERRY GALETTE

Time: 5 minutes + Baking: 40 minutes

72

serves 4

175 g (6 oz) blackberries
400 g (14 oz) ripe pears, quartered, cored and thinly sliced
30 g (1 oz/2½ tablespoons) granulated sugar, plus 1 teaspoon for sprinkling
25 cm (10 in) round of pre-rolled shortcrust pastry
1 large egg, lightly beaten

Soy-free

method

Preheat the oven to 190°C (375°F/Gas 5). Line a baking tray with a reusable baking mat.
Toss the blackberries and pears with the sugar. Unroll the pastry onto the baking tray
and mound the fruit in the centre, leaving a 3 cm (1 in) border. Fold the border
over the fruit, brush with egg and sprinkle with the remaining sugar.
Bake for 35–40 minutes until golden brown.

STRAWBERRY LEMONADE ICE LOLLIES

Time: 10 minutes + Freezing: 3 hours

makes 4–6 lollies

140 g (4½ oz) strawberries, hulled
200 ml (7 fl oz/generous ¾ cup) still lemonade

method

Purée the strawberries and lemonade in a liquidiser, then pour into
6 x 70 ml (2½ fl oz) ice-lolly moulds (or 4 x 175 ml/6 fl oz paper cups)
and freeze until set. If using paper cups, add wooden sticks after 1 hour.

FANCIFUL

No dinner party is complete without a final sweet course and elegant-looking desserts can be simple and quick to make. Presentation is key, so this is the time to get out your best serving plates and glasses. A simple jelly can be transformed into something quite regal when served in a delicate glass.

CHOCOLATE CARAMEL ICE-BOX CAKES

Time: 10 minutes + Chilling: overnight

serves 4

200 ml (7 fl oz/generous ¾ cup) double (heavy) cream
1 tablespoon caster (superfine) sugar
20 chocolate wafer biscuits (cookies) (or 10 Oreos, cream filling discarded)
1 tablespoon dulce de leche
chocolate curls, to decorate

method

Whip the cream and sugar to medium-stiff peaks. Take 4 biscuits and top each with 2 teaspoons whipped cream. Repeat until there are five layers, finishing with a layer of cream. Refrigerate overnight. Gently warm the dulce de leche in a microwave and drizzle over the ice-box cakes, then sprinkle with chocolate curls.

MEYER LEMON POSSET

Time: 10 minutes + Chilling: 2 hours

serves 4

600 ml (20 fl oz/2½ cups) double (heavy) cream
100 g (3½ oz/generous ½ cup) caster (superfine) sugar
25 ml (1 fl oz/2 tablespoons) Meyer lemon juice (about 1 lemon)
50 ml (2 fl oz/3½ tablespoons) lemon juice (about 2 lemons)
2 teaspoons grated Meyer lemon zest
handful of blueberries

Gluten-free

method

Gently heat 500 ml (17 fl oz/2 cups) cream and sugar in a saucepan, until the sugar has dissolved, then simmer for 1 minute. Remove from the heat and add the lemon juice and most of the zest. Divide among 4 x 225 g (8 oz/1 cup) ramekins or jars and chill for 2 hours until set. Whip the remaining cream to medium-stiff peaks. Spoon on top and sprinkle with the blueberries and remaining zest.

MANGO & BRAZIL NUT DREAM

Time: 5 minutes + Chilling: 1–2 hours

serves 2

1 mango, peeled, stoned and diced
300 g (12 oz/scant 1½ cups) Greek yoghurt
2 tablespoons muscovado sugar
40 g (1½ oz/⅓ cup) toasted Brazil nuts, roughly chopped

method

Fold the diced mango into the yoghurt. Divide between 250 ml (8½ fl oz/1 cup) glasses
or jars and top with the sugar. Lightly cover with cling film (plastic wrap) and chill
until the sugar melts, about 1–2 hours. Top with chopped Brazil nuts.

FIGS WITH FROMAGE BLANC & HONEY

Time: 5 minutes

84

serves 4

250 g (9 oz/generous 1 cup) fromage blanc or fromage frais
175 g (6 oz) fresh figs, sliced
4 teaspoons honey
20 g (¾ oz/1½ tablespoons) shelled pistachios, roughly chopped

method

Divide the fromage blanc or fromage frais among four plates. Scatter with the sliced figs, drizzle with honey and sprinkle over the nuts.

DECONSTRUCTED LEMON MERINGUE PIE

Time: 10 minutes

serves 4

4 tablespoons lemon curd
2 shortbread biscuits (cookies), crushed
50 g (2 oz/generous ¼ cup) caster (superfine) sugar
1 large egg white

method

Divide the lemon curd among four plates and drag the back of a spoon through it. Scatter over the shortbread crumbs. Whisk the egg white until thick and foamy, then continue whisking, gradually adding sugar, 1 tablespoon at a time, until stiff peaks form. Spoon onto the plates and use a blowtorch to lightly scorch the top of each meringue.

COEUR A LA CRÈME

Time: 10 minutes + Chilling: overnight

serves 4

175 g (6 oz/¾ cup) cream cheese
100 g (3½ oz/scant ½ cup) crème fraîche
100 ml (3½ fl oz/⅓ cup plus 1 tablespoon) double (heavy) cream
35 g (1¼ oz/¼ cup) icing (confectioner's) sugar
½ teaspoon vanilla paste
1 quantity Raspberry Coulis (see page 28)

Gluten-free

method

Whisk the cream cheese to soften. Add the crème fraîche, cream, sugar and vanilla paste
and whisk until thickened and stiff. Spoon into 4 x 10 cm (4 in) coeur a la crème moulds
(or a single 18 cm/7 in mould), lined with 3 layers of muslin. Chill overnight.
Invert onto plates and serve with the coulis.

CHEAT'S CRÈME BRÛLÉE

Time: 5 minutes

serves 4

1 quantity Vanilla Custard (see page 30), or 500 g (1 lb 2 oz) store-bought custard
8 teaspoons demerara sugar

method

Divide the custard among 4 x 175 ml (6 fl oz/¾ cup) ramekins and sprinkle evenly
with sugar. Melt the sugar under a hot grill (broiler) or use a blowtorch.
For a hard topping, chill for 10–30 minutes before eating.

PROSECCO SORBET FIZZ

Time: 5 minutes

92

serves 4

½ x 750 ml (25 fl oz) bottle prosecco
4 scoops fruit sorbet (use different fruit flavours)

Dairy-free

method

Scoop sorbets into shallow Champagne glasses. Pour over prosecco. Serve immediately.

AFFOGATO

Time: 5 minutes

94

serves 4

500 ml (16 fl oz/1 pint) tub vanilla ice cream
4 double shots espresso or 200 ml (7 fl oz/generous ¾ cup) strong coffee
20 g (¾ oz/2½ tablespoons) toasted hazelnuts, lightly crushed
chocolate curls or grated chocolate, for sprinkling

method

Scoop two balls of ice cream into each of 4 x 175 ml (6 fl oz/¾ cup) heatproof glasses
or cups. Pour over hot espresso and sprinkle with hazelnuts and grated chocolate.

CUSTARD-BAKED PEACHES

Time: 5 minutes + Baking: 40 minutes

96

serves 4

1 small peach, stoned and sliced
1 quantity Vanilla Custard (see page 30)

method

Preheat the oven to 150°C (300°F/Gas 2). Divide the custard among 4 x 175ml (6 fl oz/ ¾ cup) ramekins. Top with peach slices and place in a deep baking dish. Fill the dish with enough boiling water to reach halfway up the sides of the ramekins. Bake for 40 minutes.

INDIVIDUAL CHERRY TIRAMISU

Time: 10 minutes

serves 4

2 large egg yolks
2 tablespoons caster (superfine) sugar
300 g (10½ oz/1⅓ cups) mascarpone cheese
4 tablespoons Amaretto liqueur
1 quantity chilled Black Cherry Sauce (see page 26)
8 sponge finger biscuits
4 tablespoons Amarena cherries in their syrup

Soy-free

method

Using an electric hand mixer, beat the egg yolks and sugar until pale. Add the mascarpone and half the Amaretto and mix until smooth. Combine the remaining Amaretto with the cherry sauce. Break up the sponge fingers and divide half among 4 x 225 ml (8 fl oz/1 cup) glasses. Spoon over half the cherry sauce, followed by half the cream, then repeat the layers. Top with Amarena cherries.

MINI NECTARINE & MANGO PAVLOVAS

Time: 10 minutes

serves 4

50 g (2 oz/3½ tablespoons) mascarpone cheese
50 ml (2 fl oz/3½ tablespoons) double (heavy) cream
1 tablespoon apricot jam (jelly)
4 meringue nests
½ mango, peeled, stoned and sliced
1 nectarine, stoned and diced

method

Whisk together the mascarpone and cream to medium peaks. Fold through the apricot jam (preserve), then spoon into the meringue nests. Top with fruit.

SORBET WITH MASCARPONE & ALMONDS

Time: 10 minutes

102

serves 4

85 g (3 oz/scant ½ cup) granulated sugar
55 g (2 oz/scant ½ cup) unsalted roasted almonds, chopped
100 g (3½ oz/scant ½ cup) mascarpone cheese
125 ml (4 fl oz/½ cup) double (heavy) cream
500 ml (16 fl oz/1 pint) tub fruit sorbet

method

Heat a frying pan (skillet) over a high heat until hot. Add the sugar, shaking the pan (but not stirring), until evenly melted and golden. Add the almonds, stirring to combine, then transfer to a greased baking tray to cool. Break the cooled brittle into shards. Whisk together the mascarpone and cream to soft peaks. Top scoops of sorbet with mascarpone cream and sprinkle with the almond brittle.

QUICKEST CHOCOLATE MOUSSE

Time: 10 minutes

serves 4

260 g (9 oz) good-quality dark chocolate, very finely chopped
200 ml (7 fl oz/generous ¾ cup) just-boiled water

Egg-free

method

Place the chocolate in a heatproof bowl. Pour just-boiled water over the chocolate and whisk until completely melted. Place the bowl inside a larger bowl of iced water and whisk until the mixture resembles softly whipped cream. Immediately remove from the ice and spoon into serving dishes.

CHOCOLATE TRUFFLES

Time: 10 minutes + Chilling: 4 hours

makes 20

300 g (10½ oz) good-quality dark chocolate, very finely chopped
100 ml (3½ fl oz/⅓ cup plus 1 tablespoon) double (heavy) cream
20 g (¾ oz/generous 3 tablespoons) unsweetened cocoa powder, for dusting

method

Line a 900 g (2 lb) loaf tin (pan) with baking paper. Place the chocolate in a heatproof bowl. Heat the cream in a saucepan until hot but not boiling. Pour the cream over the chocolate and stir until the chocolate has fully melted. Return to the pan and stir over very gentle heat, if needed. Transfer to the lined tin. Chill until firm, then bring to room temperature before slicing. Toss with cocoa powder to serve.

LEMON JELLY

Time: 10 minutes + Chilling: 3 hours

108

serves 4

4 sheets leaf gelatine
300 ml (10 fl oz/1¼ cups)
    water
100 g (3½ oz/generous ½ cup)
    caster (superfine) sugar
150 ml (5 fl oz/⅔ cup) lemon juice
150 g (5 oz) raspberries

method

Submerge the gelatine in a small bowl of cold water for 5 minutes. Bring 150 ml (5 fl oz/
⅔ cup) water and all the sugar to the boil in a saucepan, then simmer for 1 minute, or until
the sugar dissolves. Gently squeeze excess liquid from the gelatine and add to the hot
mixture, stirring to melt. Transfer to a bowl, and add the remaining water and lemon juice.
Divide among four serving glasses. Chill until set, then decorate with raspberries.

CLOTTED CREAM & JAM MADELEINES

Time: 5 minutes

serves 4

8 plain madeleines
4 tablespoons clotted cream
8 teaspoons raspberry jam (jelly)

Nut-free

method

Spread the clotted cream on the madeleines and top with raspberry jam.
Divide among four small plates to serve.

TIRAMISU

Time: 10 minutes + Chilling: 2–8 hours

serves 6–8

450 g (1 lb/2 cups) mascarpone cheese
85 g (3 oz/scant ½ cup) caster (superfine) sugar
400 ml (13 fl oz/1⅔ cups) double (heavy) cream
550 ml (18½ fl oz/2¼ cups) chilled espresso coffee
1 tablespoon brandy
28 sponge finger biscuits (cookies)
grated chocolate, to decorate

method

Beat the mascarpone and sugar until smooth. Add the cream and beat to stiff peaks. Add 1 tablespoon coffee. Combine the remaining coffee and brandy in a shallow dish and dip each sponge finger into the mixture. Transfer half the fingers to a 23 cm (9 in) square baking dish. Spread with half the mascarpone, then repeat. Cover and chill for 2–8 hours. Sprinkle with chocolate.

DECONSTRUCTED TIRAMISU

Time: 5 minutes

114

serves 4

125 g (4 oz/generous ½ cup) mascarpone cheese
150 ml (5 fl oz/⅔ cup) double (heavy) cream
1 tablespoon caster (superfine) sugar
16 sponge finger biscuits (cookies)
180 ml (6½ fl oz/¾ cup) chilled espresso coffee
1 teaspoon unsweetened cocoa powder

Nut-free

method

Whisk together the mascarpone, cream and sugar to soft peaks. Place two sponge biscuits on each plate and drizzle with coffee. Dollop with cream, then repeat the layers. Dust with cocoa powder to serve.

LIMONCELLO TIRAMISU

Time: 10 minutes + Chilling: 2 hours

serves 6

1 quantity chilled Simple Syrup (see page 12)
1 tablespoon limoncello
50 ml (2 fl oz/3½ tablespoons) lemon juice, plus 2 teaspoons lemon zest
175 g (6 oz/¾ cups) mascarpone cheese
175 g (6 oz/¾ cups) whole milk ricotta cheese
25 g (1 oz/2¼ tablespoons) caster (superfine) sugar
250 ml (8½ fl oz/1 cup) double (heavy) cream
16 sponge finger biscuits (cookies)

method

Combine the syrup with limoncello and lemon juice. Beat the mascarpone, ricotta, half the lemon zest and sugar until smooth. Gradually add the cream to incorporate, then beat to stiff peaks. Dip half the sponge fingers in syrup and use to line a 16 x 25 cm (6 x 10 in) baking dish. Spoon over half the cream mixture, then repeat the layers. Chill for 2 hours or up to 1 day. Top with remaining lemon zest to serve.

Nut-free

BOURBON SLUSHIE

Time: 10 minutes + Freezing: 3 hours

serves 4

250 ml (8½ fl oz/1 cup) black tea
250 ml (8½ fl oz/1 cup) orange juice
250 ml (8½ fl oz/1 cup) lemonade
100 ml (3½ fl oz/⅓ cup plus 1 tablespoon) bourbon

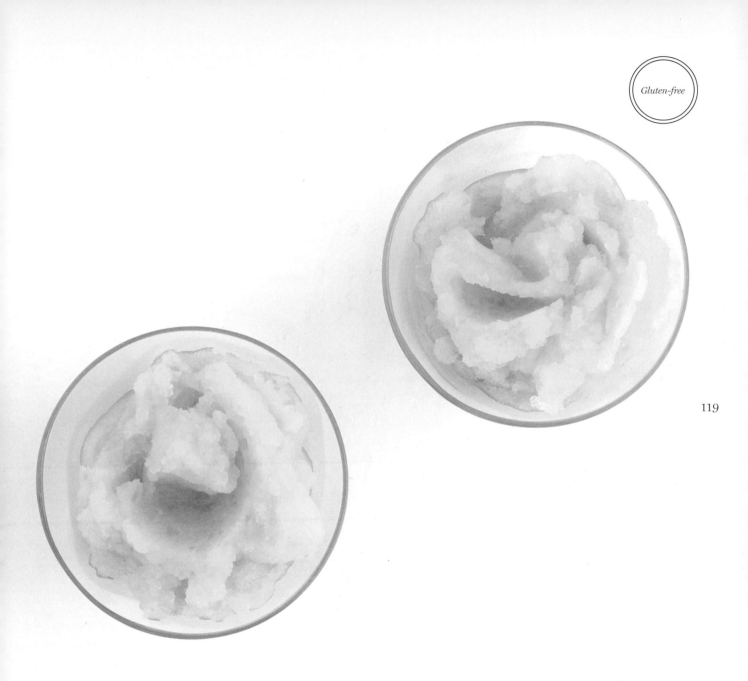

Gluten-free

method

Freeze the black tea, orange juice and lemonade in ice-cube trays. Once frozen, crush in a blender with the bourbon. Spoon into glasses to serve.

CRÈME CARAMEL

Time: 10 minutes
Baking: 35 minutes + Chilling: 3 hours

serves 4

135 g (4½ oz/⅔ cups) caster (superfine) sugar
600 ml (20 fl oz/2½ cups) whole milk
2 large eggs plus 2 egg yolks
pinch of fine sea salt
1 teaspoon vanilla bean paste

method

Preheat the oven to 150°C (300°F/Gas 2). Heat a frying pan (skillet), then add 100 g
(3½ oz/generous ½ cup) sugar, shaking the pan until it melts and turns into caramel. Divide
among 4 x 225 ml (8 fl oz/1 cup) ramekins and place in a roasting pan. Heat the milk until
hot but not boiling. Whisk eggs, yolks, salt and remaining sugar together in a bowl until
pale. Gradually whisk in the warm milk. Strain, add the vanilla and pour into the ramekins.
Fill the roasting pan with hot water to halfway up the sides of the ramekins. Bake for
35 minutes until just set. Chill for at least 3 hours. Loosen with a knife and invert
onto plates.

Gluten-free

RASPBERRY NAPOLEONS

Time: 10 minutes

serves 4

125 ml (4 fl oz/½ cup) double (heavy) cream
1 tablespoon icing (confectioner's) sugar, plus extra to serve
1 teaspoon finely chopped orange zest
12 waffle biscuits (cookies)
125 g (4 oz) large raspberries

method

Whisk the cream and sugar to medium peaks. Add the orange zest, then transfer the mixture to a piping bag fitted with a star tip. Make 3-layer sandwiches with waffles, cream and raspberries, piping between the berries. Dust with icing sugar.

VANILLA PANNA COTTA WITH POMEGRANATE

Time: 10 minutes + Chilling: 4 hours

serves 4

3 sheets leaf gelatine
500 ml (17 fl oz/2 cups) double (heavy) cream
50 g (2 oz/¼ cup) caster (superfine) sugar
1 teaspoon vanilla paste
pomegranate seeds, to decorate

method

Soak the gelatine in cold water for 5 minutes. Heat the cream, sugar and vanilla
in a saucepan, until the sugar dissolves. Squeeze excess water out of the gelatine and
add to the hot cream to dissolve; strain. Divide among 4 x 250 ml (8½ fl oz/1 cup) greased
pudding moulds and chill until set, about 4 hours. Invert onto plates and sprinkle
with pomegranate seeds.

MANGO, BLUEBERRY & PIMM'S TRIFLE

Time: 10 minutes

serves 4

2 slices sponge cake, trimmed and cut into small cubes
3 tablespoons Simple Syrup (see page 12), made with 2 tablespoons Pimm's
125 g (4 oz) blueberries
125 g (4 oz) fresh peeled mango, destoned and diced
200 ml (7 fl oz/generous ¾ cup) double (heavy) cream

method

Divide cake among 4 x 175–200 ml (6–7 fl oz/¾ cup) glasses. Drizzle the syrup over the cake and scatter over most of the blueberries and mango pieces. Whip the cream to medium peaks. Spoon on top, then sprinkle over the remaining fruit.

SORBET ICE CREAM SWIRL

Time: 5 minutes + Freezing: 1 hour

128

serves 4

500 ml (16 fl oz/1 pint) tub vanilla ice cream
125 g (4 oz/1 cup) fruit sorbet

method

Using an electric hand mixer, beat the ice cream until soft but still holding its shape.
Spoon half the ice cream into a freezerproof container. Dollop in spoonfuls of sorbet
and swirl through using a knife. Repeat with the remaining ice cream and sorbet.
Eat immediately or freeze for a firmer ice cream.

CRÊPES WITH LEMON & SUGAR

Time: 5 minutes

130

serves 4

15 g (½ oz/1 tablespoon) unsalted butter
4 store-bought crêpes, folded into quarters
4 teaspoons granulated sugar
1 tablespoon lemon zest
4 tablespoons lemon juice

method

Melt the butter in a frying pan (skillet) over a medium heat until foaming, then briefly cook the crêpes on both sides. Transfer to plates, sprinkle with sugar, lemon zest and juice and serve immediately.

ALMOND & CACAO NIB BRITTLE

Time: 10 minutes + Setting: 15 minutes

serves 4

55 g (2 oz/⅔ cup) toasted flaked almonds
20 g (¾ oz/2 tablespoons) cacao nibs
35 g (1¼ oz/2½ tablespoons) unsalted butter
85 g (3 oz/scant ½ cup) caster (superfine) sugar
3 tablespoons water
½ teaspoon coarse sea salt

method

Evenly spread out the nuts and cacao nibs on a reusable baking mat. Melt the butter, sugar and water together in a saucepan over a medium heat, until the sugar melts. Increase the heat and boil until it turns a golden colour (do not stir). Immediately pour the caramel over the nuts and nibs, and sprinkle with salt. Leave to set before breaking into shards.

DATE & COCONUT BALLS

Time: 10 minutes

134

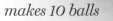

makes 10 balls

200 g (7 oz/1½ cups) pitted Medjool dates
85 g (3 oz/generous 1 cup) desiccated (dried shredded) coconut
2 tablespoons raw cacao powder

135

method

Pulse the dates, 60 g (2 oz/generous ¾ cup) coconut and cacao powder
in a food processor to combine. Squeeze together into 10 golf ball-sized balls,
then roll in the remaining coconut.

COMFORT

When it comes to desserts, comfort comes in many guises.
This chapter is full of rich, and sometimes wicked, desserts
to fulfil every need, whether it be something warm, gooey,
crunchy, creamy or just plain chocolatey.

PISTACHIO ICE CREAM SANDWICHES

Time: 5 minutes

serves 4

8 round shortbread biscuits (cookies)
4 scoops pistachio ice cream
30 g (1 oz/2 tablespoons) shelled pistachios, roughly chopped

Egg-free

139

method

Form sandwiches with the biscuits and scoops of ice cream, then roll the sides
in the pistachios.

PEPPERMINT CHOC NO-CHURN ICE CREAM

Time: 10 minutes + Freezing: 4 hours

serves 4

150 g (5 oz/¾ cup) sweetened condensed milk
300 ml (10 fl oz/1¼ cups) very cold double (heavy) cream
½–1 teaspoon peppermint extract
100 g (3½ oz) good-quality dark chocolate, chopped
handful of small mint leaves
chocolate-dipped wafers or biscuits (cookies), to decorate

method

Using an electric hand mixer, whisk together the condensed milk, cream and peppermint extract in a chilled bowl, starting on low then increasing to high, to medium-stiff peaks. Fold through the chocolate chunks and mint. Transfer to a freezerproof container and freeze until firm. Decorate with extra mint leaves and wafers/biscuits.

LUXURIOUS VANILLA RICE PUDDING

Time: 10 minutes

142

serves 4

2 x 500 ml (16 fl oz/1 pint) tubs vanilla ice cream
100 ml (3½ fl oz/⅓ cup plus 1 tablespoon) water
180 g (6 oz/1 cup) instant white rice
4 tablespoons fruit jam (jelly) of your choice

method

Melt the ice cream and water in a saucepan. Add the rice, bring to a simmer, then remove from the heat, cover and let stand for 5 minutes. Immediately spoon into bowls and top with jam.

CHOC CHERRY ICE CREAM SANDWICHES

Time: 5 minutes + Freezing: 10 minutes

144

serves 4

85 g (3 oz) good-quality dark chocolate, finely chopped
8 chocolate-coated biscuits
4 scoops black cherry and chocolate ice cream

method

Sandwich scoops of ice cream between the biscuits and freeze on greaseproof paper while you melt the chocolate. Dip the biscuits halfway into the chocolate and return to the freezer until set, about 5 minutes.

MOLTEN CHOCOLATE CAKES

Time: 10 minutes + Baking: 14 minutes

146

makes 4

200 g (7 oz) good-quality dark chocolate, chopped
100 g (3½ oz/scant ½ cup) unsalted butter, at room temperature, plus extra for greasing
3 large eggs
85 g (3 oz/scant ½ cup) caster (superfine) sugar
35 g (1¼ oz/¼ cup) plain (all-purpose) flour, sifted
unsweetened cocoa powder, for dusting

method

Preheat the oven to 200°C (400°F/Gas 6). Grease 4 x 250 ml (8½ fl oz/1 cup) pudding moulds. Gently melt the chocolate and butter in a saucepan, stirring until the chocolate has melted. Whisk the eggs and sugar together to combine. Add the melted chocolate and flour and whisk to combine. Pour into moulds, put on a baking tray and bake for 14 minutes. Immediately invert the cakes onto plates and dust with cocoa powder.

ICE CREAM SUNDAE CUPCAKES

Time: 5 minutes

148

serves 4

4 store-bought vanilla cupcakes
4 scoops vanilla ice cream
4 teaspoons chocolate fudge sauce
4 maraschino cherries

149

method

Slice rounded tops off cupcakes and discard. Scoop the ice cream in round balls
on top of the cupcakes, drizzle with chocolate sauce and top with the cherries.

BANANA FLAMBÉE

Time: 10 minutes

serves 4

30 g (1 oz/2 tablespoons) unsalted butter
75 g (2½ oz/generous ⅓ cup) light brown sugar
4 bananas, peeled and halved
75 ml (2½ fl oz/⅓ cup) dark rum
1 x 500 ml (16 fl oz/1 pint) tub vanilla ice cream
20 g (¾ oz/2 tablespoons) roasted unsalted peanuts, chopped

method

Melt the butter in a frying pan (skillet) over a medium heat. Add the sugar, stirring for 1 minute. Add the bananas and cook for 1 minute on each side. Remove from the heat and add the rum. Return to the heat, shaking the pan (it will flame up). Once the flame subsides, serve with ice cream and peanuts.

FROZEN MOCHACCINO

Time: 5 minutes

serves 2–4

150 ml (5 fl oz/⅔ cup) chilled coffee
100 ml (3 fl oz/⅓ cup plus 1 tablespoon) whole milk
4–6 tablespoons chocolate sauce, plus extra for drizzling
3 large handfuls of ice cubes
100 ml (3 fl oz/⅓ cup plus 1 tablespoon) double (heavy) cream

Gluten-free

method

Blitz the coffee, milk, chocolate sauce and ice cubes in a blender, until the ice is crushed.
Pour into glasses. Whip the cream until stiff, then spoon on top of the mochaccino.
Drizzle with extra chocolate sauce.

CHOCOLATE BARK

Time: 10 minutes + Chilling: 20 minutes

makes 420 g (15 oz)

375 g (13 oz) good-quality dark chocolate, chopped
30 g (1 oz/2 tablespoons) shelled pistachios, roughly chopped
15 g (½ oz) goji berries

Dairy-free

method

Grease a 23 cm (9 in) rimmed baking dish and line with a reusable baking mat or baking paper. Melt the chocolate in a heatproof bowl set over a pan of simmering water, then pour into the baking dish and spread evenly. Sprinkle with the pistachios and goji berries and chill until firm. Peel off the baking mat/paper and break into pieces.

SHORTCUT APPLE CRUMBLE

Time: 10 minutes

156

serves 2

25 g (1 oz/2 tablespoons)
   unsalted butter
1 tablespoon lemon juice
40 g (1½ oz/3¼ tablespoons)
   golden caster (superfine) sugar
300 g (10½ oz) apples, peeled,
   cored and cut into 1 cm (½ in) pieces
40 g (1½ oz/scant ½ cup) granola
½ quantity Vanilla Custard (see page 30)

157

method

Sauté the butter, lemon juice, sugar and apples for 5–7 minutes, until softened and lightly caramelised. Spoon into bowls, top with granola and pour over the custard to serve.

CHOCOLATE FONDUE

Time: 5 minutes

158

serves 4

1 quantity Chocolate Ganache (see page 20)
selection of strawberries, chunks of sponge cake, pretzels, frozen grapes and marshmallows, for dipping

method

Warm the ganache over a low heat, then divide among 4 small ramekins.
Serve with the dipping ingredients and some small skewers.

CHOCOLATE BISCUIT CAKE

Time: 10 minutes + Chilling: 1 hour

serves 4

50 g (2 oz/3½ tablespoons) unsalted butter
75 g (2½ oz/scant ¼ cup) golden syrup
150 g (5 oz) good-quality dark chocolate (or a combination of milk and dark), chopped
100 g (3½ oz) digestive biscuits (graham crackers), lightly crushed
50 g (2 oz) dried apricots, roughly chopped
40 g (1½ oz) raisins
30 g (1 oz/¼ cup) toasted Brazil nuts, chopped

method

Melt together the butter, golden syrup and chocolate in a saucepan. Fold in the remaining ingredients, transfer to a 15 cm (6 in) tart ring lined with cling film (plastic wrap) and place on a baking sheet. Chill until firm, then slice into wedges to serve.

CHOCOLATE TOASTS WITH CRÈME FRAÎCHE

Time: 10 minutes

serves 2

½ baguette, sliced diagonally into 1 cm (½ in) thick slices
25 g (1 oz/2 tablespoons) unsalted butter, softened
125 g (4 oz/½ cup) warmed Chocolate Ganache (see page 20)
4 tablespoons crème fraîche

method

Butter the bread on both sides, then add to a frying pan (skillet) set over a medium heat, cooking until toasted on both sides. Remove from the heat and pour over the ganache, turning the toasts to coat. Pile onto plates and top with crème fraîche.

WHITE CHOCOLATE MOUSSE

Time: 10 minutes

serves 2–4

100 g (3½ oz/⅔ cup) white chocolate buttons
125 ml (4 fl oz/½ cup) double (heavy) cream
2 large egg whites
½ quantity Raspberry Coulis (see page 28)
8 biscotti

Soy-free

method

Melt together the white chocolate and cream very gently. Whisk the egg whites to stiff peaks, then fold one-third into the chocolate mixture. Fold in the remaining whites, then divide among 4 x 125 ml (4 fl oz/½ cup) glasses or bowls. Top with the coulis and add biscotti soldiers on the side. Serve immediately or chill.

ALMOND BRIOCHE WITH BLUEBERRY SAUCE

Time: 10 minutes

serves 4

2 large eggs
2 tablespoons whole milk
1 tablespoon granulated sugar
4 thick slices brioche
125 g (4 oz/1½ cups) flaked almonds
30 g (1 oz/2 tablespoons) unsalted butter
1 quantity Blueberry Sauce (see page 24)
crème fraîche, to decorate

method

Whisk together the eggs, milk and sugar. Dip the brioche slices into the egg mixture, turning to fully coat, then press on the almonds. Melt the butter in a non-stick frying pan (skillet) set over a medium heat and cook the brioche until golden brown on both sides. Transfer to plates, spoon over the sauce and dollop with crème fraîche.

NO-BAKE CHEESECAKE

Time: 10 minutes + Chilling: 2 hours

serves 6–8

100 g (3½ oz) chocolate wafer biscuits (cookies) (or Oreos with the cream filling removed), finely crushed
50 g (2 oz/3½ tablespoons) unsalted butter, melted
225 g (8 oz/1 cup) cream cheese, at room temperature
2 tablespoons granulated sugar
60 ml (2 fl oz/¼ cup) very cold double (heavy) cream
½ teaspoon vanilla bean paste
1 quantity Blueberry Sauce (see page 24)

method

Combine the biscuit crumbs and butter and press into a 450 g (1 lb) loaf tin (pan) lined with baking paper so that the paper overhangs on 2 long sides. Use an electric hand mixer to beat the cream cheese and sugar until smooth. Add the cream on low speed until incorporated, then increase the speed to medium and beat until stiff. Stir in the vanilla, then spread evenly over the crumb base. Chill for 2 hours. Top with sauce.

Nut-free

RASPBERRY & HAZELNUT BROWNIE CAKE

Time: 10 minutes + Baking: 25 minutes

makes 12

250 g (9 oz/1⅔ cups) good-quality dark chocolate chips
175 g (6 oz/¾ cup) unsalted butter, cut into small pieces
3 eggs, at room temperature
150 g (5 oz/¾ cup) caster (superfine) sugar
100 g (3½ oz/1 cup) ground hazelnuts or ground almonds
50 g (2 oz/½ cup) unsweetened cocoa powder
140 g (4½ oz) small raspberries

Gluten-free

method

Preheat the oven to 180°C (350°F/Gas 4). Line a 23 cm (9 in) square baking tin with baking paper. Melt 175 g (6 oz/1 cup) chocolate with the butter. Use an electric hand mixer to beat the eggs and sugar until thick and pale. Add the melted chocolate, mixing on a low speed, to combine. Fold in the ground nuts, cocoa, remaining chocolate and raspberries. Pour the mixture into the tin. Bake for 25 minutes. Cool completely before serving.

EASY APPLE TART

Time: 10 minutes + Baking: 30 minutes

172

serves 4–8

100 g (3½ oz/½ cup) caster (superfine) sugar
35 g (1¼ oz/2 generous tablespoons) unsalted butter, cubed
pinch of coarse sea salt
350 g (12 oz) crisp apples, about 2 (such as Cox, Pink Lady, Granny Smith or Braeburn),
    peeled, cored and sliced 5 mm (¼ in) thick
300 g (10½ oz) pre-rolled puff pastry, trimmed into a 24 cm (9½ in) circle (5 mm/¼ in thick)

method

Preheat the oven to 200°C (400°F/Gas 6). Heat a 20 cm (8 in) ovenproof frying pan (skillet), add the sugar and cook, shaking the pan, until golden brown. Remove from the heat and add the butter and salt. Arrange the apple slices in the caramel and return to the heat for 2 minutes, spooning the caramel over. Drape the pastry over the top, pushing the excess inside with a wooden spoon. Bake for 30 minutes until golden. Rest for 5 minutes, then invert.

PECAN TURTLES

Time: 10 minutes + Chilling: 30 minutes

174

makes 8

50 g (2 oz/scant ½ cup) toasted pecan halves
8 chewy caramels, halved
100 g (3½ oz/⅔ cup) white chocolate buttons

Egg-free

method

Preheat the oven to 180°C (350°F/Gas 4). Arrange the pecans in 8 clusters (about 4 per cluster), 5 cm (2 in) apart on a baking sheet lined with a reusable baking mat. Top each cluster with a caramel half. Place in the oven until just melted, about 2–3 minutes. Melt the chocolate, then spoon over and chill until set.

GINGERY PLUMS WITH TOASTED CAKE

Time: 10 minutes

176

serves 4

25 g (1 oz/2 tablespoons) unsalted butter
50 g (2 oz/¼ cup) granulated sugar
25 g (1 oz) fresh ginger, peeled and finely grated
1 star anise
450 g (1 lb) assorted plums, stoned and cut into wedges
4 slices sponge cake, toasted
100 g (3½ oz/½ cup) crème fraîche

Nut-free

method

Melt the butter in a large frying pan (skillet) over a medium-high heat. Add the sugar, ginger and star anise and stir to combine. Add the plums, tossing occasionally until starting to caramelise, about 4 minutes. Spoon over slices of toasted cake and top with the crème fraîche.

BANOFFEE PIE

Time: 10 minutes

178

serves 4–8

125 g (4 oz) digestive biscuits (graham crackers), crushed
75 g (2½ oz/⅓ cup) unsalted butter, melted
110 g (3¾ oz/⅓ cup) dulce de leche
1 large banana, peeled and sliced
150 ml (5 fl oz/⅔ cup) double (heavy) cream
chocolate curls, to decorate

method

Mix together the biscuits and butter and press into a 15 cm (6 in) pastry ring on a lined baking tray. Spread the dulce de leche over the base, then top with bananas. Whip the cream to medium peaks, then spoon over the bananas. Top with chocolate curls.

NUTTY CHOCOLATE BANANA ICE CREAM

Time: 5 minutes

serves 4

4 small-medium frozen bananas
100 g (3½ oz/⅓ cup) Nutella® chocolate spread
20 g (¾ oz/3 tablespoons) unsweetened cocoa powder
20 g (¾ oz/2½ tablespoons) toasted hazelnuts, lightly crushed

method

Purée together the bananas, Nutella® and cocoa powder in a food processor. Spoon into bowls and top with hazelnuts to serve.

ICY FUDGE POPS

Time: 10 minutes + Freezing: 2 hours

makes 4–6 pops

150 g (5 oz/½ cup) Nutella® chocolate spread
300 ml (10 fl oz/1¼ cups) coconut milk (vigorously shaken to combine solids and liquid)

method

Whisk together the Nutella® and coconut milk and divide among
4 x 125 ml (4 fl oz/½ cup) ice lolly moulds or cups (or 6 x 70 ml/2½ fl oz/⅓ cup moulds).
If using cups, freeze for 1 hour, then push in wooden sticks.
Return to the freezer until solid.

SNOW CONES

Time: 5 minutes

serves 2

6 large handfuls of ice cubes
4 tablespoons fruit-flavoured syrup

Nut-free

method

Very finely crush the ice then divide between cones or cups and drizzle
with syrup to serve.

CHOCOLATE & CANDIED GINGER FUDGE

Time: 10 minutes + Setting: 4 hours

186

makes 18

1 x 397 g (14 oz) tin sweetened condensed milk
200 g (7 oz) good-quality dark chocolate, finely chopped
20 g (¾ oz) crystallised ginger, chopped
¼ teaspoon coarse sea salt flakes

Gluten-free

method

Heat the condensed milk to barely simmering in a saucepan, about 5 minutes
(do not boil). Remove from the heat and add the chocolate, stirring until the chocolate
is melted and smooth. Transfer to a 900 g (2 lb) loaf tin (pan) lined with baking paper.
Sprinkle with ginger and salt. Chill until set and slice to serve.

FIZZY ORANGE FLOAT

Time: 5 minutes

serves 4

500 ml (16 fl oz/1 pint) tub vanilla ice cream
500 ml (17 fl oz/2 cups) fizzy orange drink
½ orange, cut into small triangles

method

Scoop the ice cream into 4 x 300 ml (10 fl oz/1¼ cup) glasses and pour over the fizzy orange drink. Cut small slits in the orange pieces and hook onto the sides of the glasses to serve.

INDEX

191

ACKNOWLEDGEMENTS

A book contains many moving parts and this book would not be what it is without the hard work of Catie Ziller, Kathy Steer and Alice Chadwick. Thank you to the talented Lauren Volo whose pictures bought these recipes alive, Jade Zimmerman for being an amazing assistant and even better friend. Many, many thanks to Valrhona (the king of chocolate makers) for making my desserts taste so good, and to Häagen-Dazs for all the delicious ice cream to work with.

Finally, to my family and my world, Don, Charlie and Poppy – even on the days we all end up in tears, I still love you more than chocolate cake.

First published by © Hachette Livre (Marabout) 2016
The English language edition published in 2018 by Hardie Grant Books,
an imprint of Hardie Grant Publishing

Hardie Grant Books (London)
5th & 6th Floors
52–54 Southwark Street
London SE1 1UN

Hardie Grant Books (Melbourne)
Building 1, 658 Church Street
Richmond, Victoria 3121

hardiegrantbooks.com

Text © Anna Helm Baxter 2018
Photography © Lauren Volvo 2018

British Library Cataloguing-in-Publication Data. A catalogue record for this book is available from the British Library.

10-Minute Desserts by Anna Helm Baxter

ISBN 978-1-78488-184-9

Publisher: Catie Ziller
Photography: Lauren Volvo
Food Stylist: Anna Helm Baxter
Designer and illustrator: Alice Chadwick
Editor: Kathy Steer

For the English hardback edition:

Publisher: Kate Pollard
Publishing Assistant: Eila Purvis
Editor: Emily Preece-Morrison

Colour Reproduction by p2d
Printed and bound in China by Leo Paper Group

Social Psychology **Matters**

Wendy Hollway, Helen Lucey and Ann Phoenix

WITHDRAWN

The Open University

OPEN UNIVERSITY PRESS
McGraw - Hill Education

Published by

Open University Press
McGraw-Hill House
Shoppenhangers Road
Maidenhead
SL6 2QL

in association with

The Open University
Walton Hall
Milton Keynes
MK7 6AA

First published 2007.

Edited and designed by The Open University.

Typeset by The Open University.

Printed and bound in the United Kingdom by CPI, Bath.

This book forms part of an Open University course DD307 *Social psychology: critical perspectives on self and others*. Details of this and other Open University courses can be obtained from the Student Registration and Enquiry Service, The Open University, PO Box 197, Milton Keynes MK7 6BJ, United Kingdom: tel. +44 (0)870 333 4340, email general-enquiries@open.ac.uk

http://www.open.ac.uk

ISBN 0 33522 103 3/ISBN 978 0 3352 2103 5 (pb)

ISBN 0 33522 105 X/ISBN 978 0 3352 2105 9 (hb)

1.1

Contents

Preface

The editors of this book would like to thank all the chapter authors for their original contributions to the book. In addition, because this book was produced for The Open University's Social Sciences course DD307 *Social psychology: critical perspectives on self and others*, the editors would like to acknowledge the special contributions from colleagues at The Open University: other members of the DD307 course team, Karen Hagan, Mary Horton-Salway, Caroline Kelly, Darren Langdridge, Bianca Raabe and Stephanie Taylor; External Assessor, Valerie Walkerdine; Associate Lecturer and Student Critical Readers, Sally Ann Gallagher, Geoff Harris, Marie Ann Lavelle, Harriette Marshall, Kate Pearson, Anna Sarphie, Annette Thomson; Course Manager, Ann Tolley; Editorial Media Developer, Kathleen Calder; Media Project Manager, Lynne Downey; Copublishing Media Developer Margrit Bass; Psychology Department Office Manager, Lynda Preston; and the secretarial team from the Psychology Office in Social Sciences, Sarah Pelosi and Elaine Richardson.

Wendy Hollway, Helen Lucey and Ann Phoenix

Introduction

Navigating social psychology

by Ann Phoenix, The Open University

Contents

1   Introduction: navigating social psychology

The issues that lie at the heart of social psychology are endlessly fascinating. Questions of how to understand ourselves, other people and everyday social interaction, are not just absorbing, but consequential. This is because the publication of social psychology research can suggest how social issues can best be dealt with. The popularisation of social psychology also has an impact on what we expect from other people and how we treat them and ourselves.

The discipline of social psychology has proliferated over the last century so that a wealth of topics has been studied using a variety of methods and theories. This makes the theories and history of the discipline important areas of study in themselves. Yet this very diversity means that it is difficult for anybody interested in social psychology to get a good overview of it without help in finding ways to navigate its material, methods and theories. This book is designed to help with that task. It provides an overview of social psychology, including its substance, theories and methodologies, and takes stock of current social psychology, indicating ways in which it has changed and continues to change. In order to identify the routes social psychology is pursuing, the authors of this book trace its roots and present examples of how key social psychology perspectives address real life social experiences. A careful engagement with the history of the discipline shows that social psychological knowledges, methods and theories change because society changes, and because social psychologists transform the ways in which they think about their discipline, what they choose to study and how they study it. Some of those changes result from influences from other disciplines and from other countries (see Chapter 1). This dynamism is, at least partly, responsible for the freshness of social psychology's approaches and subject matter. It would be inaccurate, however, to assume that these shifts all contribute in a straightforward and incremental way to progress towards one, agreed view of the discipline. In practice, different areas of social psychology take different perspectives on what it means to be a person and on how social psychological knowledge is best produced.

These differences in perspective are not accidental. The major divisions in social psychology arise because social psychologists take different positions on two central and basic questions: epistemology and ontology. Epistemology is concerned with the nature, sources and limits of knowledge; in other words, it is about how we know what we think we know, and how certain we can be that the social world is actually how we think it is. Ontology is concerned with the nature of being and existence; it is about the assumptions we use to characterise human beings and what it means to be human. This may seem esoteric, particularly since published research results generally do not mention either position. Yet all research starts from both an epistemological and an ontological position, and social psychologists disagree about which are the most fruitful approaches. Both epistemology and ontology are discussed in detail in Chapter 1.

As a result of differences in epistemology and ontology, research findings from social psychology cannot simply be added together to increase understanding of the experience of being a person in today's world. For this reason, *Social Psychology Matters* does not simply present topics side by side as if they are equivalent. Instead, it is innovative in that it highlights up-to-date research on contemporary social psychological issues, but does so by introducing the theoretical and methodological perspectives that inform social psychology, showing clearly which approaches are being used to address the topics presented. This book situates its treatment of social psychology consistently in the history of how it became what it did and therefore how it engages with the variety of its subject matter. It considers how the emphasis on well-established social psychological topics shifts over time, and discusses how topics that fit the subject matter of social psychology, but have largely been ignored, are beginning to be addressed and why they are fruitful. This includes looking at how its methodologies formed and the effects these have on the discipline.

This book provides tools for critical analysis of social psychological ideas and methods by unpacking the theories and methods that underpin the study of particular areas of social psychology and by showing how research in one perspective can be critiqued from another perspective. It reflects on the nature of social psychology and demonstrates what high-quality research looks like from different perspectives, as well as how it is produced and interpreted. Overall, the book explores the significance of social psychology in the twenty-first century and the contributions it can and does make to understanding people in their social worlds. The title is deliberately ambiguous to reflect the fact that the book discusses both matters of social psychology and the ways in which social psychology matters. The chapters are written by social psychologists eminent in their fields.

1.1 The structure of the book

In order to foreground history, theory, epistemology and methods in social psychological treatment of its subjects, the first two chapters of *Social Psychology Matters* aim to situate social psychological knowledges. They provide a framework for understanding the context, history and paradigms that have produced the contemporary discipline and that constitute the conditions for its future development. These two chapters set out the history of the discipline and its methodological debates; they also present two sets of structuring devices or organising themes that readers can use as tools to examine the topics and research presented throughout the book. These analytical overviews of the content of social psychology can be applied to any social psychological research the reader encounters later.

We call the first of these structuring devices 'interrogative themes' in order to highlight the analytical purchase they allow for readers to ask probing questions about social psychological topics. These interrogative themes consist of four critical concepts which can be used to interrogate and analyse social psychology. They have been chosen because they help to provide a framework for conceptualising and analysing the intersecting relationships between individuals and society – i.e. social psychology's object of study.

These four interrogative themes are:

- power relations
- situated knowledges
- individual–society dualism
- agency–structure dualism.

Each of these is introduced, explained and discussed in detail in Chapter 1. Together, they help to elucidate the ways in which epistemology and ontology underpin, and are produced, in social psychological work. The cumulative effect of these four themes is to teach students how to step back from the immediate substance of the social psychological topics presented and to recognise how, why and in what context they are produced, as well as how they themselves are productive of theory, knowledge and practices. This goal informs the structure of the book's chapters. It is worth noting that the themes are referred to in slightly different ways by different chapter authors (as they are in social psychology more generally). For example, 'dualism' is sometimes referred to as 'dichotomy' or 'binary terms', and when its opposite is discussed, some authors use the word 'unitary', whereas others use 'monism'. Similarly, 'society' is sometimes replaced by 'the social'. However, meanings are clear in the context of the chapters and these different usages have deliberately not been unified in order to promote familiarity with a variety of ways in which social psychological concepts are used. The aim is to facilitate wider reading of social psychological work where readers have to be alert to the particular meanings of terms in their academic context.

The second set of structuring devices consists of the presentation of four perspectives that characterise different contemporary social psychologies and their associated methodologies. These are: cognitive social, discursive psychological, phenomenological and social psychoanalytic perspectives. They are introduced in Chapter 2.

Following the first two framework-setting chapters, the book applies the interrogative themes to five social psychological topics using different perspectives. Each chapter presents both the substance of research in the topic it addresses and showcases ways in which at least two perspectives have dealt with it. Thus each chapter presents at least two theoretical approaches and their associated methodologies, as well as highlighting those of the four main themes that are relevant and discussing appropriate work from other perspectives which illuminates the topic. The choice of chapter topics reflects contemporary concerns that show how social psychology knowledge reflects changes in society and efforts to address these (e.g. the chapters on families and on prejudice and conflict reduction). The choice of topics is also governed by our belief that these are all issues that present an enduring challenge to social psychology because the discipline requires that individual and social explanations are brought together (thus posing a challenge to individual–society dualism and raising questions about agency and the constraints of social structures).

Three of our topics have a long history of being recognised as central to social psychology: notably, emotions, and prejudice and conflict in psychological social psychology (PSP), and self in sociological social psychology (SSP). Two chapters explore areas that are surprisingly little researched in social psychology, but in which work is beginning (families and embodiment). Generally these have been regarded as 'belonging' to other parts of psychology or other disciplines. By including them, we are making a case for social psychological treatment of these areas. It is not that the subject of 'families' has not been addressed in social psychology in the past. For example, the social psychologist Jerome Bruner (1990) analysed family discussions of their members' pasts. However, families as a topic is commonly addressed in developmental psychology and is also a sociological topic, but has been little developed in social psychology. Similarly, the influential identity theorist Erik Erikson (1974) theorised the importance of the body for human experience of space and time, arguing that our upright stance means that we can symbolise: behind (e.g. symbolising things we leave behind); ahead (things we aim for); above (what we look up to); below (what is beneath us); right and left. Despite this, 'embodiment' has been more frequently discussed in biological psychology and has only relatively recently received sustained attention in the social sciences.

Throughout, the book encourages reflection on the experience of being a person in a social world. It poses challenging questions about how we come to know what we know about ourselves and other people, and allows critical engagement with the different perspectives. The book ends with a short concluding chapter.

1.2   The chapters

Chapter 1, 'Social psychology: past and present', by Wendy Hollway introduces over one hundred years of social psychological history. It aims to provide a framework for understanding the origins of social psychological theories, methods and topics and the changes these have undergone. It shows how time and place are intertwined by presenting the somewhat different traditions established in the USA and in Europe and how these have influenced each other. Donna Haraway's notion of *situated knowledges* is presented as an apt interrogative theme for analysing the historical and geographical location of social psychological knowledge.

The relevance of the other three interrogative themes used in the book is set out in this chapter. For example, the discussion of how the experimental method became pre-eminent in social psychology, debates about 'crisis' in social psychology and the emergence of feminist social psychology show the centrality of *power relations* to epistemology in the discipline. At the heart of all these debates are ontological divisions. The chapter demonstrates how social psychology has been characterised by dualistic thinking about whether the focus of attention should be on individuals or on society, and whether people have agency in their lives or are determined by the social structures in which they live. These dichotomies are generally referred to as *individual–society dualism* and *agency–structure dualism* (which is also debated in sociology). They relate to the division between social psychology that has been largely influenced by psychology (PSP) and what has been more influenced by sociology (SSP). The chapter argues that this dichotomous thinking is unhelpful.

Chapter 2, 'Methods and knowledge in social psychology', by Wendy Hollway starts by demonstrating that methods do not just reveal a social world as it already is, but actively produce knowledge. Hollway introduces the four perspectives chosen as examples for the book (cognitive social, discursive psychological, phenomenological and social psychoanalytic) and their related methodologies. In order to give a clear and concrete example of the similarities and differences between the four perspectives, four social psychologists (each an expert in one of the perspectives) analyse the same newspaper headline. The chapter then discusses the dominance of the scientific method in PSP, particularly in North America, and its place in the power relations that produced social psychology.

The sections that follow discuss the predominant quantitative traditions in social psychology: the experimental method and social psychometrics. These sections apply two of the four course themes: power relations and situated knowledges. A now famous set of social psychology experiments conducted by Stanley Milgram in the 1960s and 1970s – on obedience to authority – is examined in detail. Hollway places the research in its post-war historical context. She makes clear that knowledge produced from experiments such as Milgram's is situated within particular sets of power relations. The final section of the chapter discusses how the dominance of the 'scientific' method in social psychology has led some qualitative researchers in the SSP tradition to be overly concerned with sample size and statistical issues of generalisation. Hollway argues that different research questions require different methods and different strategies of sampling and generalising. Methodological choices, therefore, have to be theoretically informed.

Chapter 3, 'Families', by Helen Lucey examines the first under-researched social psychological topic presented in the book by exploring how and why family relationships are an important topic for contemporary social psychology. Families have been the focus of considerable attention in developmental psychology, where they are viewed as sites of causes and outcomes. For example, developmental psychology has been influential in shaping normative ideas about what constitutes 'good' practices in families and in informing health, welfare and educational interventions into 'unhealthy' families. Instead, the focus in social psychology is on families as dynamic and changing, on diversity between families, and on the meanings and experiences associated with particular family forms for those within and outside them. The chapter uses the interrogative theme of situated knowledges to highlight the ways in which psychological ideas that influence commonsense and professional ideas about all mothers and fathers are produced in particular historical and geographical contexts.

The chapter discusses the ways in which families are changing demographically (and so are historically located) as parents more frequently separate and re-partner and as more families develop transnational links. The chapter then presents the principles of a critical discursive psychological perspective before examining a piece of discursive psychological research on the gendered division of household labour. The second social psychological perspective examined is social psychoanalytic, and its principles are illustrated through research on the place of sibling relationships in identity processes. The chapter addresses the interrogative themes of power relations, situated knowledges, agency–structure and individual–society dualism.

Chapter 4, 'Emotion', by Brian Parkinson argues that 'emotion resists dualistic positioning on the individual–society axis' and that emotions are distinctively social psychological because they 'play out in the course of interpersonal episodes' that are themselves located within broader cultural contexts. The chapter demonstrates that an everyday issue such as emotion continues to puzzle social psychologists and, as a result, has generated numerous theories and methods for studying it. The chapter reflects this diversity, while presenting detailed examinations of both experimental and discursive psychological approaches.

The chapter discusses the early philosophical beginnings of concern with emotions that focused on subjective feelings. The later historical move into an experimental perspective marked a shift to objectively measurable components, such as facial expressions and physiological responses. However, the chapter argues that the future of emotion research may require better ways of specifying both verbal (discursive) and nonverbal aspects of emotion. It shows the relevance of the interrogative themes of agency–structure, individual–society and situated knowledges. It demonstrates that experimental social psychologists have continually made refinements to their epistemology and ontology in order to engage with the complexities of a topic such as emotion: they are theoretically and methodologically dynamic. This dynamism reflects the fact that, while the cognitive social psychological approach to emotions has been dominant in social psychology for a long time, it has not ossified, but continues to renew itself.

Chapter 5, 'Self', by Wendy Hollway first places some of the many terms that refer to self in the historical context of changes in understanding of self that have influenced social psychology. The first section concludes with a summary of all the binary terms (*either* this *or* that) that have characterised arguments about how the self is made up. The chapter then moves from broad theoretical accounts of self to examples of how the self has been researched empirically as a social psychological topic. This reflects the principle of situated knowledges: that is, the idea that the situation in which knowledge about the self is produced makes a difference to how selves are understood. The first methodological section illustrates the ways in which a phenomenological approach assumes a knowing, self-conscious self, while the second examines the ways in which a social psychoanalytic approach assumes a hidden, defended self. Research from these two perspectives is compared to see what they have in common and how they differ in relation to research on the self. The final section of the chapter returns to the binaries that have been used to understand the self and discusses if and how some of these can be transcended.

Chapter 6, 'Prejudice, conflict and conflict reduction', by John Dixon starts by locating studies of prejudice and conflict in their social and historical contexts. It shows that there have been ontological shifts in how prejudice has been conceptualised in social psychology – away from viewing it as primarily the result of abnormal individual psychological development to seeing it as being understandable rather than *sense-less*. The first social psychological perspective evaluated is discursive psychological. Dixon presents an analysis of how accounts of political violence by a Protestant and a Catholic activist help to sustain 'incompatible constructions of the political realities of the Northern Ireland situation'. The second perspective considered is cognitive social. Dixon presents the contact hypothesis, which has been the dominant approach to conflict reduction, and considers its limitations. The chapter ends by using insights from discursive psychology to interrogate cognitive social approaches and to suggest new questions that social psychologists need to address to move forward an issue that is crucial for many societies.

The chapter addresses in detail the ways in which the area has been dogged by a focus on the individual side of the individual–society dualism. Although many social psychologists acknowledge the cultural and political determinants of our everyday relationships, much social psychological work on prejudice has treated it as individually, rather than socially, produced. The chapter identifies elements that are necessary for a more reflexive, varied and contextualised social psychological approach to conflict and conflict reduction.

Chapter 7, 'Embodiment', by Linda Finlay and Darren Langdridge, the final, issue-based chapter, addresses a topic that has been under-researched in social psychology – embodiment. It starts by critiquing mind–body, individual–society and agency–structure dualisms as they have been applied to thinking about the body. It argues that the body, self and society are necessarily interconnected and so the study of the body should not be left to biology. The interrogative themes of individual–social and agency–structure are, therefore, central to this chapter and an example of the concept of 'body projects' is introduced to illustrate these themes. The first social psychological perspective presented is discursive psychological, with a particular emphasis on the way Michel Foucault theorises discourse. Research on eating disorders and on transgenderism is used to highlight the socially and historically located nature of discourses, their power relations and the ways in which discourses help to constitute the body and body practices.

The second social psychological perspective addressed is phenomenological. This approach makes central the ways in which bodies are experienced. Finlay and Langdridge present the details of a phenomenological study of embodiment in order to give insights into the phenomenological method. Both discursive and phenomenological approaches are evaluated critically for their utility in the study of bodies and embodiment.

Chapter 8, 'Conclusion: social psychology matters', by Wendy Hollway draws together the ways in which social psychological knowledge is situated, and summarises the arguments that have been made in the book about the interconnectedness of epistemology, methodology and ontology. The final part uses the device of posing and answering what Hollway calls 'insistent questions'. In doing so, it ensures that various issues raised throughout the book concerning the interrogative themes, the historical specificity and plurality of social psychological perspectives are succinctly summarised.

Overall, this book demonstrates why social psychology matters by discussing in depth a range of social psychology issues. It does so in accessible language and with the use of carefully chosen examples that support readers in the process of analysing social psychological research critically. We hope that you enjoy it.

References

Bruner, J. (1990) *Acts of Meaning: Four Lectures on Mind and Culture*, The Jerusalem-Harvard Lectures, Cambridge, MA, Harvard University Press.

Erikson, E. (1974) *Dimensions of a New Identity*, The Jefferson Lectures in the Humanities, New York, W.W. Norton.

Chapter 1

Social psychology: past and present

by Wendy Hollway, The Open University

Contents

> **Learning outcomes**
>
> By the end of this chapter, you should be able to recognise different traditions in social psychology and situate them:
>
> - geographically (in the USA, the UK and continental Europe)
> - historically (in their period of origin and influence)
> - methodologically (uses of a variety of qualitative and quantitative approaches)
> - in terms of their disciplinary origin (psychology or sociology).
>
> You should also understand the idea of stepping back from the substance of social psychology in order to:
>
> - notice the power relations involved in producing social psychological knowledge
> - ask whether knowledge claims have been appropriately situated in the contexts in which they apply
> - recognise where explanations focus exclusively on individual or social factors and try to include both
> - identify assumptions about agency or the determining influence of social structure and recognise when these are mutually exclusive.

1   Introduction

In its modern form, social psychology has existed – by one estimate – for about 100 years. A centenary marks a good point to assess it and to consider why it takes its current form in the UK. However, to claim that social psychology is a particular age involves making some assumptions about what social psychology is. Traditionally, the book by the British psychologist William McDougall, *Introduction to Social Psychology*, published in 1908, is identified as the start of modern social psychology in the UK. In that same year, an American sociologist called Edward Alsworth Ross published a book called *Social Psychology*, but this did not achieve the same status as McDougall's work. However, William James, a medically trained American philosopher and Harvard Professor of Psychology (until 1897), began work on his book *Principles of Psychology* in 1878. This was eventually published in 1890, and treated many important social psychological topics. Clearly then, identifying the beginning of the discipline in its current form is not straightforward, so let us look more generally at changes in the intellectual climate of the time in order to discover the conditions for the emergence of what we now call 'social psychology'.

Until the early twentieth century, psychology was a branch of philosophy. This means that ideas about human beings formed part of the thinking, theorising and writing of philosophers, no doubt based partly on their own experience. James's *Principles of Psychology* is an example of this tradition, before the growth of what we now call 'Social Sciences'. As a philosopher, he was not concerned with distinctions between his subject matter and psychology or sociology. His work ranged across these areas and, perhaps because he was not constrained by disciplinary boundaries, still influences social psychology.

However, by the beginning of the twentieth century, science had somewhat displaced philosophy as it was generally believed that new branches of knowledge could, by following scientific methods and principles, arrive at the kind of certainties on which progress could confidently be built. Science had transformed Western cultures' understanding of the physical universe. Its spectacular successes, including advances in agriculture, transportation, medicine and hygiene, gave it an almost religious status: that is, beliefs in the authority – even the infallibility – of science were widespread and powerful. In this climate, it is not surprising that some wanted to use these powerful methods to understand and influence the world of people. By conducting experiments in laboratories, the early scientific psychologists believed that they could establish psychological principles that were as secure as physical ones.

A similar move, also at the start of the twentieth century, led to the establishment of modern sociology, based on the wish to understand and influence society. However, whereas society cannot easily be operationalised (translated into the protocols demanded of experiments) in the laboratory, individual behaviours could be, or so it was thought. Early psychological experiments largely focused on perception and memory.

From the perspective of scientific psychology, contemporary social psychology originates with the first experiments on a social psychological topic. This is often set just before the First World War when a German called Walter Moede (1920) wrote a pamphlet on 'Experimental group psychology'. He purposely opposed the nineteenth-century European tradition of 'crowd psychology' (associated with Gustave Le Bon, 1908 [1896]) which was more philosophical. The experiments he suggested involved setting up groups in the laboratory in various controlled ways so that the effects of group membership on thinking and feeling could be established. Moede influenced Floyd Allport, whose series of investigations at Harvard University in the 1920s into whether group membership influences people's judgements definitively launched North American experimental social psychology. The idea of 'social facilitation' (that an individual's performance could be facilitated or impaired by the presence of others) remains one of the core topics of experimental social psychology. By 1924, Allport's book *Social Psychology* (1924) generalised the use of experimental methods for the first time to a broader range of social psychological questions. According to Edward Jones (1985) by the mid-1970s social psychology had become, from these roots, 'largely a North American phenomenon' (p. 47).

The European antecedents of social psychology included not only French crowd psychology (Le Bon, 1908 [1896]), but German 'Völkerpsychologie', espoused by Wilhelm Wundt, who started as a keen proponent of laboratory psychology in the 1860s (another candidate date, then, for the start of social psychology!). In his view, laboratory experiments were appropriate for addressing elementary mental functions such as perception, while Völkerpsychologie addressed 'those mental products created by a community of human life'. Wundt concluded that these could not be explained in terms 'merely of individual consciousness since they presuppose the reciprocal action of many' (Wundt, 1916, p. 2, quoted in Graumann, 1995, p. 301). Hence Wundt established a core principle of differentiation between individual and social psychology. A journal taking this sociocultural approach was established as early as 1860 (*Zeitschrift für Völkerpsychologie und Sprachwissenschaft*), dedicated to a 'psychology of societal man and of human society' (Graumann, 1995, p. 302): a fitting early definition of social psychology. Although this tradition did not survive directly, the more philosophical German tradition has continued to influence one version of European social psychology which places greater emphasis on units larger than the individual (notably groups), theory building, naturalistic methods of inquiry and the interpretation of meaning. In summary, it is clear that what we identify as the start of social psychology depends on what we regard as its core definition.

1.1   Summary

Section 1 has been about the beginnings of social psychology as a discipline and the influences that led to its emergence. Depending on what criteria are used, the discipline of social psychology is at least one hundred years old. There is not a clear-cut answer to the question of when it began because it depends on whether we look at its emergence in the scientific tradition or at how it continued to be a topic within philosophy. We have looked at the influences leading to the emergence of scientific psychology, the most significant development in the history of psychology, and have seen when experimental social psychology emerged from this tradition. Finally, the example of early German social psychology was used to illustrate geographical differences and identify the products of different traditions. It is clear that what we identify as the start of social psychology depends on what we regard as its core definition. Since this definition is contested, however, it is worth exploring the key variations further.

2   Two social psychologies

In the UK, the major contender for the title of mainstream social psychology is experimental social psychology, influenced as it has been by the North American tradition. In the *Blackwell Encyclopedia of Social Psychology*, Miles Hewstone and Antony Manstead, the British editors, define social psychology as 'the scientific study of the reciprocal influence of the individual and his or her social context' (1995, p. 588). But what is meant by 'scientific' here? A narrow definition might confine science to the laboratory, whereas a wider one would accommodate rigorous social psychological research in natural settings: for example, systematic observation and recording. Hewstone and Manstead make their position clear when they conclude that 'one can, at least, predict that social psychology will remain an empirical, primarily experimental, discipline, notwithstanding new challenges to its hard-earned scientific respectability' (1995, p. 594). Now, the second part of this prediction – the primarily experimental character of social psychology – looks less sure, especially in the UK. Whereas social psychology remains largely empirical, there has been a huge growth of research taking place in natural settings, using designs based not on experiment but on individual and group interviews, observations and analyses of spontaneously generated conversation and text.

So far my discussion has centred on the social psychology that emerged as a branch of psychology. This meant that, like psychology, it aspired to scientific status and was based on the individual as its conceptual object (an individualist paradigm). It is these two prior commitments that have shaped the dominant social psychology of the twentieth century. However, social psychology had the potential to be, not a branch of psychology, but an interdiscipline, trying to go beyond reductionist conceptions of both a psychological and a sociological nature. One of the themes of this book is how an effective social psychology can transcend the widespread tendency in the social and human sciences to reduce it to *either* individual *or* social explanations; a tendency usually referred to as individual–social dualism.

It is predictable perhaps that as a result of this pervasive dualism there has been a split in social psychology. In North America there are two social psychologies generally referred to as psychological social psychology (PSP) and sociological social psychology (SSP). (To complicate matters, SSP is often regarded as micro-sociology.) The psychological version is focused on the individual: 'PSP focuses on psychological processes of, and seeks to understand the impact of social stimuli on, individuals, and adopts a primarily experimental methodology ... [It] is the dominant field, in terms of impact, the amount of work published, graduate students trained and control over publications'. In contrast, 'SSP concentrates on the reciprocity of society and the individual, sees its fundamental task as the explanation of social interaction, and relies methodologically on naturalistic observation and surveys' (Hewstone and Manstead, 1995, p. 589). Examples of work in this tradition are symbolic interactionism and ethnomethodology (see Section 3.4). There is very little cross citation between these two areas and 'little or no overlap was found in research methods; textbooks, journals read, cited or published in; and academic departments in which doctorates were awarded' (Wilson and Schafer, 1978, quoted in Hewstone and Manstead, 1995, p. 589).

Contemporary British social psychology is creatively, if ambiguously, placed between mainstream North American and European traditions. Increasingly during the last twenty-five years, some distance from the North American experimental and individualist paradigm has developed, first through the influences of European traditions and second through the influence of sociology's work on interaction, language and identity. European traditions in social identity theory were brought into British psychology departments through Henri Tajfel's social group research (see Chapter 6). He summed up the European emphasis in the following terms: 'social psychology can and must include in its theoretical and research preoccupations a direct concern with the relation between human psychological functioning and the large-scale social processes and events which shape this functioning and are shaped by it'. Despite this aspiration, however, research in this tradition remains experimental and, as such, remains at the individual level (Tajfel, 1981, p. 7, quoted in Hewstone and Manstead 1995, p. 590). This observation raises important questions about the available methodologies in social psychology and their effects on its theoretical perspectives and objects of research (see Chapter 2). Certainly the dominance of the experimental tradition has reinforced social psychology's concentration on the individual and made it harder to hold in view the multiple ways in which individuals are socially situated.

The existence of two American social psychologies, one psychological, one sociological, has a recent parallel in British social psychology. This division was remarked on by the psychology panel of the Research Assessment Exercise (RAE) in 2001. The RAE takes place every five or six years and is a government-led evaluation of all research taking place in British higher education institutions. On British social psychology, the panel concluded:

> Unlike almost any other country, social psychology in the UK is divided into two camps. While there is a fair representation of conventionally empirical (and often experimental) social psychology, there is also an unusually strong representation of 'critical' social psychology in which discourse analysis or conversation analysis dominate. This diversity should be enriching and distinctive, but there appears to be little communication between these two camps. If UK social psychology is to profit from its distinctive composition, the conventional and critical areas need to find effective ways of communicating and collaborating.
>
> (HERO, 2001)

The approach to British social psychology called 'critical' in the quotation is, among other things, distinguished by its largely qualitative research in everyday social settings. It criticises how complex research questions can become reduced by turning them into laboratory-based questions (see Chapter 2). Critical social psychologists prefer to work with the complexity of people's experiences and meanings in their changing worlds. The critique is also partly about the idea of the individual that has tended to underpin experimental and quantitative social psychology.

2.1   Summary

In this brief treatment, I have described two origins of the major differences in social psychology: one disciplinary (emerging from either psychology or sociology) and one geographical (based primarily in North America or Europe – although there has been a lot of traffic between the two continents). The idea of 'individual–social dualism', and how it is reflected in the two social psychologies, was introduced. I showed how this dualism is also reflected in the current shape of social psychology in the UK. The differences in method referred to by the RAE panel have been a salient theme and are dealt with in detail in Chapter 2. However, in both disciplinary traditions and on both continents there have been many, often diverse, developments over the course of a century. The development of social psychology has been influenced by a series of critiques, which will be detailed further in Section 3.

3   Social psychology: roots and routes

In this section we trace the developments in social psychology from the early twentieth-century history already charted through to the current situation in UK social psychology, where there is a plurality of perspectives and methods unparalleled in its earlier history. The first three subsections below all focus on the development of psychological social psychology, since it is this history that has had the most long-standing and profound influence on what we see as social psychology today. Subsections 3.4 and 3.5 trace the influences from outside psychology; respectively from the American sociology called symbolic interactionism and the European traditions, German and French, which took account of social groups in shaping individual experience and action. The final two subsections (3.6 and 3.7) examine the impact of these and other critical trends in philosophy, social theory and other social sciences on contemporary social psychology in the UK.

3.1   Measurement without experiment

Not long after the establishment of experimental psychology, just before the First World War, another quantitative tradition emerged: psychometrics, meaning the measurement of psychological characteristics. It was claimed to be a revolution in psychology: 'a complete change can be traced in our science' said Hugo Munsterberg (1913, p. 10). There was already interest in measuring people's physical characteristics and comparing these to those of the whole population. Psychometrics, like experimental psychology, measured the individual extracted from his or her social context. Unlike experimental psychology, by developing measures for intelligence and personality, it had an applied emphasis right from the start.

Box 1.1   The Psychological Corporation

On 17 February 1922 the *New York Times* announced the new Psychological Corporation, whose aim was described as 'the application of psychology to business'. It referred to the 'impetus ... applied psychology received during the war when intelligence and other tests were designed to determine the fitness of soldiers'. The *New York Times* article continued 'Some of the backers of the Psychological Corporation believe that it would be possible to increase by $70,000,000,000 the national wealth each year by properly fitting every man, woman and child to the kind of work each could best perform'
(Journal of the National Institute for Industrial Psychology, 17 February 1922, vol. I, p. 76)

There was a parallel to these developments in psychological social psychology. Social psychometrics, the measurement of reported attitudes, opinions, beliefs and behaviours, soon followed general psychometrics. Today it is probably the most commonly practised form of social psychology and this is because of its applied emphasis. With a measuring device of this kind, whole populations can be sampled to discover prevailing attitudes and behaviours in areas of concern, such as young people's views on smoking and their reported smoking behaviour. Not surprisingly, the recent area called health psychology consists predominantly of research based on social psychometrics, often useful to, if not funded by, governments and retail or campaign organisations.

Box 1.2   The social distance scale and stereotyping

In the late 1920s, the American social psychologist Emory Bogardus developed the 'social distance scale', one of the first attitude scales (see Bogardus, 1933). It assessed attitudes toward various racial and ethnic groups on a set of questions varying according to social distance. For example, it asked 'Are you willing to permit X to live in your country?' and 'Would you permit your child to marry X?'. This period in North American history was a time of great waves of immigration from Europe, which created widespread interest in how immigrants were to be integrated.

A parallel strand of research, laboratory-based, used first-year Princeton undergraduates (presumably they were mainly white, male and middle class) to study beliefs about people from a variety of national and ethnic groups (Katz and Braly, 1933). Thus began the tradition of social psychological research into stereotyping (see Chapter 6 of this book), and the use of undergraduates as representative of people more generally.

Both of these early traditions took individuals as their objects and units of study. Allport was quite explicit about this. At the beginning of his influential book *Social Psychology* he points out that, although readers might expect social psychology to be about social relations, his goal was to explain social behaviour in terms of individual behaviour 'to adhere to the psychological (that is the individual) viewpoint'. He justifies this by arguing that 'only within the individual can we find the behaviour mechanisms and the consciousness which are fundamental in the interactions between individuals' (1924, p. v). We can see in this an early – and influential – statement of the principle informing North American *psychological* social psychology.

3.2   Social intervention or science

Whereas the First World War influenced the growth of psychometrics, the Second World War encouraged social psychology. In 1979, Dorwin Cartwright claimed that the turmoil leading up to this war and the war itself were 'the most important single influence on the development of social psychology up to the present' (1979, p. 84). The persecution of Jews and other groups defined as inferior made salient pressing global problems about conflict among groups, racial hatred, national identity, authoritarianism and leadership. More prosaically, the American government was interested in how to maintain morale among both troops and the domestic population. In practical terms, scores of Jewish intellectuals, trained in German theoretical traditions, fled Europe and made their homes in the USA and, to a lesser extent, the UK.

Box 1.3   Kurt Lewin

When Hitler became Chancellor of Germany in 1933, Kurt Lewin, a Jewish German social psychologist who was visiting the USA in the early 1930s, decided to remain there. He was a lifelong advocate of the idea that psychology should be relevant to social reform. During the Second World War, he worked on ways to change people's food habits. He analysed the effects of group participation in decision making and evaluated psychological warfare activities. Later, and until his death in 1947, he was involved in research designed to change prejudice and improve intergroup relations. He is probably best known for his field study, undertaken in 1939, of three different styles of leadership: autocratic, democratic and *laissez-faire* (see Lewin et al., 1939). These categories influenced social science thinking and interventions, for example, in management training, and also entered common-sense language, for example, in relation to parenting styles. Lewin also introduced the term 'action research' to describe research engaged in intervening in real social problems.

Despite Lewin's influence, a split was developing in American social psychology between those who believed in a social psychology dedicated to social reform and those who believed that it should be a neutral and objective science. With his death, there remained few influential voices advocating the integration of theory, research and social action. 'A split developed that widened into a chasm' (Deutsch, 1975,   p. 2). The outcome was an academic social psychology that held application and action in low esteem and remained isolated within the universities. 'A perusal of the major social psychology journals of the 1950s and 1960s reveals a concentration of research on topics such as attitudes, communication processes, group processes and leadership, almost exclusively within a laboratory setting' (Pancer, 1997, p. 153). Methodologically the picture was even starker: 'By 1965, the experimental approach was the queen of methods. In fact, in some quarters it was vaguely disrespectful to even consider using any other method' (Hendrick, 1977, p. 20, quoted in Pancer, 1997, p. 153). Seventy-five per cent of the articles published in three major social psychological journals in 1980 and 1985 were based on investigations which used American undergraduate students as the sole research participants. Only 17 per cent of the studies used non students (Sears, 1986, quoted in Pancer, 1997, p. 157). This picture is still reflected in most North American social psychology textbooks, despite the challenge to the dominance of the experimental method in social psychology that was looming.

_____ *Pause for reflection* _____

What are the potential problems of basing psychological knowledge on almost exclusively undergraduate populations? What age groups are probably not included? What other groups? For what kinds of research might it be appropriate and inappropriate?

3.3   The crisis in social psychology

In 1967, an American social psychologist called Kenneth Ring published an article in the *Journal of Experimental Social Psychology* entitled 'Experimental social psychology: some sober questions about some frivolous values'. It was the first salvo in an attack on the values of experimental social psychology that continued throughout the 1970s. Ring distinguished three kinds of social psychology: a humanistic action-orientated one (the kind that Lewin espoused and that lost out in the post-Second World War split), a scientific social psychology conducted largely in the laboratory and uninterested in social relevance, and a 'fun and games' social psychology that engaged in clever experiments and produced counter-intuitive findings of questionable relevance. Ring concluded that social psychology was 'in a state of profound intellectual disarray' (1967, p. 119). Over the following decade, this came to be called 'the crisis' in social psychology.

Two charges dominated the next decade of criticism of social psychology. The first decried the use of experimental methods that manipulated variables, deceived participants and produced reductive and irrelevant findings (for example, McGuire 1973; Silverman, 1977). The second objected to the individualism of social psychology (Sampson, 1977; Steiner, 1974). Edward Sampson linked social psychology's individualism to the American cultural ideal of 'self-contained individualism' in which 'a substantial burden of personal and social responsibility for success and failure is placed on the individual within an individualistic perspective' (Sampson, 1977, p. 779).

There are different positions about the crisis and its effects. One historian of the period who favours experimental social psychology maintains that there was never really a crisis and that changes were not needed (Jones, 1985). Others believe that improvements in the sophistication of methods resolved the crisis (Reich, 1981). Perhaps the crisis faded but informed a new generation of critiques of psychology based on the allegation that it fosters a dehumanising vision of human beings and that it ignores real world settings. Both of these allegations were aimed at psychology in general, but they have particular relevance for social psychology. It is to these that we now turn.

3.4   Sociological social psychology

Earlier in this chapter, I distinguished between psychological and sociological social psychology (PSP and SSP) and since then we have followed the fortunes of the former in North America where its influence largely originated. Before moving to consider Europe, it is worth reviewing the emergence (also in the

USA) of SSP, because this has had considerable influence on the current critical qualitative tradition in the UK. Its origins go back to William James (1981 [1890]) and his thinking about social selves.

George Herbert Mead, who taught at the University of Chicago between 1893 and 1931, is the most prominent early theorist in sociological social psychology, especially in symbolic interactionist theory, which is almost synonymous with early SSP (Mead, 1934). The name 'symbolic interactionism' already tells us that the emphasis in this theory lies in two related claims: the importance of symbols for understanding individuals (especially language) and of interaction.

Box 1.4   The Chicago School

I knew that G.H. Mead was part of the 'Chicago School' and that this is an influential tradition in Sociology, so I decided to pursue my questions, not through the books on my shelves, but on the web. This is how I did it. It's simple. Try it yourself to see what you find. First I 'Googled' three words: Chicago School sociology. One result was as follows: (http://en.wikipedia.org/wiki/Chicago School (Sociology)). There I found a reference to a paper by Howard Becker, a later sociologist of the Chicago School, called 'The Chicago School – so called'. Becker said that G.H. Mead was one of the founders of the first period of the Chicago School, in the 1920s and 1930s, as a result of which it came to be more or less equated with symbolic interactionism. The second period of its fame was after the Second World War. Most Chicago School researchers pursued ethnographic work in natural settings, but Becker cites the case of William Ogburn, a largely statistical sociologist, who was influential in persuading the American government that what it needed from sociological research was 'quantitative, empirical in a narrow sense and scientific in an equally narrow sense' (Becker, 1999, p. 3). (You can also find this article on Becker's homepage: home.earthlink.net/~hsbecker/.)

For the purposes of this chapter, I draw two points from this web reading. The first is that sociology was afflicted, like social psychology, by arguments between quantitative and qualitative research. The second is that sociologists of the symbolic interactionist school (like Becker, but see also Garfinkel and Goffman below) have addressed a subject matter that is social psychological.

In Mead's view, because the social system precedes any given individual, individuals are always already immersed in language as they engage in experience and action. Moreover, it is through language that a person internalises the role of the other. Thus the self is made up not only of an 'I', the subject of language, but also a 'me', positioned as the object of other people's meanings and, through internalisation, one's own. This distinction between I and me (which actually originated with William James in 1890) is basic to symbolic interactionist theory of the individual and the self, which has contributed to the idea of a person formed through symbolically based interaction with others and therefore inevitably social (see Chapter 5).

Methods in SSP have varied and included self report measures, but most research has been carried out in natural settings. Harold Garfinkel famously got his students to go back home at the end of term and act as if they were lodgers rather than family members (Garfinkel, 1967). Not surprisingly, this behaviour was bizarre and disturbing to the parents (such research would probably not pass ethical procedures now). The idea was to produce 'normative disruption': that is, experiments to reveal the unstated rules of social roles by breaching them. Garfinkel conducted a series of so-called 'breaching experiments'. They were a key strategy in ethnomethodology, which is the study of lay methods used in everyday life to make sense of what is happening. The idea that people were situated in social contexts was modified to emphasise the idea of 'definition of the situation'. In other words, it was not people's actual situation that mattered, but how they defined it: meaning was the key to people's action in social situations.

Box 1.5   Being a marihuana user

Howard Becker analysed extracts from interviews with marihuana users and concluded that 'an individual will be able to use marihuana for pleasure only when he goes through a process of learning to conceive of it as an object which can be used in this way' (Becker, 1972 [1967], p. 508). He went on to compare his conclusions with 'those [theories] which ascribe marihuana use to motives or predispositions rooted deep in individual behaviour'. In contrast, he says, 'the evidence makes it clear that marihuana use for pleasure can occur only when the process described above [that is, learning to conceive of the activity in a particular way] is undergone and cannot occur without it'. In a direct critique of static individualistic theories, Becker compares his conclusions with the kind of theories about individuals which assume that people have a stable and consistent makeup, ways of responding that predetermine their actions in a given situation. In contrast, his explanation of individual action here is not based on assumptions of a static and asocial individual with inherent dispositions and motivation, but one where individual experiences are derived from social meanings, themselves largely shaped by language.

Following in the tradition of the Chicago School, Erving Goffman (1959) emphasised the influence of interaction in forming the self. His approach was based on the idea that, choose it or not, everyone is giving out impressions of self to others who are necessarily seeking these. This is the basis of all interactions, which in turn produce selves (see Chapter 5). With his detailed attention to how interaction is kept going, he introduced forms of interaction analysis which have informed current discourse and conversation analysis.

_____ *Pause for reflection* _____

At this move from one historical epoch to another, I have paused to notice a change in my own frame of reference. It is a change from 'history' to 'experience' (from information about the past that I have learned about, to the actual encounters I have had and which have influenced my values). I can go to my bookshelf and pick out copies of some of the key texts. I warm further to my task! What is your personal relationship to this material?

Even the older history and the differences of opinion that it holds will reverberate through your value system and leave feelings of 'pro' and 'anti' at various points. As we move closer to the contemporary state of British social psychology, influenced by movements that may well have influenced your life, such as feminism, remember to pay attention to your subjective responses to the ideas.

3.5 European social psychology

In 1989, the *European Journal of Social Psychology* had a special issue on the state of social psychology. In the introduction, two European social psychologists, John Rijsman and Wolfgang Stroebe, evaluated the scene. They reviewed the American 'crisis' and remarked:

> It is certainly no coincidence that the ascent of European social psychology as a strong force in the field also happened during the seventies. By sapping the self-confidence of North American social psychology, the crisis made researchers receptive for new and different solutions which Europeans were ready to provide. Thus, the work on intergroup conflict of Tajfel and his colleagues in Bristol and the research on minority influence by Moscovici and his colleagues in Paris had an immediate impact on the field and stimulated a great deal of further research on both sides of the Atlantic. These were the first examples of post-war research traditions that had originated in Europe being taken up by Americans. But while the theoretical ideas were new, the research conducted to test these ideas was completely traditional.
>
> (Rijsman and Stroebe, 1989, pp. 340–1)

Their last point is a significant one and means that there is one further important step to document in the recent transformations of British social psychology: the move from experimental to field methods.

Just before moving on there, though, it is worth reproducing in some detail Rijsman's and Stroebe's characterisation of the two social psychologies at the end of the 1980s. First, they defined the difference between the old and new paradigms in terms of their adoption of a 'natural science approach': 'Central to this paradigm is the hypothetico-deductive approach and the belief in internal causal mechanisms that can be traced through rigorous empirical research' (Rijsman and Stroebe, 1989, p. 341). They cite Rom Harré (a British philosopher pursuing social psychological topics) and Kenneth Gergen (an American social constructionist) as exponents of the new paradigm who, although they differ in other ways, agree in rejecting these starting points. They go on to describe a new epistemology (theory of knowledge) in which theory and truth have a different status:

> Truth is no longer the revelation of the world as it is to privileged observers and theory the best description of this truth by privileged writers. No, theory and truth become forms of discourse which reflect the embeddedness in social practice of those who speak and which invite others to engage in similar forms of social life.

> Theories therefore are no longer judged on their accuracy about the previously
> hidden world, but on their social intelligibility and power to invite forms of
> conduct which enact the truth that they project on the world.
>
> (Rijsman and Stroebe, 1989, p. 341)

Their conclusion points to the radical effect of this shift on social psychology:
'This self reflexive attitude towards science also led them [the exponents of the
new paradigm] to redefine the topic of social psychology and the meaning of
research in it'. They go on to characterise this new paradigm:

> Social behaviour, they propose, should itself be seen as the discursive activity
> leading to the construction of meaning, and we are invited to study things like the
> ideological function of thought, rules of conversation, configurations of content
> etc. Of course, the research practices appropriate for such an endeavour are
> certainly not confined to experimentation, which itself is seen as a rhetorical
> device in the scientific claim of truth.
>
> (Rijsman and Stroebe, 1989, p. 341)

This is a useful description of the more recent social psychology that has
burgeoned on the British scene, ushered in by Jonathan Potter's and Margaret
Wetherell's classic book *Discourse and Social Psychology: Beyond Attitudes
and Behaviour* (1987; and see Chapter 2 of this book for further detail). They
introduced discourse analysis into social psychology, drawing on two different
traditions, one European and the other American. European discourse analysis
originated in the work of Michel Foucault, whose historical work studied the
emergence and effects of discourses (systems of meaning), such as madness,
punishment and sexuality. This macro, socio-historical approach was
complemented in the work of Potter and Wetherell (1987) by drawing from
the American SSP tradition which focused on micro interactions and the
production of meanings in everyday interaction.

Potter and Wetherell based their introduction of discourse into social
psychology on a trenchant criticism of the way that the concept of attitude had
come to dominate social psychology. This was a concept that located attitudes
in the minds of individuals. So where else do meanings come from? Potter and
Wetherell located them in the social world, outside the mind, calling them
discourses. These are used by people in everyday interaction and written
texts. They concentrated not on mental or linguistic structures but on
processes, on what people do with language and discourse and the effects that
they achieve with it. They challenged the assumption that people use
language simply to communicate messages from one mind to another. Rather,
people use language in ways that construct versions of the world of objects,
subjects and social relations. These constructions (like 'attitudes') are not fixed
but changing, depending on the context of use. Potter and Wetherell
introduced the idea of 'interpretative repertoires' (from Gilbert and
Mulkay, 1984), a concept that helped to make the concept of discourse (very
general and used in many different ways) more amenable to empirical
research. They defined interpretative repertoires as 'basically a lexicon or
register of terms and metaphors drawn upon to characterize and evaluate
actions and events' (Potter and Wetherell, 1987, p. 138).

Did you notice, reading through the history so far, that all the influential names (until we got to Margaret Wetherell) were those of men? There had been some women working in social psychology, but they were scarce. What effects might this have had on social psychology? From the 1980s, in the UK, this changed with the influence of feminism.

Figure 1.1   Influential figures in social psychology. From left to right: Mead, Allport, Lewin, Garfinkel and Wetherell

3.6   Feminist social psychology

Until the development of 1970s feminism, the history of psychology had been one in which women, researched almost exclusively by male psychologists, were treated as the 'other' and their difference from the male norm often regarded as problematic. For example, the American developmental psychologist Lawrence Kohlberg (1958), researching moral reasoning, proposed a model involving six sequential stages. The sixth – universal ethical principles – represented the highest achievement of moral development. His theory was largely based on boys and the main characters in his moral dilemmas were men. According to Kohlberg, far fewer women than men reached the highest stage of moral development. With the development of feminism, Carol Gilligan's work on women's moral reasoning was able to question Kohlberg's findings at every level (Gilligan, 1982). She pointed out that Kohlberg regarded as inferior the kinds of moral reasoning based on situated relationships, as opposed to abstract principles which were more often used by men. Her work, followed by many other feminists, has led to a climate in which women's morality can be valued in its own right, rather than be judged by so-called universal standards that were based on male norms.

In considering research on moral development, I have introduced an example that, strictly speaking, is located in developmental, not social psychology. But doesn't it sound like a social psychological topic? The artificial divisions within and between disciplines and sub-disciplines can be unfortunate in the way that they imply a separation; one that is undesirable for studying real world issues which do not come discipline-shaped.

The example of Gilligan's work illustrates the interrelationship among the three challenges that feminist psychology represented to the traditional versions of psychology and social psychology. Wendy and Rex Stainton Rogers (2001, p. 147) summarise these as follows:

- challenges to psychology's epistemology – its assumption about what constitutes knowledge

- challenges to psychology's modes of enquiry – the methods and approaches psychologists use to gain empirical evidence

- challenges to psychology's subject matter – the topics and issues it studies.

Feminist psychology is social, as a glance through the volumes of its influential international journal *Feminism and Psychology* will demonstrate. Its origins were also explicitly political, 'informed by the political goals of the feminist movement' (Wilkinson, 1997, p. 247), and these goals boiled down to two things.

According to Sue Wilkinson, first, women should be listened to by social psychology researchers. Women were omitted in many major studies (like Kohlberg's, and also Erik Erikson's work (1980) on lifespan development). If women were to have their voices heard and respected, this would involve a change of methods too, from ones that tightly set the terms of the research exchange to methods that were open to receiving the meanings and experiences of women without constraints. This has meant a significant, although not total, shift from quantitative to qualitative research methods.

Second, 'feminism recognizes the need for social change on behalf of women' (Wilkinson, 1997, p. 248). Wilkinson regrets the fact that, as feminist psychology has entered the mainstream professional institutions, it has lost sight of social change for women as a primary goal. She instances the battle over naming that took place in the Psychological Societies of most of the English-speaking countries (UK, USA, Australia, Canada and New Zealand) where the term 'Feminist Psychology' was not allowed, and the sections were usually called 'Women and Psychology' or 'Psychology of Women' instead (as in the case of the section in the British Psychological Society, established in 1987). She argues that:

> Much of 'psychology of women' challenges neither the institutions and practices of psychology, nor the dominant conceptions of women which the discipline constructs and promotes. It does not engage with the damage psychology has done to many women's lives, nor does it struggle to end psychology's continuing oppressions.
>
> (Wilkinson, 1997, p. 248)

An important example of this damage has been the way that mainstream psychology pathologised femininity, from women's reproductive capacities (Ussher, 1989) to psychological characteristics (see Box 1.6), in effect going along with the dominant wider beliefs that women were inferior to men.

Box 1.6   Psychology constructs the Female

In 1968, in a classic early feminist intervention into the politics of psychology, the American psychologist Naomi Weisstein argued that women are characterised by psychology as:

> Inconsistent, emotionally unstable, lacking in a strong conscience or superego, weaker, 'nurturant' rather than productive, 'intuitive' rather than intelligent, and, if they are at all 'normal', suited to the home and the family. In short, the list adds up to a typical minority group stereotype of inferiority.
> (Weisstein, 1993 [1968], p. 207, quoted in Wilkinson, 1997, p. 251)

———————————————— Pause for reflection ————————————————

Weisstein was writing nearly forty years ago and I wonder if it is still true of psychology's constructions. What does it suggest about the two-way traffic between wider (in this case, sexist) beliefs in society and the assumptions that exist within the discipline?

What Wilkinson says raises the issue of how social change occurs. My view of change – within psychology as within any institution – emphasises the processes. I see it happening gradually, with reversals and resistances, and not predictably in one direction as feminism or other political causes would like. In this light, I see enormous changes in social psychology that have been partly achieved by the wide variety of feminist perspectives that abound. For example:

- The question of power relations within research has become very prominent. Although this is most evident in qualitative research, it has begun to affect other paradigms too. Ethical practices in research have been transformed (see Chapter 2 in this book).

- The principle of listening to people's meanings and experiences is central to the shift in research paradigms that has taken place and has been a guiding factor in qualitative research design. This has had certain problems as well as strengths. It promotes reluctance to do anything with the accounts that women (and other groups) provide and can lead to descriptive data analysis that hardly goes beyond the data themselves.

- The subject matters of social psychology are now more likely to derive from real world issues again, especially questions of how inequalities are reproduced and resisted at the psychological and group levels.

- The idea of the autonomous individual, criticised as a very masculine notion, has been influentially contested. There is a new emphasis on relationship and its centrality to the self.

More broadly, attention to the status of women in psychology puts difference on the agenda – and not only gender difference. Those connected to ethnicity, class and sexuality could be approached in similar ways. None of these achievements are the sole responsibility of feminist social psychology, as will become clear in the following section.

3.7 Critical social psychology

In the late twentieth century, there was a fashion in social science theory for arguments that emphasise the change from previous world views: postmodernism, poststructuralism and postcolonialism are significant exemplars. These have been taken up by critical psychology. The idea of 'critique' or 'critical' always begs the question of what went before what is being critiqued. Modernism means many different things, but in psychology, like philosophy, it referred to an Enlightenment view of 'man' that dominated in Western thought from the seventeenth century. This model of human being was based not only on a masculine ideal but on a white middle-class European notion of human qualities. Rational knowledge was pre-eminent. Critiques of the treatment of the individual in psychology point out that psychology's notion of the individual has not only assumed but reproduced the belief that individuals are autonomous agents, unitary and singular and rationally governed by conscious intention.

Poststructuralism, closely associated with the work of Foucault (for example, Foucault, 1970; Gordon 1980), has been influential in questioning the 'truth' of the notion of the individual as it has been passed down to us. *Changing the Subject*, a British-authored book, provided an early and influential critique of psychology from this perspective:

> Our aim is to demonstrate that the individual is not a fixed or given entity, but rather a particular product of historically specific practices of social regulation. We do not accept the innocence of theory, especially when it seeks impunity in the name of science. All theory is conditioned by historically specific circumstances and has definite effects on social existence.
>
> (Henriques et al., 1984, p. 12)

The idea of self-contained, self-defining individuals has been comprehensively challenged from many different starting points (see Chapter 5 in this book). The critique quoted above, emphasising the way individuals have been formed within practices of social regulation, has been applied to psychology through the idea of the 'psy complex'. This refers to all the ways that the discipline of psychology (and related areas like psychoanalysis) has been involved in shaping people's practices and understandings of themselves through its expert knowledge and recommendations to governments and other institutions. Nikolas Rose's (1990) work is exemplary. He argues that

> Our intimate lives, our feelings, desires and aspirations seem quintessentially personal ... our mental states, subjective experiences and intimate relationships offer themselves as perhaps the only place where we can locate our real private selves. There is, no doubt, much comfort to be afforded by such a belief. But it is profoundly misleading.

Our personalities, subjectivities, and 'relationships' are not private matters, if this implies that they are not the objects of power. On the contrary, they are intensively governed.

(Rose, 1990, p. 1)

Rose considers in detail the way that the 'psy' disciplines were central in how this regulation of subjectivities was accomplished in factories, business organisations, the military, schools and homes.

Box 1.7   From the 'individual' to 'subjectivity' in social psychology

Through changing research methods and questions it is possible to generate alternative visions of the individual. Critical social psychology is largely in agreement in emphasising the following ways of thinking about individuals as:

- socially and historically located (situatedness)
- relational (influence of others within the self)
- dynamic and conflictual (change and tensions among people's plural identities)
- embodied (bodies expressing social meaning)
- discursive (positioned in socially available meanings and practices).

Since the individual is the object that defines the discipline of psychology, this is a radical move indeed. To signal the critique of the whole notion of the individual, a different term is usually employed: subjectivity. This is often confusing to psychologists who understand it as a derogatory term, the opposite of objectivity. In *Changing the Subject*, which introduced the term subjectivity (along with poststructuralism) to psychologists, it was summed up as follows: 'we use subjectivity to refer to individuality and self-awareness – the condition of being subject – but understand in this usage that subjects are dynamic and multiple, always positioned in relation to discourses and practices and produced by these' (Henriques et al., 1984, p. 3).

The humanist individual of modernism – which was the idea of the individual adopted by most twentieth-century psychology – was an agent. In other words, modernism saw human beings as having free will, exercising intention, making decisions and acting on them, albeit in the context of constraints. This account is called into question by an emphasis on people as being formed by social structures and positioned in discourses and practices in such a way that opportunities to exercise agency are almost non-existent. Therefore, the new 'post' tendencies in social theory question this account. Yet if power relations and discourses position people so influentially, where does their agency reside? How do they exercise choices? This illustrates how the dualism of agency and structure in social and psychological explanations continues to dog social psychology too (see Section 4.4).

These critiques have also asked the elusive question of what social psychology should be achieving or aspiring to achieve. A value question of this kind is sometimes taken to be outside the scope of intellectual enquiry, the idea being that knowledge is important for its own sake and can be disinterested. This position has been challenged by theories of knowledge that emphasise the impossibility of knowers – for my purposes here, scientists and researchers – being able to stand outside their locations in history, culture and power relations. Foucault's legacy has been to document the specific ways in which all knowledge has effects that, because of the power relations that are inseparable from it, bear on people's lives, regulate their actions and infuse their characters. Social psychology is, of course, no exception. Indeed, because of its adherence to scientificity and the authority that goes with it, and because of its policy relevance, social psychology's effects can be very powerful. One example is social psychology's influence on how prejudice is understood (see Chapter 6 in this book) and its implications for how to regulate it. In this light it is inadequate to plead scientific neutrality. Rather it behoves social psychologists, like all knowledge producers, to enquire deeply into what factors shape their endeavours and what effects these have. One of the themes throughout this book is therefore that of power relations.

3.8   Summary

In Section 3, the main new trends in social psychology were explored under seven different headings. While focusing on the UK, the influences from the USA and continental Europe on trends in British social psychology have also been shown. The emphasis has been on the diversity of approaches and methods and the outside influences that have affected the discipline at different times – such as the Second World War; and the political critiques that emerged in the 1960s. The section introduced the method of social psychometrics and what it has in common with the experimental method in social psychology. I identified the main features in the growth of American psychological social psychology, tensions between laboratory-based and socially involved research, and the growing dominance of the experimental approach. The key features of 'the crisis' in social psychology, and its subsequent effects, were introduced. I also looked at the range of challenges that feminist social psychology has posed to the established discipline and at its subsequent influences.

4   Four interrogative themes

The transformations occasioned in British social psychology as a result of these historical trends and criticisms that started over thirty years ago have led to the identification of four overarching themes that run throughout this book: power relations, situated knowledges, individual–society dualism and agency or structure in explanations of human action. We call these 'interrogative themes' in order to emphasise the way in which we hope to use them: namely, to interrogate a set of value issues that permeate social psychology and otherwise might not get noticed, yet have effects that matter. As we introduce the substantive topics that social psychology concerns itself with, we shall highlight one or another of these interrogative themes when they appear most relevant to the topic. This will help you, the reader, to step back from the information and begin to understand how it came to be and how it is linked to the wider forces at work in its production.

4.1 Power relations

I have already summarised the argument that power relations are central in the way that all knowledge gets produced, interpreted and taken up. Foucault changed the understanding of power from something that is a property of certain individuals or positions to a dynamic that is present in all relations, all practices and all knowledges. It is a two-way dynamic, not just something that the powerful impose on the powerless. In this view, power is not equated with oppression; indeed, it is 'positive', not in the value judgement sense but in the wider sense that it has effects. Whether these effects are beneficial or malign (or both) is an empirical question that has to be addressed in relation to the specific case.

At what levels do we therefore need to attend to power relations in social psychology? Traditionally, when science was defined as neutral and therefore outside power relations, power was not addressed at all and, as has been argued widely since, could be exercised all the more unaccountably for its invisibility. Questions of power were first raised in relation to the deception of subjects (as participants were called at the time) in the name of science: for example, in Stanley Milgram's (1965) work (see Chapter 2 for a detailed exploration). The specific focus was on power relations between the scientist and participants, many of whom performed, as they believed, sadistic and harmful acts on the instruction of the scientist. Ethical guidelines in social psychology are hugely influenced by this rather shameful aspect of its history. A more routine example is the use of stooges, members of a team of experimenters instructed to act as if they are a subject in the experiment in order to establish one of the experimental conditions. For example, in studies of compliance, stooges give wrong answers in order to see if subjects will go along with them.

However, these power relations are only the most obvious and accessible. Radical psychologists first pointed to the objectification and stigmatisation of, for example, mental health patients by psychologists and psychiatrists. Similar critiques have been aimed at clinical psychoanalysis, because of the expert power of the analyst to interpret the patient's experience. The question of who has the power to interpret people's experience applies to all social psychological research. It is a political and ethical question because in the process of giving meaning to events and accounts, we evaluate them. Since it is impossible to avoid this process, we need to be careful how we base interpretations on evidence. Also, we must interrogate how that evidence and those meanings came to be produced; within what assumptions and power relations. In this book we try to hold in mind the many levels at which power relations operate when we situate our topics historically and critically.

4.2   Situated knowledges

One specific way in which power operates in the production of knowledge is through the over-generalisation of claims based on findings that necessarily are situation-specific. The emphasis on knowledge that is situation-specific leads to use of the plural: different knowledges produced in different situations. Donna Haraway's (1991) coinage of the term 'situated knowledges' captures these principles. Once aware of this issue, you will notice how often experiments based on a sample of North American college students are used to make universal claims about, for example, conformity, helping behaviour, cognitive bias or interpersonal attraction. These claims are widespread, not by mistake, but because they are legitimated by a coherent set of principles governing the use of statistical samples. The idea is that if you derive a sample whose numbers and distribution are statistically valid, then the social location of your participants will not affect your findings, especially since – as we have seen in the American experimental tradition – the focus is on individual cognitions, which are assumed to have a kind of universality. These principles derive from physics, on which early psychological experiments were based (and called 'psychophysics' in the early twentieth century). When inanimate physical objects were manipulated in the laboratory, it could reliably be assumed that the consequent effects were generalisable to all other objects of the same category with the same properties (although physics has since modified this assumption).

Box 1.8   Demand characteristics

An example of demand characteristics in interview methodology came to my attention just recently in conversation with a social psychologist researching into lesbian and gay lifestyles. In response to a research literature that foregrounds the differences from the assumed norm in lesbian and gay lifestyles (gay bars, AIDS, assisted reproduction, the threat of homophobia), she wanted to find out about their ordinary everyday lives: in other words, about ways in which they probably did not differ from heterosexuals. She chose a sample of adult gay men and lesbians and encouraged them to talk in open-ended ways without specifying a research question. When she analysed themes in the resulting data, they were about issues specific to being lesbian or gay, such as discrimination and coming out at work. I wondered if this was to do with the fact that they all knew that she was specifically interviewing gays and lesbians and therefore focused on these topics. The participants knew because research ethics requires that researchers give advance information about the area of their research, but in doing so, she necessarily framed their responses. It would have been difficult to change the 'demand characteristics' of the interview without either talking to interviewees drawn from a more general sample and being very non-specific about her research purposes (would it have still qualified as informed consent?) or emphasising why she wanted to know specifically about their everyday lives (running the risk of even more explicit demand characteristics!).

The identity of the researcher also plays into demand characteristics. If interviewees knew that the interviewer was herself lesbian, they might be more likely to talk about aspects of their lives that were clearly affected by this aspect of their identity. On the other hand, they might feel more constrained by someone they see as an insider who might be more, not less, judgemental because of her own commitments. And if they assumed that she was heterosexual, would the danger be that they would leave aside those aspects of their lifestyle associated with being lesbian, perhaps assuming that the researcher would not understand their experiences?

Perhaps it now seems obvious that people do not behave like objects in the laboratory. However, social psychology, because of its adherence to a scientific paradigm, has been slow to take into account the many and complex ways in which researching people cannot rely on natural science methods. The key difference is that people, unlike inanimate objects, negotiate meaning in relation to their situation with other participants in the setting. The concept of demand characteristics (see Box 1.8) describes cues in the experimental setting that can lead to bias. Likewise, experimenter effects refer to ways in which researchers act unintentionally to affect outcomes. The introduction of these ideas into experimental psychology testifies to the limitations of the ideas of objectivity and control in experiments with people. However, they are only a partial acknowledgement of the dynamics of the experimental setting. Although this problem has been most acute in experimental social psychology, it also affects interviewing and observation methods.

Clearly knowledge production needs to be situated at the level of each and every piece of research. Who is providing the data? What have participants been told about the research? What do they make of what they have been told? What differences in social identity may be salient in the relation between researcher and researched (sexuality – as in the case above – sex, 'race', age, class, occupational role, for example) and with what effects? What are the salient features of each participant that situate them socially, and what difference will this make to how they make sense of the research task? It also needs to be situated at the level of historical changes in culture, values and salient social issues (in the making of which social psychology may or may not have had a hand).

One of the implications of this argument is that methods are highly influential in the knowledges that are produced. Acknowledging the importance of situated knowledges also means situating social psychology within a set of broad historical changes, as this chapter has done. There is a tendency to see science as an endeavour that progresses through building up a series of findings into general principles that apply permanently. Even if this were a safe assumption for the natural sciences, it is certainly not the case for social psychology, whose object is a constantly changing one. Moreover, to complicate matters further, social psychology affects how people make sense of their everyday lives and so changes the very terrain that it is meant to understand.

The 2006 replication on UK television of the Milgram obedience to authority experiments, conducted originally in 1971 in the US, provides an example. (I discuss Stanley Milgram's experiments in detail in Chapter 2 of this book.)

Derren Brown, a popular magician and hypnotist in the UK, staged the principal experiment in his television show *The Heist* (2006), reproducing a version of the social psychology of obedience for millions of viewers. This made widely available the message that, despite obvious ethical objections, the average person would harm someone if they were under instruction from a person in authority. People apply such messages to themselves and to others and they are disseminated into the wider culture. Some of the participants in the 2006 television show had heard of the original experiments and this would have affected the way in which they made sense of their participation in the replicated experiments, whether it was to believe that their obedience to authority was normal and unavoidable, or whether it was to prove the original findings were wrong in their case. In addition, wider cultural knowledge about obedience to authority would have been indirectly affected by the dramatic findings of the Milgram experiments, even for those participants who had not heard of them.

_____ *Pause for reflection* _____

You might be tempted to conclude that the principle of situated knowledges means that social psychological research is invalid. What other conclusions could you draw? I think that there are still criteria by which better and worse knowledge can be evaluated. These require a continual and open process of debate. To generate this, researchers need to situate themselves and their approaches, to acknowledge the messiness of their data and the provisionality of their conclusions.

4.3   Individual–society dualism

The theme of whether individual or society is privileged in the explanation of social psychological phenomena is an enduring one deriving from the wider dualism of explanations that have characterised Western thought since the Enlightenment. We have seen it, for example, in the American split between psychological and sociological social psychology, and more recently in Europe between cognitive and discursive explanations of social behaviour. The dualism is evident throughout the history that has been traced in this chapter. We saw it in Wundt's distinction between individual consciousness and community life (Section 1) and again at the beginning of Section 2 where Hewstone and Manstead define social psychology in terms of the individual, an entity that reciprocally interacts with social context. Twentieth-century social and human science was continually compromised by this dualism. I drew attention to it above when discussing the early influential text in Allport's *Social Psychology* (1924). Individual–society dualism often manifested in a reduction of explanation to either biological (often genetic) or social causes. Sometimes 'both/and' explanations also suffer from this dualism because they behave as if there is no other level of explanation, only an 'interaction' between biological and social factors. Genuinely social psychological explanations get squeezed out.

Box 1.9   Heredity versus environment in the intelligence debate

The example of intelligence is one of the most politically significant debates and was particularly salient in the 1960s and 1970s. Psychologists who believed in the influence of a genetic component to intelligence, such as Hans Eysenck in the UK and Arthur Jensen in the US, argued with those – often sociologists – who believed that the influence of a growing child's environment was so important as to nullify any direct genetic influence. The political stakes were high. If genetic predisposition to intelligence is only alterable in small ways, educational policy would concentrate on categorising children early. This was the assumption built into the 11-plus examination, obligatory for English, Welsh and Northern Irish children at age eleven from 1944 and still retained in some areas (phased out in Northern Ireland in 2008). By the 1960s, the examination was largely based on IQ tests on the basis of which children were sent to grammar, technical or secondary modern schools. Different curricula were delivered, based on the assumption of static ability. If social influences on intelligence (or more widely on educational achievement) were so strong as to mean that improved opportunity could affect intelligence, then governments should be directing resources into programmes such as Sure Start (as the New Labour government is doing at the time of writing). Sure Start consists of a set of locally based initiatives, now extended to cover all of England, targeted at children of pre-school age. Its aim is to provide early learning experiences in the belief that children's later social and intellectual abilities will be enhanced. The original idea was pioneered in the USA during the 1970s.

The intelligence debate became bogged down in its dualistic terms and the argument came to centre on what proportion of intelligence could be attributed to genetics and environment, as if complex, multiple and multi-directional effects could be quantified in this way. Neither genetics nor environment are psychological concepts (the first is biological, the second, sociological). One social psychological concept potentially useful for under-standing intelligence is anxiety, which I believe has quite powerful effects on shutting down people's capacity to think. Anxiety is rooted in the specific settings in which people perform and embodied as a result of their unique life history of coping with self-threatening experiences.

The intelligence debate illustrates an important feature of social psychology as an interdiscipline: its function as a 'bridge' between understanding of individuals (often reduced to biology and cognitions) and of society can feel more like a war zone, sandwiched between a rock and a hard place. In other words, the dualism that characterises thinking about people (which inevitably means people in their social surroundings) has tended to leave little or no space for concepts and principles that reduce neither to genetics, evolution or cognition on the one hand, nor to social structures, ideology or language on the other. The concepts of meaning and experience can help to populate this new ground, because of their quality of being definitively neither inside nor outside the person. This book aims to carve out such a space, which is truly social psychological.

4.4   Agency or structure in the explanation of action

Agency or structure is the twin problem of individual–social dualism; one that has been a source of continuing but unresolved debate in social theory. The binary terms 'agency' and 'structure' mirror the terms 'individual' and 'society' in the following way: if individuals are seen as relatively independent of social influence, they can be theorised as agents of their own destinies. Indeed, Western philosophy has traditionally seen individuals as the source of free will and of conscious intentional choice. On the other hand, if social structures are overwhelmingly influential in individual action, people's choices and desires would be irrelevant. Traditionally, social theory placed such emphasis on the power of social structures in governing people's actions that this led to social determinism.

As part of the critique of social determinism, explanations depending on the influence of structures, which tend to be very static in their implications, have often been replaced by an emphasis on dynamic processes. This makes it easier to focus on change. The explanatory shift from structures to processes can apply equally to social psychology and sociology. For example, instead of being seen primarily in terms of given and relatively static social structures, relationships, such as marriage, or psychological structures, such as sex differences, can be seen as continually in flux. The effect might be to bring into focus relationships of choice, such as friends and sexual partners. It suggests the importance of studying, for example, the negotiation of gender difference within ongoing relationships of all kinds.

Of course, agency and choice are always exercised within specific and complex constraints, both external and internal. An enduring challenge for social psychology is to be able to understand the dynamic tension between desires and actions that are relatively free and ones that are heavily constrained by circumstances, rather than to fall into assumptions on either side of the agency–structure binary. This interrogative theme will help us remain aware of the dangers which, like individual–society dualism, have strong political and ethical implications.

4.5   Summary

The purpose of Section 4 is to help you to step back from the substance of social psychology in order to situate it critically in its wider context. The following four themes, which are pursued throughout this book, introduced ways of interrogating the subject matter of social psychology:

1   the power relations involved in producing social psychological knowledge;

2   the way in which knowledge claims result from how they are situated;

3   the idea that explanations too often focus exclusively on individual or social factors;

4   the dualistic assumptions about agency or the determining influence of social structure.

5   Chapter summary and conclusion

This chapter has provided an exploratory history of social psychology, a history orientated by the question: why does social psychology take the forms that it does now in the UK? However, the chapter started by addressing how we decide what social psychology is. The answer to that affects how we identify the origins of the study of social psychology.

─────────────────────── *Pause for reflection* ───────────────────────

Now, at the end of the chapter, ask yourself why you think that McDougall (not Ross or James) is commonly identified as the originator of UK social psychology.

───

Social psychology turns out to be not just a moving target but a multiple and internally divided one. In the learning outcomes at the beginning of this chapter, the dimensions of difference within social psychology were identified as:

■   geographical – between Europe and the USA (with the UK wetting its feet somewhere in the middle of the Atlantic!)

■   disciplinary – between psychology, with the individual as its object and unit of study, and sociology, emphasising the influence of social collectivities

■   methodological – between qualitative and quantitative (including experimental methods and social psychometrics).

The chapter has traced the changes in fortune of the various social psychologies representing these differences: the dominance of American quantitative psychological social psychology and the crisis; symbolic interactionism in sociological social psychology and the emergence of an identifiably European social psychology. These are discussed with particular reference to their legacy for contemporary UK social psychology, divided into 'conventional' (experimental) and 'critical' (qualitative).

UK social psychology is distinctive in the strength of its critical, qualitative tradition. We have explored these developments in detail in this chapter, noting the earlier influences of 'the crisis' and European social psychology on feminist and critical social psychology: salient themes were their critiques of method, of theory of the individual and the treatment of political implications in the traditional discipline.

The charting of this history led to showing how social psychological knowledges reflect the workings of four interrogative themes:

1   *power relations*, within the institutions of the discipline and outside

2   the *situated character of knowledges* in wider currents of thought, belief and practice

3   *individuality*, casting light on the nature of individuality and the person in his or her *social* setting

4   *agency*, casting light on people's agency, their capacity to take action
       within the constraining and enabling *structures* and currents of social life
       within which they are positioned.

Social psychology has a unique position in the social and human science
disciplines because it is the single area of enquiry whose responsibility it is to
understand the interface between individuals and the social worlds that they
inhabit. How do people affect their external world, and how do these worlds
affect the people who inhabit them? These questions could hardly be more
important. If social psychology claimed, for example, that outside influences
determined who we are and what we do, the political, policy and humanistic
implications would be very different from those based on claims that
individuals have an unquenchable capacity for agency, creativity and
resistance to social and political influence. Social psychology has the potential
to be an interdiscipline, hampered by neither an exclusively individualistic
(psychological) nor social deterministic (sociological) perspective on people's
experience, meanings, relations and actions. The two dualisms discussed
above have made this difficult. The dynamic state of UK social psychology is a
good sign that this challenge remains alive.

References

Allport, F.H. (1924) *Social Psychology*, Boston, Houghton Mifflin.

Becker, H.S. (1972 [1967]) 'Becoming a marihuana user' in Manis, J.G. and
Meltzer, B.N. (eds) *Symbolic Interaction: A Reader in Social Psychology*,
Boston, Allyn and Bacon, pp. 498–508.

Becker, H.S. (1999) 'The Chicago School, so-called', *Qualitative Sociology*,
vol. 22, no. 1, pp. 3–12.

Bogardus, E. S. (1933) 'A social distance scale', *Sociology and Social Research*
3, pp. 265–271.

Cartwright, D. (1979) 'Contemporary social psychology in historical
perspective', *Social Psychology Quarterly*, vol. 1, pp. 82–93.

Deutsch, M. (1975) 'Introduction' in Deutsch, M. and Hornstein, H.A. (eds)
Applying Social Psychology, Hillsdale NJ, Lawrence Erlbaum, pp. 1–12.

Erikson, E. (1980) *Identity and the Life Cycle*, New York, W.W. Norton.

Foucault, M. (1970) *The Order of Things: An Archaeology of the Human
Sciences*, London, Tavistock.

Garfinkel, H. (1967) *Studies in Ethnomethodology*, Englewood Cliffs, NJ,
Prentice Hall.

Gilbert, N. and Mulkay, M. (1984) *Opening Pandora's Box: A Sociological
Analysis of Scientists' Discourse*, Cambridge, Cambridge University Press.

Gilligan, C. (1982) *In a Different Voice: Psychological Theory and Women's
Development*, Cambridge, MA, Harvard University Press.

Goffman, E. (1959) *The Presentation of Self in Everyday Life*, New York, Doubleday.

Gordon, C. (1980) *Power/Knowledge: (Foucault) Selected Interviews and Other Writings*, Brighton, Harvester, pp. 1972–7.

Graumann, K. (1995) 'History of social psychology' in Hewstone, M. and Manstead, A.S.R. (eds) *Blackwell Encyclopaedia of Social Psychology*, Oxford, Blackwell, pp. 301–6.

Haraway, D.J. (1991) *Simians, Cyborgs and Women: The Reinvention of Nature*, London, Free Association Books.

Hendrick, C. (1977) 'Social psychology as an experimental science' in Hendrick, C. (ed.) *Perspectives on Social Psychology*, Hillsdale, NJ, Erlbaum, pp. 1–74.

Henriques, J., Hollway, W., Urwin, C., Venn, C. and Walkerdine, V. (1984) *Changing the Subject: Psychology, Social Regulation and Subjectivity*, London, Methuen.

Higher Education and Research Opportunities in the United Kingdom (HERO) (2001) *British Psychology in 2001* [online], www.hero.ac.uk/rae/overview/docs/UoA13/doc (Accessed 12 September 2006).

The Heist, Channel 4 television programme, 4 January 2006.

Hewstone, M. and Manstead, A. (1995) 'Social psychology' in Hewstone, M. and Manstead, A.S.R. (eds) *Blackwell Encyclopaedia of Social Psychology*, Oxford, Blackwell, pp. 588–95.

James, W. (1981 [1890]) *Principles of Psychology*, Cambridge, MA, Harvard University Press.

Jones, E. (1985) 'Major developments in social psychology during the past five decades' in Lindzey, G. and Aronson, E. (eds) *The Handbook of Social Psychology. Vol. 1: Theory and Method* (3rd edn), New York, Random House, pp. 47–107.

Katz, I. and Braly, K. (1933) 'Racial stereotypes of one hundred college students', *Journal of Abnormal and Social Psychology*, vol. 28, pp. 280–90.

Kohlberg, L. (1958) *The Development of Modes of Moral Thinking and Choice in the Years 10 to 16*, Chicago, University of Chicago Press.

Le Bon, G. (1908 [1896]) *The Crowd: A Study of the Popular Mind*, London, Unwin.

Lewin, K., Lippitt, R. and White, R.K. (1939) 'Patterns of aggressive behavior in experimentally created "social climates"', *Journal of Social Psychology*, vol. 10, no. 2, pp. 271–301.

McDougall, W. (1908) *Introduction to Social Psychology*, London, Methuen.

McGuire, W.J. (1973) 'The yin and the yang of progress in social psychology: Seven Koan', *Journal of Personality and Social Psychology*, vol. 26, pp. 446–56.

Mead, G.H. (1934) *Mind, Self and Society*, Chicago, University of Chicago Press.

Milgram, S. (1965) 'Some conditions of obedience and disobedience to authority', *Human Relations*, vol. 18, pp. 57–76.

Moede, W. (1920) *Experimentelle Massenpsychologie*, Leipzig, Hirzel.

Munsterberg, H. (1913) *Psychology and Industrial Efficiency*, Boston, Houghton Mifflin.

Pancer, M. (1997) 'Social psychology: the crisis continues' in Fox, D. and Prilleltensky, I. (eds) *Critical Psychology: An Introduction*, London, Sage, pp. 150–65.

Potter, J. and Wetherell, M. (1987) *Discourse and Social Psychology: Beyond Attitudes and Behaviour*, London, Sage.

Reich, J.W. (1981) 'An historical analysis of the field' in Bickman, L. (ed.) *Applied Social Psychology Annual Vol. 2*, Beverley Hills, CA, Sage, pp. 45–70.

Rijsman, J. and Stroebe, W. (1989) 'The two social psychologies or whatever happened to the crisis?', *European Journal of Social Psychology*, vol. 19, pp. 339–44.

Ring, K. (1967) 'Experimental social psychology: some sober questions about some frivolous values', *Journal of Experimental Social Psychology*, vol. 3, pp. 113–23.

Rose, N. (1990) *Governing the Soul: The Shaping of the Private Self*, London, Routledge.

Ross, E.A. (1908) *Social Psychology*, New York, Macmillan.

Sampson, E.E. (1977) 'Psychology and the American ideal', *Journal of Personality and Social Psychology*, vol. 35, pp. 767–82.

Sears, D.O. (1986) 'College sophomores in the laboratory: influences of a narrow data base on social psychology's view of human nature', *Journal of Personality and Social Psychology*, vol. 51, pp. 515–30.

Silverman, L. (1977) 'Why social psychology fails', *Canadian Psychological Review*, vol. 18, pp. 353–8.

Stainton Rogers, W. and Stainton Rogers, R. (2001) *The Psychology of Gender and Sexuality*, Buckingham, Open University Press.

Steiner, I.D. (1974) 'Whatever happened to the group in social psychology?', *Journal of Experimental Social Psychology*, vol. 10, pp. 94–108.

Tajfel, H. (1981) *Human Groups and Social Categories: Studies in Social Psychology*, Cambridge, Cambridge University Press.

Ussher, J. (1989) *The Psychology of the Female Body*, London, Routledge.

Weisstein, N. (1993 [1968]) 'Psychology constructs the female, or the fantasy life of the male psychologist (with some attention to the fantasy life of his friends the Male Biologist and the Male Anthropologist)', *Feminism and Psychology*, vol. 3, no. 2, pp. 195–210.

Wilkinson, S. (1997) 'Feminist psychology' in Fox, D. and Prilleltensky, I. (eds) *Critical Psychology: An Introduction*, London, Sage, pp. 247–64.

Wilson, D.W. and Schafer, R.B. (1978) 'Is social psychology interdisciplinary?', *Personality and Social Psychology Bulletin*, vol. 4, pp. 548–52.

Wundt, W. (1916) *Elements of Folk-psychology*, London, Allen Unwin.

Zimbardo, P., Haney, C., Banks, W.C. and Jaffee, D. (1975) 'The psychology of imprisonment: privation, power and pathology' in Rosenhan, D. and London, P. (eds) *Theory and Research in Abnormal Psychology*, New York, Holt, Rinehart and Winston, pp. 271–87.

Chapter 2

Methods and knowledge in social psychology

by Wendy Hollway, The Open University

Contents

> **Learning outcomes**
>
> By the end of this chapter you should:
>
> - understand the principle and implications of the claim that methods produce knowledge
> - recognise the differences and similarities between the four approaches to social psychology used in this book
> - appreciate the relation between these approaches and their associated methodologies and methods
> - be familiar with the different principles on which these four approaches are based, including those between qualitative and quantitative social psychology
> - be able to situate examples of social psychological research (Milgram's experiments on obedience and the tradition of attitude measurement) in their historical contexts and appreciate their effects on social psychology.

1 Introduction

The striking impression left by the history of social psychology traced in the previous chapter is that the dominant tradition was conditioned by principles of method, rather than by subject matter. Perhaps this is not surprising, because twentieth-century psychology was founded on a methodological principle, namely that it must be scientific. For psychology, this meant experimentation and measurement, and psychological social psychology (PSP) was bound by these principles too. Sociological social psychology (SSP) was different, in that it was part of a (minority) tradition that tended to be qualitative, as well as quantitative, and many studies were devised in naturalistic settings.

1.1 Aims

This chapter:

- provides worked examples of the four approaches used in this book (cognitive social, social psychoanalytic, discursive psychological and phenomenological)

- explores the differences and similarities of the four approaches

- takes a classic study and examines its rationale, ethics, setting and power relations

- traces changes in the ways that social psychological research has been pursued

- examines the principles on which the four approaches have been based

- contrasts some of the principles that distinguish quantitative and qualitative methods.

Let us begin with the proposition that methods produce knowledge. What I mean by this is that methods do not just reveal knowledge that is already there; rather, they play an active role in how social psychological phenomena are foregrounded or rendered invisible, how they are framed, construed, organised and understood. Consequently, the methods available to social psychology have the potential to reflect the richness and complexity of people's lived experience in its setting, but they may also limit, constrain and distort it.

In Section 2, specific examples of four different approaches to social psychological method are introduced. This enables us to see the different knowledges (in this case about emotions) that each method produces. The methods selected in this book are only four of a much broader menu of possibilities. They are experimental, psychoanalytic, discursive and phenomenological. Four social psychologists, each a specialist in one of these methods, apply their particular method to work on the same example, a newspaper headline extracted from a journalist's interview with an Iraqi family in which the father and husband had died while imprisoned during the country's occupation by American and British troops (Spears et al., 2005).

In order to illustrate the complex ways that power relations influence the production of knowledge, in Section 3 I examine the centrality and effects of measurement in mid twentieth-century (predominantly North American) social psychology. This critical review takes us as far as 'the crisis' in the mid 1970s, and helps to explain the subsequent major paradigm shift in social psychology: from the almost total monopoly of quantitative methods to the current position in the UK of a proliferation of qualitative methods. This position is reflected in the methods illustrated in Section 2.

Sections 4 and 5 contain details of the two predominant quantitative traditions in social psychology. Two of the four themes set out in Chapter 1, Sections 4.1 and 4.2, are particularly useful for this purpose: analysing the power relations that are involved in the production of knowledge (and which therefore implicate methods), and applying the principle of situating the knowledge that methods produce. I first focus on a particular criticism that emerged during 'the crisis', namely that PSP largely failed to understand that experiments were undertaken in a social setting, which had significant effects on how the results should be interpreted. This also provides an illustration of the importance of situating knowledge. In Section 4, I pursue this through a detailed evaluation of the North American social psychologist Stanley Milgram's famous (and infamous) experiments on obedience to authority, which were conducted in the 1960s. In Section 5, I examine attitude and opinion measurement – probably the most widely used approach in social psychology. In Section 6, I discuss one of the contentious principles that generates disagreement between quantitative and qualitative methods in social psychology: the question of sample size and its effects on the generalisability of results.

2   Four social psychological methods

In this book, we have chosen four social psychological approaches, used variously in each chapter to illustrate the different approaches to social psychology that they represent. Each one is associated with a particular methodology and these tend to have different labels. The pairs of approach and methodology are as follows:

- cognitive social approach – statistical methodology

- social psychoanalytic approach – social psychoanalytic or psychosocial methodology

- discursive psychological approach – discourse analytic methodology

- phenomenological approach – phenomenological methodology.

Several practical methods are associated with each approach. Basically this gives us a three-fold scheme for approaching our chosen social psychological methods. First, the approach represents a perspective on how the object of social psychology is understood, a theory of being, or *ontology*. Second, each ontology suggests a particular approach to knowing about this object, or *methodology*. Third, each methodology and ontology gives rise to *methods* that follow from its perspective. These are set out with details on the history and focus of analysis in Table 2.1. You will probably find it useful to return to the table when you have read this chapter which expands on the points contained in Table 2.1, and also, for reference, at various points throughout the book. The grid represents a very condensed summary of the approaches, details of which will arise throughout the book and gradually make more sense

The terminology can be confusing and it is impossible to fix it too rigidly because, as you can see from the 'History' row in Table 2.1, none of these features stands still over time and development always proceeds unevenly, with separate parts moving at varying rates and in different directions. For example, we have labelled one approach 'Cognitive social' because, since the 1970s, this has been the dominant ontological paradigm in PSP. But it was preceded by the dominance of the behaviourist paradigm, and both have been wedded to statistical methods. The object of the experimental method is behaviour. When the behaviourist paradigm was largely overtaken by the cognitive paradigm, a statistical method able to find out about cognitive processes was required and as a result the cognitive social approach drew on social psychometrics as well as retaining experiments. But when the idea of attitudes (located in the mind) was challenged (see Box 2.7 in Section 5) and replaced with the idea of discourse, the analysis of written and spoken text became appropriate. If this sounds chaotic, it is perhaps because the production of knowledge is not a smooth process. We have used the term 'Unit and focus of analysis' in Table 2.1, but the term 'unit of analysis' is also used to describe the phenomena that is being studied. The different terms can be understood as emphasising different meanings, with 'unit' being more in line with a cognitive social emphasis on variables, whilst 'focus' is a broader way of viewing the object of study and is therefore more appropriate for the other three perspectives. You may find it helpful to regard it as a welcome sign

Table 2.1   Approaches to social psychology

	Cognitive social	Discursive psychological	Phenomenological	Social psychoanalytic
Theory of the person (ontology)	The information-processing individual in a social context	The socially-constructed, situated, contingent identity	The experiencing embodied individual in relation with others	The conflicted psyche in dynamic relation with the external world
Methodology and description	Statistical (quantitative, through controlled conditions, scientific paradigm)	Discourse analytic (qualitative, through textual and conversation analysis)	Phenomenological (qualitative, through rich description of experience)	Social psychoanalytic or Psychosocial (qualitative, through interpretation of what is unsaid as well as said)
Methods	Experimental, social psychometric	Conversation analysis, Foucauldian discourse analysis	First-person written account of experience, interview, literary text	Case study, free association narrative interview, observation
History	Dominant in PSP, emerged from the critique of behaviourism in the mid twentieth century	Emerged in the 1970s with the linguistic turn, and influenced by SSP	Originated in the philosophy of Husserl in the late nineteenth/early twentieth century	Limited to use in the clinic and not an area of academic study until the late twentieth century
Unit and focus of analysis	Individual cognitions in controlled social conditions	External world of discourse, its meanings and effects	Detailed description of social experience derived through the senses	Internal world of psyche in relational settings and its effect on actions

of a dynamic social psychology which tolerates the complexity and fluidity of knowledge.

To put some flesh on the skeleton provided in Table 2.1, each approach is now exemplified, based on an analysis of the same data. To underline the point about complexity, it is worth emphasising that the writers of each example are not representing a set approach because each exists in diverse forms and every researcher's position is, in some regard, idiosyncratic.

2.1   Four approaches to a headline about hate

The following extract, 'Three views on hate', is reproduced from a special feature in *The Psychologist* (the monthly magazine of the British Psychological Society) in September 2005. The feature emerged from the work of a group called 'Dialoguing across Divisions in Social Psychology', convened by Wendy Hollway and Anthony Manstead. It represents three methodological approaches to the empirical social psychological study of emotion, which correspond to three of the methodological approaches that we feature in this book. This extract is followed by 'Phenomenological social psychology', Darren Langdridge's work on a fourth approach, which was commissioned in order to complete the treatment of this particular topic from our four perspectives.

THREE VIEWS ON HATE

On 24 May 2004 *The Guardian* published a story about an Iraqi family, a mother and her children. The woman's husband, and children's father, had died mysteriously in detention during the American/British invasion. The newspaper headline quoted the woman's response – 'I will always hate you people'.

Mrs Izmerly's response, extreme emotions, unequal power and national, global and group conflict are part of the territory social psychology covers. We want to use the story as a way of exploring what social psychology offers and to probe the differences between three core approaches – the experimental, the psychoanalytic and the discursive. Each author speaks from their particular perspective within each of these broad approaches.

Experimental social psychology
Russell Spears

Where do you begin to devise an experiment to gain insight into this headline? This reminded me of a conference I recently attended called 'Why neighbours kill', an interdisciplinary meeting of political scientists, sociologists and social psychologists. After diverse talks on genocide in Rwanda, the Balkans, and Cambodia, by people who had actually been there and talked to the survivors, I was starting to feel a bit uneasy that my little package of 2 x 2 designs (with no killing in sight) might come over as ever-so-slightly trite. This was not helped by a well-known 'experimental' social psychologist (who shall remain nameless) who boldly announced before my talk that he would not insult the audience by presenting experiments on such a grave topic.

So what is the use of experiments on such extreme emotions? First, however real and high-impact these examples are, they remain what psychologists often disparagingly call 'anecdotal'. There is a serious point here: empirical evidence is the lifeblood of psychology, and experiments provide the control to assess causal relations and patterns among variables that may not be apparent to the naked eye. Although few would doubt the evidence of exclaimed hatred from the headline, this is only the first step to understanding it.

I will try to explain why I think an experimental approach can be useful, and perhaps even necessary, to answer key questions about feelings of hatred. Let's take the research I talked about at the conference, conducted with Colin Leach, on the topic of *Schadenfreude*: pleasure felt at another's failure or downfall. Although not the same as hate, *Schadenfreude* is closely related and can be fuelled by hatred. It can explain pleasure in an enemy's demise, and the failure to stop, or even the tendency to participate in, some of the extreme acts associated with conflict.

However, *Schadenfreude* is rarely openly expressed like hatred. Nietzsche noted that *Schadenfreude* is an opportunistic emotion that relies on a third party for the rival's demise, and this can make it less legitimate, for example, than direct victory over the rival. Open gloating in such circumstances can also be dangerous if the rival retains power (hence Arafat's concern at the open gloating of some Palestinians about 9/11). So how do we detect *Schadenfreude* if it is not legitimate to express it? Experimental techniques can help us.

In our research we have employed a 'bogus pipeline' technique in which we attach a sensor to participants and tell them that this can detect their true emotions (rather like a polygraph). Although this is not actually connected to anything, we find that people are most honest and show more *Schadenfreude* towards a hated rival as a result. More generally, experiments allow us to detect causal relations (e.g. that threats to identity can incite *Schadenfreude*) and meaningful patterns among variables (e.g. that the pain caused by threats to identity predicts *Schadenfreude*).

Of course we cannot reproduce in the lab the conditions that foster the kind of hatred that motivates some people to become suicide bombers (nor would we want to for obvious ethical reasons!). However, we can model some of the proposed processes and test implications of theories. In other research we have tried to show that the disempowering conditions of stable low status can be associated with more aggressive forms of discrimination. This reflects a 'nothing to lose' strategy of the hopeless and helpless, epitomised by our headline.

The point about experiments is that they offer depth of explanation, enabling us to dig beneath the surface, and to investigate the psychological processes that are not always visible or accessible in direct accounts. Experiments are particularly good at getting at the parts that other methods cannot reach: they are useful in telling us things that people either don't want to reveal, or can't. This may be because they are ashamed to admit to them (e.g. malicious emotions like *Schadenfreude*) or are not even aware of them (e.g. unconscious thoughts and desires, or patterns of behaviour that are only apparent at the group level, through the lens of the experimental panopticon). As with all methods, these need to be treated with interpretative care, but they provide explanation that goes beyond conscious accounts and surface appearances.

The claim that experimentalism is the only show in town is a dangerous one, however. While some advocates of the experimental approach are wont to claim scientific superiority, this is not inherent in the method itself, and experiments (or quantitative psychology more generally) can be seen as complementary to other approaches. To confine oneself to experiments is surely partial and unhealthy (a bit like a dietary fad). Returning to the conference example, it would have been foolish to see myself in a contest with political scientists about the causes of genocide in Rwanda. To admit only experimental evidence here would be absurd. But to deny their utility when they can sometimes 'tell us more than we know' is equally ludicrous. Rather, we had different parts of the jigsaw, relating to different levels of explanation, and the choice of methods was contingent on this analysis. In the spirit of methodological pluralism (or unholy alliances), experiments could complement discursive approaches (by digging beneath the discourse) and supplement psychodynamic approaches (by uncovering unconscious processes).

[Social] psychoanalysis
Wendy Hollway

I stare at a headline: 'I will always hate you people' and monitor my feelings, grabbed by the picture of Mrs Izmerly and her three children. It conjures in me a knot of knowledge, belief and feelings about the Iraq war. I am furious with Bush (and Blair) and regularly have a tussle between my hate and my better judgement when it comes to how I feel about American people in general. I feel guilty when I read in the main text that the daughter accuses all British citizens, as well as American citizens, of being complicit in this war because we live in a democracy. There are some powerful group constructions going on even in the six words of the headline and I do not – cannot – stand outside of them. I am British, in this instance to my shame. I start here because I believe that social psychologists should reflect on their own subjective responses to any issue on which they conduct an inquiry in order to clarify where their commitments might lie.

It is not only my meaning frames that will shape the analysis of this headline however. If the journalist did not choose the words, he certainly framed the story, and it is always within a frame that meaning is achieved. I know immediately that this family of an Iraqi man were expressing their hatred of what the coalition was doing in Iraq. After reading the article, I could see that this case was framed in terms of the terrible effects that such treatment has on the reputation, acceptance and, ultimately, purpose of the coalition's presence in Iraq. The theme of hatred in the main heading was mirrored in the final sentence quoting one daughter: 'I won't allow myself to rest until I have got revenge for him'. Meaning and interpretation are co-productions; in this case the interviewees, the journalist (perhaps editors) and me.

Psychoanalysis is one of the few theoretical perspectives in social psychology that does not shy away from hate, understands it and takes it seriously. There is no established psychoanalytic method in social psychology because psychoanalysis is a clinical method not a research method. I have used psychoanalytic principles to inform my understanding of individuals (ontology) and how research can come to know them (epistemology). There is no single accepted way of doing this, but it informs my mode of interviewing (see Box 2.1).

Box 2.1   A [social] psychoanalytic perspective

The free association narrative interview method reaches beyond structured interviewing, which is dominant in qualitative research and runs the risk of constraining interviewees within assumptions provided by the questions. This method can elicit deeply felt and difficult emotions, possibly conflictual, as well as taken-for-granted issues like identity and identifications, so it fits well with this subject.

> To guard against eliciting generalisations (like the headline) or common discourses, questions are open but specific, eliciting a narrative grounded in actual events. Main questions could include 'Can you tell me about your life under Saddam's regime?' and 'Can you tell me about your husband's life?' The simplicity of these questions belies the complexity and richness they give rise to in the context of an attentive and respectful relationship with the participants.
>
> The resulting narratives are developed by follow-up questions, the ordering and wording of interviewees, based on the principle that the researcher should elicit participants' experiences, meaning and free associations, imposing as little as is possible of their own. Because meaning is achieved in the context of the wider whole (the gestalt principle), the material is not broken up (as is common) for analysis. Analysis of data involves, among many other things, noticing signs of the affect and potential conflict interviewees show in their narratives.

If I wanted to do research on this topic, how would I go about it? What research questions would I choose of the many possibilities? Each is made possible by the salient ideas in a given approach. Social identity theory, for example, will be interested in the construction of group identity in the 'we', or 'I' and 'you people'. A social psychoanalytic approach takes account of the feelings and investments that are involved in such constructions – the inner psychic contributions to meaning – and recognises that these are negotiated in relational, discursive and wider social contexts. So here, hate is a dynamic kindled in Iraqi–Anglo–American relations in the current context of the actions of coalition forces in Iraq. Of course this is a gloss on a situation with a very complex history in respect of relations between Islam and Judaeo-Christianity, but it informs understanding of the affective loading on a category like 'you people'. In summary, the research question is not an innocent, neutral tool but an intervention that already carries a payload of meaning that will shape the knowledge produced from the research.

Until the research question is clarified, decisions about design are premature. It affects what we take as the unit of analysis. It could be the headline, the whole media text, the existing interviews from which the story was constructed, or new interviews with this family or other families specifically set up for research purposes.

Should it be based on a single-case interview? This question raises the issue of how extrapolation ('generalisability') can proceed from one or few cases. On the other hand, how many interviews is enough? What is the justification for needing a number that is amenable to statistical analysis? Is it that one case does not provide 'proof'? In the case of this extract, the phenomenon of Iraqi hate comes as no surprise. If the question is how widespread it is, the design goes in a survey-based, quantitative direction. If it is what makes some Iraqis hate and not others, the design must be comparative.

My purpose is to understand more deeply what it means to 'hate you people', how it has come about and its likely effects. Such questions require qualitative methods because only these can understand experience and meaning. One case will provide the depth and can be extrapolated using theoretical understandings of hate and group relations as long as this is restrained by careful contextualisation. This makes it appropriate, in principle, to conduct one or more in-depth interviews to establish the specificity and detail of this woman's hate in the context of her life history and especially of the treatment of her husband. In practice, there might be political and cultural barriers. The analysis would then take what I call a psychosocial direction, which means I would look at how Mrs Izmerly's account of her experience (never separable from emotions) draws on actual events and makes something unique of them in her inner world. In terms of generalising from single-case data, the approach is one of theoretical extrapolation.

This method provides data concerning the complexity of a person's meanings and their relation to specific experiences. Like experimental social psychology, it goes beyond 'conscious appearances and surface accounts', although incorporating a complexity and attention to particularity which that cannot achieve. Unlike the discursive approach, its focus is the person who speaks, rather than the text, which in my view is a central location for emotion.

Discursive social psychology
Derek Edwards

My first reaction to the headline, and the story beneath it, is that of an ordinary reader. It is a powerfully evocative report. But rather than exploring my emotions, or developing my stance on Iraq, finding people to interview, or devising experiments on how emotions are caused, I start to get interested in the report itself. This is not a pursuit of deep, underlying significances, but rather, of how specific words, descriptions and accounts are assembled and put to work.

A common objection to discursive psychology (DP) is that it only analyses discourse, when there are other, more important things to do. We are turning away from the events themselves, whether in the world or in the psyche – in this case death, politics and hatred. Yet to take an immediate interest in those matters is also to turn away from the actual object presented for analysis, the newspaper report, which is also real. Discourse is both real and important. If it were not for discourse there would be no politics, no war in Iraq, no understanding of what is happening there, nobody to quote, nothing to say. So there is no immediate requirement to use the report as a point of *departure* and do some other study instead. Our immediate focus is on reports themselves, how they provide for causal explanations, invoke psychological states (see Box 2.2), and build implications for politics and policy.

Box 2.2   Examining everyday emotion

Discursive psychology (DP) examines, among other things, how people deploy commonsense psychological ideas. Rather than taking those ideas out of context and finding that they amount to a messy, contradictory and inaccurate theory of mind, we explore how people actually put them to use in their everyday lives, when accounting for actions and events.

In a relevant study of emotion discourse (Edwards, 1999), talk from relationship counselling was analysed along with newspaper reports in the aftermath of Princess Diana's death. A *Sun* editorial said: 'In the depths of his grief, Diana's brother is entitled to be bitter about her death.' Analysis focuses on how this formulation selects emotion rather than, say, judgement as his reaction (her brother, Earl Spencer, had produced a heavy rebuke of the role of the press in her death), and names that emotion *grief* rather than, say, *anger*. Conceptually, grief's object would be Diana's death, whereas the object of anger would be (in this context) the activity of the press. Similarly, *bitter* evokes a disposition within Spencer, and perhaps a motive for producing emotive criticisms, whereas *anger* directs attention to its object and cause – the press and their paparazzi.

> Very briefly, these kinds of observations reveal a range of functional uses of emotion terms including, in the case of the *Sun*'s editorial, how to deflect attention from a criticism of their own journalistic practices onto the psychological state of the critic. Everyday emotion talk turns out to be very precise when examined inside the real-life practices where it is used, and for which it is surely designed.
>
> Source: Edwards (1999)

Out of such an analysis may come further questions, and the need for more materials. But those materials will probably be more discourse rather than an experiment, survey, or even a depth interview designed to probe the psyches of the participants. In DP there is a preference for collecting discourse as we find it, rather than doing research interviews. The reason is a basic conception (and observation) of how discourse works. Everyday discourse deals not only with its obvious topics, but also with the conditions of its production. It is always situated, indexical, sequentially relevant, always of and for its context, and always doing something. Research interviews are the basis of a great deal of qualitative research, especially where the aim is to discover how people think on some chosen topic. But interviews inevitably usurp the circumstances in which people ordinarily say things in and for living their lives.

Apart from uses of emotion words, and other items from the commonsense psychological thesaurus, DP examines how psychological business is generally handled and managed when people talk together. One specific topic, again starting with our newspaper headline, might be how direct quotation works ('I will always hate you people'). What are the general characteristics and uses of direct quotation? What does it do? In what discourse contexts, at what junctures, and in the performance of what kind of activities, do people actually produce quotes of what other people say? Does it have regular characteristics, types, functions and occasions? In fact there is already plenty of work on this (by writers ranging from Goffman and Bakhtin, to the detailed conversation analysis of Elizabeth Holt and Robin Wooffitt), and it turns out to be more interesting and systematic than we might imagine. Rather than formulating, as independent variables, a range of theoretically generated types of quotations and measuring their effects, we find order in the ways that quotations are actually used.

From DP's perspective the tendency of psychologists to turn the world into causal factors and variables, and get them under laboratory control, often seems inappropriate. Experimentation conforms to (some) canons of scientific research but it also, especially in social psychology, seems based on an assumption that the everyday world of social activities is actually a complex mix of causal factors and variables, rather like the relationship between physics experiments and the world outside the laboratory. In DP the social world is already orderly and intelligible precisely because people make it so – that's how it works. Experimental social psychology is also grounded in an understanding of how social life works, but not in systematic observation and analysis of it. Further, DP is not a preliminary, 'natural history' phase of research that will eventually generate experiments. Rather, our methods are adequate and appropriate to the phenomena. The orderliness we find is that of actions oriented to norms, rather than effects stemming from causes. It seems weird to treat discourse and social interaction in the same way as one would a chemical reaction.

(Spears et al., 2005)

Phenomenological social psychology
Darren Langdridge

Being presented with a newspaper piece such as this makes me feel somewhat uncomfortable and I find myself immediately wanting to make contact with the human beings behind the story, in particular the family directly affected by the conflict in Iraq. Why is this so? Well, very simply because as a phenomenological social psychologist I am primarily interested in experience. Experience is at the heart of all of the many different forms of phenomenological psychology and I believe should also be at the heart of all forms of psychology. Of course, this story was not the sole production of the family at the centre of the story. Indeed, I wonder how much it was their production at all. But for me, whilst the newspaper article may be the focus here, the story that is most important, if I wish to understand the hatred being felt, is the story of the family living in the shadow of the conflict in Iraq.

A phenomenological approach to social psychology is first and foremost a descriptive enterprise. Description is often thought unimportant in psychology, with its ready desire to explain the phenomena it studies, but description, especially here when dealing with the extremes of human emotions, is vital if we are to stand any chance of *understanding* experience. But before I begin to work with my participants and their concrete descriptions of experience, I must first of all work with what I bring to the analysis and engage in the phenomenological process known as epoché [see Box 2.3].

Box 2.3   Epoché

Epoché is a key part of the phenomenological method but is perhaps also the most controversial and most misunderstood. Husserl, the founder of phenomenological philosophy – which forms the basis of phenomenological psychology – argued that it was necessary to bracket off one's natural attitude (or everyday way of perceiving the world) in order to discern the essence of the 'things in their appearing'. The process of bracketing (epoché) is of course an imperfect one and this was recognised by the existential phenomenologists (Heidegger, Sartre and Merleau-Ponty in particular) who argued that Husserl was mistaken when he thought it possible to take a 'God's eye view'. They argued instead that all experience is grounded in our embodied being-in-the-world and that while we may seek to bracket off some aspects of our way of seeing the world (for instance, in the scientific natural attitude) it is impossible to assume a 'view from nowhere' (Ricoeur). This therefore suggests a need for a reflexive approach to the research process, attending to our role in co-constructing the experience being described, that is continuous and ongoing.

In all phenomenological psychological methods, data are normally collected through first-person written accounts or interviews. At all times, the rush towards explanation is avoided and instead projects focus on describing the experience, elaborating all the qualities that were previously hidden from view. The aim is always to identify those structural qualities that are invariant across the experience, as well as those that are more idiosyncratic, focusing on the reasons but not causes behind the phenomena in the hope of providing new insights that (perhaps) enable us to effect change.

2.2   Similarities and differences

There are many features deserving of comment in the examples above of the four approaches, but in this section I will discuss their similarities and differences. Although some of these arise from the predictable distinction between qualitative and quantitative approaches, others do not. However, something that they all have in common is reflexivity, or the researchers' preparedness to put themselves in the picture of knowledge production. In the social psychoanalytic and phenomenological perspectives, this is mentioned explicitly as a desirable part of the method, but both the writers of the other approaches put themselves 'in the picture' too. Each writer is also explicit about the way in which his or her particular approach is appropriate to the object of his or her analysis.

A difference that cuts across the qualitative and quantitative divide is about whether the object of analysis is hidden from view. Russell Spears highlights this as an advantage of the experimental method, and it is central also to the free association narrative interview method which draws from the psychoanalytic concept of unconscious dynamics. Even phenomenological psychology, whose object of analysis is conscious experience, aims to elaborate qualities previously hidden from view through rich description. But in contrast to these three, discourse analysis is not interested in underlying significance, but in words. Whereas discourse analysis is interested in emotion terms, social psychoanalysis looks for emotions themselves (even if these are hidden), while the object of phenomenological analysis is the emotions that people are aware of and can therefore describe. Social psychoanalysis and the experimental method look for causes of actions, but discourse analysis explicitly rejects this, and phenomenology is content to focus on experience, not its causes nor its motives.

The issue that most clearly differentiates quantitative from qualitative approaches is control: control of the research setting. While the other three approaches seek ecological validity by researching in social settings, experimental social psychology 'models' social processes in order to control them. However, within the qualitative approaches there are differences in emphasis. Discourse analysts prefer to collect discourse as it can be found, although they also conduct interviews. As Derek Edwards suggests, debates continue about the status of the research interview and whether, when and how it differs from ordinarily occurring conversations.

The social psychoanalytic and phenomenological approaches both rely on eliciting experience, often grounded in a narrative of actual events. Narrative is becoming an overarching theme in qualitative social psychology, partly because of the critique of structured interview techniques on the grounds that they dictate the terms in which participants can give their accounts. When interviews are relatively unstructured, participants have a tendency to give accounts in narrative form (Mishler, 1986). Indeed, it has been argued (e.g., Polkinghorne, 1988) that narrative is the fundamental form in which people make sense of their experience and their life, so much so that some say that identity is a product of the way people narrate, or create a story about, their lives.

Box 2.4   On becoming a mother

The following example illustrates how ontological and methodological principles were followed through in research design, starting with a set of research questions. What happens to women's identities in the process of becoming mothers for the first time? How do ethnicity, 'race', culture, religion, age, social class and gender intersect with motherhood identities? What can we learn from first-time mothers about embodied, unconscious, taken-for-granted and practical aspects of identity formation and change, and what role is played by processes of identification? These are the questions posed in a study I undertook with Ann Phoenix.

We chose qualitative methods because we needed to focus on meaning and experience and keep this situated in the specific and varying contexts of each woman's life. Because we believed that identity is greatly influenced by life history, we selected a narrative interviewing technique and a method of data analysis that do not break up a woman's narrative. (Use of content analysis, or code and retrieve methods, removes extracts from the surrounding context of their story.) The chosen method is called 'Free Association Narrative Interviewing' (FANI). It is an appropriate method to apply because it was informed by a particular theory of identity, namely that research participants (like people in general) are not aware of everything that makes up their identities or motivates their actions and relationships. This must therefore be taken into account in the methods of data production and analysis. Free associations are elicited and suggest emotionally meaningful connections of which the interviewee might be unaware.

Being interested in the embodied and relational nature of the experience of new mothers, we realised that any interview method would be limited by its dependence on the talk of the research participants. Hence we used in parallel a psychoanalytic observation method originally developed to understand early infant–mother relationships (Reid, 1997).

Both of these are in-depth methods and necessarily limit sample size (thirty mothers interviewed up to three times, six of whom were also involved in once-per-week observations in their homes). Because identity formation unfolds over time, both interviewing and observation took place over the first year of the baby's life. Such samples require theoretical sampling principles. Because we were interested in understanding a range of culturally different responses to the universal phenomenon of becoming a mother, we chose our interviewees from different ethnic groups. Nonetheless, we chose our participants from the same London borough, so that their current context was similar at least in terms of welfare provision and services.

Qualitative social psychological research argues for the importance of the principle of reflexivity. The psychoanalytic observation method builds in a weekly seminar at which each observer presents notes from their observation and hears about the others' work. It is recognised that everyone has powerful feelings about motherhood and infant dependency (we have all been dependent on our mothers or primary caregiver as infants) and researchers are no exception. With the help of a trained group leader, observers use their subjective responses as a means of analysing and interpreting the observational data. The provision of a group helps to bring many subjectivities to bear on the same data and so opens it out to different interpretations, cultural knowledge and personal family dynamics.

2.3   Historical change

All four approaches illustrated in this chapter are the products of changes during social psychology's history. The history of psychoanalysis dates back to the mid nineteenth century, but its methods and training were conducted in the context of medicine. As a research method in social science, social psychoanalysis is very young indeed. (To call it psychoanalysis would be inappropriate because that refers to a clinical psychotherapeutic practice. For this reason, its use in social psychology, which is conducted in non-clinical settings, is often referred to as 'psychosocial'.) Discourse analysis was introduced into social psychology in the 1980s (see Box 2.7 in Section 5). It drew its inspiration broadly from the linguistic turn in European social science (a new emphasis on language, discourse and culture as central to understanding the psychosocial world) and also from the SSP of symbolic interactionism (see Chapter 1) with its emphasis on everyday talk and interaction. Its types vary from the macro (e.g., Michel Foucault's analysis of historical shifts in discourses such as madness and how these analyses construct and regulate people's behaviour) to the micro (e.g., conversation analysis (CA), which dissects the minutest details of conversational interaction). Phenomenological psychology has a longish history in philosophy (Edmund Husserl, its originator, lived from 1859–1938) and always had a place in the kind of psychology that never relinquished its roots in philosophy and did not espouse quantitative methods. Recently this rather marginal tradition has been subject to new interest. The experimental approach has the longest history within the discipline, but it changed considerably, both as a response to the 'crisis' (see below) and the later 'linguistic turn' (see Chapter 1, Section 3.5, for an example). So now it is time to retrace some historical steps and examine the forces during the twentieth century that led to the dominance of scientific methods, and what undermined this to produce the present plurality of social psychological approaches.

X: A've [I've] bin rait [right] depressed miseln [myself] this week. An' fuckin 'boored [bored] aht'a [out of] mi [my] mind. Ah just an't got a fuckin' thing to du [do]. It is strange, it just meks mi s' [so] upset. It's like beein' fuckin' ill, I feel sick an' I an't [haven't] bin [been] rait [right] fo' weeks. A'm just wastin' all mi life an' the'r in't a fuckin' thing Ah' can du. That's why Ah stay in bed su [so] late. Ah dun't wanna get up to feel su fed-up. [Pause] It meks mi feel strange inside ... [pause]

S: What du yer mean?

X: Ah feel different, especially when Ah g' [go] aht [out]. Like Ah'll gu' [go] fo' a video or sumaht [something] an' when Ah'm [I'm] the'er Ah feel worried an' threatened a bit, like, an' Ah sort'a can't decide which t'ave, then Ah'll get 'ome an' Ah dun't [don't] wanna watch it but Ah'm boored an' Ah need sumaht t' du. So Ah watch it! But Ah dun't enjoy stuff at moment.

S: Du things not seem t' matter to yer?

X: No. Nowt [nothing] seems rait t' mi, not like it wo [was]. It's awful in it, gettin' older, fo this! That this is it. Signin' on', crap jobs ... [Pause] ...n' money ... this place! [Laughs]

```
 1  S:  So were you put in that situation then?
 2  D:  No coz I – I – I picked who I hung a – hung about with very
 3      carefully, but – well not carefully but I just happened – you know
 4      like attracts and you hang about with people who are like
 5      yourself [(                                    )]
 6  S:           [Who are] not 'laddish' then?
 7  D:  Yeah I was lucky to - > but there was still the laddish< (1.0) er
 8      only -only as far as – as drinking went definitely coz I – I was in
 9      (.) – I was on like two or three of my group were big drinkers and it was
10      'you've got to match pint for pint at the same rate of drinking
11      as I do or else you're a queer, or else you're weak, or else you're a
12      Southerner' you know and that's [(all this)]
13  S:                                  [Did they] actually say that?
14  D:  Oh yeah! all the time mm [(          )]
15  S:                           [Yet you] hung around with
16      these people?
17  D:  No well I was doing it to others as well you know [it's all] =
18  S:                                                    [really?]
19  D:  = it's a – it's a – it's a – a hive mind (.) you know=
((lines omitted))
27  D:  and it's – it's like a group mind and everybody (.) thinks the
28      same and talks the same and you have the same phrases and
29      you have the same likes and dislikes.
```

Dad was always a family man. He didn't go off and play golf on Sundays, or anything like that. Um, he was always around the home, yeah. Great sense of – of family, and supporting Mum, and the children, and, um – and work with the church. He was like me, a practical man. He did a lot of jobs round the house and that, and – But, no, he never felt it was right to, um, sort of work all week, and then at weekends go off and play golf on a Sunday. You know, leave the wife again with the family and that, so – ...He helped us with our homework if we wanted help with the homework. And if we were – I don't know, repairing our pushbikes or something, he would do that. He let us use his garage and his tools. If we wanted to learn how to use them, he'd show us how to use the tools in the garage. Um, as I say, he always helped us with homework. If I had a problem, I always felt I could go and ask him. More like technical things like Maths, and things like that. I always remember the day he explained to me how an internal combustion engine worked.

RP Do you think of yourself as being English, or white?

Bob Um, I do think of myself as a British person, a British citizen but I, I don't think of myself as any other race because I was born in England, which makes me English, so I'm not nothing else, I wouldn't try and be nothing else.

RP Right Do you think some boys do they want to be something else?

Bob Yeah, Yeah, try and act hard or try and talk in a, like some people like try talkin' like a Jamaican accent or =

RP = Do they?

Bob Yeah and like kiss their teeth like Africans, like Afro-Caribbean do, try and copy them.

RP This is English boys tryin' to be like that White English boys?

Bob Yeah. Some do. Yeah.

RP So why is that then? Why do they try and be like that?

Bob Dunno because they look as ... quite hard people and if they try and, if they act like that then they're gonna, people are gonna think oh look they look hard. Don't look at them else they're gonna start trouble. So that s probably why. (14-year-old white boy)

Figure 2.1 Four examples of transcription styles emphasising different aspects of the spoken interview

2.4   Summary

In this section, you have been introduced to four social psychological approaches to research: experimental, psychoanalytic, discursive and phenomenological, of which the last three are qualitative. Each was applied to the same example from the social psychology of emotion, specifically the question of researching hate. The examples show how different approaches will produce different knowledges because of the ways that they frame their object of analysis. Similarities and differences among the four methods were discussed, notably their approaches to the reflexivity of researchers, the hiddenness of the object and the principle of control.

3   The experimental approach and the crisis

It is widely recognised that nineteenth-century natural science became powerful through its success at prediction and control, and that this was decisive in shaping twentieth-century psychology and social psychology. Prediction and control have been (partially) achieved in social psychology, notably through attitude and opinion measurement and the use of statistical methods for generalisation. Kurt Danziger, a leading American historian of psychological methodology, agrees on this success:

> There is no question that it [the 'reigning', that is, statistical methodology] can be very effective in the context of specific practical problems that involve questions of limited scope which require an unambiguous answer. These are problem-solving situations with a rather similar structure to those in agriculture and industry in which the basic approach of the standard methodology of statistical design and inference was first developed. In this kind of context the assumptions of the methodology have a certain practical utility.
>
> (Danziger, 1985, p. 11)

Danziger goes on to argue in detail that the assumptions of statistical methodology can be extended to low-level 'unambitious' theorising 'without raising too many problems', but that they are inappropriate for testing other theories whose properties are not congruent with those that the methodology has imposed on the data. Danziger instances several approaches in social psychology where there is a 'disjunction between the aims of a theoretical system and the theoretical assumptions of statistical methodology' (Danziger, 1985, p. 7). He mentions Kurt Lewin's field theory, Piagetian and Gestalt psychology, and then specifies two of the methods that are foregrounded in this book – psychoanalysis and phenomenological psychology – as particularly at odds with the principles of statistical methodology.

——————————————— Pause for reflection ———————————————

Having read the examples of the four psychological approaches in Section 2, can you work out what the disjunctions are in the cases of social psychoanalysis and phenomenological psychology? You may find it helpful to consult Table 2.1.

Danziger concludes that there are three prevailing methodological beliefs that are 'ripe for revision':

> (1) that statistical inference provides the only valid procedure for relating data and theory; (2) that the rules about what constitutes valid evidence are independent of theory and are fixed for ever; (3) that the structure of theory must be accommodated to the structure of methodology and not vice versa.
>
> (Danziger, 1985, p. 13)

Danziger argues that the social conventions that were established in order to achieve a consensus among quantitative researchers about the production and interpretation of psychological research data were no more valid than those that preceded them, which, although experimental, were case based (see Section 6). However, 'by the second decade of the twentieth century, the ground rules for the production of numerical psychological data were well enough established to be utterly taken for granted' (Danziger, 1990, p. 149). The question of the inferences that could be drawn from statistical data remained tricky, but:

> this way of putting the question had the advantage of converting a fundamental question about the scientific project of psychology into an essentially technical question that could be solved by the adoption of a few conventions governing the use of certain technical devices. The work of producing quantitative data could then proceed as though there were not unanswered questions about the psychological reality that these data represented.
>
> (Danziger, 1990, p. 149)

The consolidation of the experimental method could not have been achieved without the institutional power of university departments (to recruit and promote, to control syllabuses and graduation), publishers and editors (to accept or reject journal articles and book proposals) and funding bodies (to support some kinds of research at the expense of others). There continued to be a widespread attachment to the experimental method even when its blind spots and weaknesses became evident, and an increasing number of social psychologists voiced their concerns that a crisis confronted social psychology.

Box 2.5   Methodology and the crisis in social psychology

The crisis in social psychology resulted from the feeling that social psychology had become irrelevant. The primary blame for this was placed on the detrimental effects of the experimental method on the questions that social psychology could ask and the issues that it could address. The first phase of the critique, in the 1960s, involved some important, but limited, criticisms of the experimental method, notably by Martin Orne (1962) pointing to the effects of demand characteristics (cues, often unwitting, in the experiment, that belie its neutral status and can lead to bias in results) and Robert Rosenthal (1966) on experimenter effects (ways in which experimenters act, again unintentionally, that affect results).

By the 1970s, the critique was more profound: it was claimed that experiments often lacked validity (Tajfel, 1972), posed serious ethical questions (Kelman, 1972) and could not offer knowledge that remained relevant over time (Gergen, 1973). Kenneth Gergen (1978) challenged the central principle of experiments, namely that they can definitively reveal cause—effect relationships between independent variables (those that are manipulated in the experiment) and dependent variables (those that are measured as outcomes or effects). Gergen argued that by isolating these as variables, they are taken out of the context of everyday life within which they derive their meaning (which changes over time). Danziger emphasised the way in which the topics of psychology were 'consistently redefined to fit the Procrustean bed of a very limited range of allowable procedures' (1996, p. 17). Silverman, in an article called 'Why social psychology fails' (1977) summed up the problem as follows: 'The failure of social psychology to develop substance and direction has been due primarily to our misguided vision that complex social phenomena can be fruitfully studied by experimental laboratory methods' (Silverman, 1977, p. 353). The result was 'short-term, low-impact studies' (p. 354).

3.1 Summary

This section has documented the influence of the scientific method on PSP, focusing on the North American context. The increasing dominance of a rather rigid set of procedures had detrimental effects on social psychology, which were central to the 'crisis of social psychology' in the 1970s. The section has also shown a salient feature of the power relations that produced social psychology: the power of scientific method.

4 The experimental setting: obedience to authority

Borrowed from a natural science model, the setting of the psychological experiment was assumed not to affect the behaviour of 'subjects'. Rather it was expected to be neutral, as were subjects' interactions with researchers. According to Danziger, '[psychology's] first century was nearly over before it began to dawn on its practitioners that they operated in a micro-social context that might well have a crucial influence on the results of their investigations' (1996, p. 26). Social psychology was a little more alert than the rest of experimental psychology to this principle, as befits a subject area that is meant to be about the study of individuals in their social setting. Nonetheless, progress has been halting. Stanley Milgram's experiments show both the increasing sophistication and the limitations of the experimental method in social psychology in the early 1960s (Milgram, 1963, 1965).

BOX 2.6 Milgram's experiments

In an extensive and thorough series of studies, which were performed in the 1960s under many different conditions, Milgram required experimental subjects to administer electric shocks to people who were, in fact, Milgram's accomplices. The studies purported to be about the effects of punishment on learning. Participants ('subjects') were told to increase the voltage whenever the 'learner' made a mistake. The main measure used in the study was the point at which the 'assistants' stopped delivering electric shocks on a 30-point incremental scale of intensity. If they subjected the 'learners' to shocks all the way through the scale to the maximum level, they were designated 'obedient'; if they refused to continue to administer electric shocks at any earlier point, they were regarded as having disobeyed. Although no actual shocks were administered, stooges in the various experiments could either be seen or were heard to react as if they had received electric shocks. When participants objected to administering the shocks (which most did), they were told to continue and this instruction became increasingly stern and insistent. Milgram commented later that it was striking how many subjects raised increasingly agitated objections to what they were being required to do but continued to obey (1977, p. 117). Although the proportion of participants proceeding to give the highest level of shock varied under different conditions (e.g., immediacy of the victim to the participant administering the shocks and the authority of the experimental context), Milgram found that more than 60 per cent continued to administer the highest level of shock on the display, even, for example, when they heard the (supposed) recipient begging them to stop, screaming in pain and eventually going silent.

As an adjunct to the main experimental method, Milgram kept detailed observational records and conducted interviews with participants afterwards, in addition to a debriefing session. They received a follow-up questionnaire about their participation after one year which 'confirmed [Milgram's] impression that participants felt positively toward the experiment' (Milgram, 1974, p. 195).

_____ *Pause for reflection* _____

The disturbing nature of Milgram's results has ensured that this is probably the best known (and some would say most notorious) item of knowledge in the whole of social psychology. Does this point to another kind of power relation: one in which a certain (perhaps over-simplistic) distillation of Milgram's findings is continuously reproduced because it is horrific? Does the sensational value of the results affect how they have been evaluated historically? In this light, how can Milgram's findings best be summarised?

4.1 Power relations in the production of knowledge

Milgram's study is used to show that people are prepared to submit to authority even when to do so is cruel and probably harmful. By creating this experiment, Milgram gave scientific authority to knowledge about a general phenomenon he called 'obedience to authority', and his findings are transmitted as social psychological 'fact'. I shall now analyse the different kinds of power relations that contributed to Milgram's study. Power relations are always expressed in concrete social ways and I shall pay particular attention to Milgram's research as situated knowledge. Criticisms of this study have been both in ethical and substantive terms.

The authority of the institutional context and the power relations between the researcher, his or her assistants and participants are exemplified quite starkly. In experiments, these are often taken for granted and go unexamined, but not so in Milgram's case. For example, when, in early feedback interviews, he learned that the experimental setting, the 'elegant Interaction Laboratory' at Yale University (1974, p. 16), was lending authority to the research instructions, Milgram first moved down to the basement and then to a nearby town devoid of any university associations. It made a difference, but not a 'significant' one: 'as it turned out, the level of obedience in Bridgeport, although somewhat reduced, was not significantly lower than that obtained at Yale' (48 per cent as opposed to 65 per cent) (Milgram, 1977, p. 116).

Pause for reflection

Do you think that the reduction from 65 per cent to 48 per cent is insignificant? I don't. It means that under half of the participants disobeyed – seventeen fewer in every hundred. This example is useful in thinking about how statistical 'facts' only have meaning through interpretation. If Milgram had wished to emphasise the difference in these two sets of results, the headline story that has been passed down in social psychology might have been different.

Milgram was interested in the three-party situation 'in which one agent commands another to hurt a third', which he regarded as a significant theme in human relations (Milgram, 1977, p. 102). This experiment took place in the context of the North American post-Second World War interest in the conditions under which Hitler led Germany into an aggressive war, why the nation had supported him and, in particular, why soldiers carried out orders which enabled the genocide of Jews and others in the death camps. 'Perhaps all organized hostility may be viewed as a theme and variation on the three elements of authority, executant and victim' (Milgram, 1977, p. 102). Thus Milgram's experimental power relations reflected a social situation which he wished to explore. In Milgram's study, the participants' responses were predetermined by the researcher (with phrases instructing the participants to 'please continue'; 'it is absolutely essential that you continue'; 'you have no other choice, you must go on'); they were required to follow orders. Importantly then, the standard experimental set-up of researcher, assistants and subjects was not just a convention for Milgram (accompanied by predictable but usually unremarked power relations). He claimed explicitly that 'we are not dealing with the personal power of the experimenter ... but with the consequence of social structure for action' (Milgram, 1977, p. 131).

> What the experimental situation does is to condense the elements present when obedience occurs in the larger world such that the essential ingredients are brought into a relatively narrow arena where they are open to scientific scrutiny. The power of the situation derives from the fact that we are able to see, and the subject can experience, the concurrent operations of antagonistic forces that in the larger world rarely impinge on him at the identical instant.
>
> (Milgram, 1974, p. 26)

In this respect, Milgram's experimental design is one of remarkably few that passes Gergen's test: 'the real task of the experimenter is to find or create a social context in the experiment that is appropriate to test a hypothesis concerning the effects of manipulating the key construct of theoretical interest' (Gergen, 1978, summarised in Hewstone et al., 1997, p. 44).

Although the design of Milgram's experiment encompassed an interest in the feelings of participants, this interest did not extend to anticipating any problems and questioning whether ethically such experiments should have taken place. Milgram was asked about this in a later interview. The interviewer prefaced his question with comments about 'the present ethical standards of "informed consent"' and asked whether Milgram would now go ahead with an experiment where 'the subjects were going to be exposed to a certain amount of stress' (he instanced 'ordering somebody to get shocked'). Milgram replied: 'before you do the experiment, you don't know there will be stress' (Milgram, 1977, p. 97). Such naivety is startling, but Milgram's stance can be partially understood when it is recognised that experimentalists were trained to cultivate an atheoretical approach: that is, to avoid making prior assumptions, even when they were soundly based.

_____ *Pause for reflection* _____

Milgram's response made me wonder whether he ever applied his interest in the three-party power relation to himself. He was the senior researcher who devised the experiment and wrote the script of the 'assistants'. Did he ever identify sufficiently with the subjects to understand the extremity of what he was putting them through? Now identification is seen in some quarters of qualitative psychology as a necessary and useful mode of understanding. In the experimental tradition, it was regarded as a weakness, compromising objectivity.

_____

Observations during the experiment demonstrated the stress: 'There were powerful reactions of tension and emotional strain in a substantial proportion of the participants. Persons were observed to sweat, tremble, stutter, bite their lips, and groan as they found themselves implicated' (Milgram, 1977, p. 112). In one case the experiment had to be stopped because a participant's seizure was 'so violently convulsive' (p. 113).

Here in the twenty-first century, social psychologists assure each other this would not be allowed to happen, and indeed the use of deception is one reason why experimental social psychology has attracted strong criticism since the 1970s. The regulation of research ethics is now strict. At the time there was an implicit value that scientific knowledge was a greater priority than protecting participants from trauma, and hence it is important to locate Milgram's studies in their historical context. Nonetheless, ethical criticism was swift to follow, one of the first examples being expressed in an article by Diana Baumrind in 1964 in which she questioned whether adequate measures had been taken to protect participants. Milgram had been sufficiently interested in ethics during his doctoral dissertation in 1960 to have given his Norwegian participants, after an experiment about group conformity, a short questionnaire in which one question asked: 'Do you feel now that the experiment was ethical or unethical?' The vast majority ticked the response 'neither ethical nor unethical' and 'many indicated that they did not understand how one could use these terms in connection with a scientific experiment' (Milgram, 1977, p. 175). One said: 'Every scientific experiment is beyond ethics'. This is an indication of a very different ethical climate from the one that is now formalised and widely disseminated in social psychology. In Milgram's time, research ethics were subordinated to what was regarded as a wider good: scientific knowledge.

Rom Harré (1979) put an alternative interpretation on the power relation in the laboratory and came to a different substantive conclusion regarding Milgram's experiment:

> It was not an experiment about obedience. It was an experiment about trust. This becomes clear when it is seen that the transcripts reveal that nearly every one of the subjects, at a point where the supposed learner was showing signs of distress, protested against the procedure they had been told to carry out. At this point they were reassured by the assistant [...] Under the conditions of trust that obtained between the subject and Milgram's assistant [...] they now believed their actions were not going to affect the learner at all, other than in the beneficial way of improving his capacity to learn.
>
> (Harré, 1979, p. 105)

Harré's argument was based on an experiment by Donald Mixon (1971) who, by manipulating the interpretations and beliefs which participants brought to the experiment, demonstrated that their trust or not in the researcher's reassurances dramatically affected their preparedness to carry on.

Although Milgram insisted (in italics in the original text) that 'one must always question the relationship of obedience to a person's sense of the context in which he [sic] is operating' (Milgram, 1977, p. 115), he did not introduce the issue of trust. Yet trust is one response to power, and the trust that nobody would be harmed invoked by the research scenario could have been crucial in producing Milgram's outcome.

In stressing context, Milgram recognised, at least in principle, the importance of one criticism of experiments that followed in the 1970s (Gergen, 1973); namely that meanings are always socially situated. Yet by the time Milgram had tailored his question to suit laboratory conditions, his operational model of obedience to authority was undertheorised: there is obedience and there is a belief that one should not harm others: the experiment asked what happens when these come into conflict. This resembles what Danziger called a low-level theory. The meanings of obedience and disobedience to different participants are not included in the investigation, even in the brief case illustrations that Milgram provided (Milgram, 1974, Chapter 5). Thus the part that trust might play in obedience was limited to varying the institutional setting from a more to a less prestigious one. Mixon's and Harré's arguments about trust raise the question not only of different interpretations of 'facts' (experimental results), but of the meaning of research scenarios and how these affect the behaviour of participants.

We can evaluate the obedience experiments from the perspective of situating knowledge as follows. Milgram improved on traditional methods in three ways:

- he acknowledged and, in a limited way, used the social relations of the laboratory and paid attention to the effects of various settings and conditions

- the structure of the laboratory relations paralleled those relations of authority in the larger world that he was researching, thus giving the experimental setting ecological validity

- he supplemented the behavioural emphasis of the experiment with several qualitative methods.

On the other hand:

- the averaging and universalising tendency of statistical analysis has meant that the 40 per cent or so (and in certain conditions, over half) of the participants who disobeyed have been rendered almost invisible in social psychology

- the meanings that participants made of the situation in which they were placed did not inform his analyses

- his espoused 'objective' position above and beyond the real relations of research left Milgram incapable of reflecting on his own position in the three-way power relations in which he was so interested, or from taking an ethical stance towards the subjects' distress through identification.

ACTIVITY 2.1

In the following list I have summarised what I regard as the main points from Milgram's experiments that illustrate, at many levels, the two interrogative themes – power relations and situated knowledges. As you read each point below, ask yourself how it illustrates these themes. Then place each point in order based on how importantly you think it affects the validity of Milgram's experiments as social psychological knowledge.

- Short, necessarily simplified, summaries are reproduced over time and are in danger of leading to a clichéd understanding of original work if primary texts are ignored.

- The post-Second World War context led to some questions being salient, which moulded the development of social psychology.

- Experiments give scientific authority and the status of facts to the knowledge they produce.

- The experimental setting affected the numbers of participants who obeyed and disobeyed.

- Milgram's emphasis on the proportion of participants who obeyed, positioned within the generalising statistical principles of his quantitative method, rendered virtually invisible the participants who disobeyed.

- The three-party relations of authority in the experiment reflected social settings of great political significance.

- The scientific paradigm's principle of objectivity probably informed Milgram's naivety about participants' stress and, coupled with contemporary beliefs about the primacy of scientific enquiry over ethics, discouraged him from protecting participants on ethical grounds.

- Milgram's interpretation of participants' behaviour in terms of 'obedience to authority' illustrates the application of a particular understanding which excluded others – for example, trust, which has different implications for understanding moral conduct towards others.

4.2   Summary

In this section I have examined in detail Milgram's experiments on obedience to authority in order to unpack the complex issues involved in a rigorous use of the experimental method on a topic of social and political significance. I have placed the research in its historical context, both in respect of ethical practices and scientific beliefs. The purpose of this section was to show the many and varied ways in which knowledge about obedience to authority was produced, how the knowledge was situated and within which set of power relations.

5   Social psychometrics: the case of attitude research

By the end of the 1920s 'it was becoming increasingly clear ... that the attitude concept was the distinctive domain of social psychology and that the development of reliable and valid attitudinal measures was an important contribution to the growing identity of the field' (Jones, 1985, p. 60). Attitude research continues to be highly influential in social psychology and suffers from many of the same weaknesses as the experimental method. The study of attitudes has taken a variety of forms, as befits such a broad and inclusive concept. However – and this will come as no surprise by now – attitude research has been dominated by measurement. It has tended to have an applied emphasis and its usefulness is not based on theoretical insights but on the technological efficacy of its methods. Predictably, in quantitative attitude research, the methodology has determined the theory (as with experimental social psychology), rather than the other way around.

Carl Graumann, a historian of social psychology, comments (1988, p. 14): 'for the historian the many techniques of attitude measurement that have been developed since the mid 1920s are less interesting than the growing certainty, reconfirmed by each new technique, that "attitudes can be measured"' (as Louis Thurstone entitled his article in 1928, having devised the first attitude scale). This enhanced the scientific status of social psychology. However, according to Danziger, the new technical language meant an impoverishment: in contrast to many centuries of natural language which had built up rich and complex ways of understanding the subtleties of people's social behaviour, 'a world of collectively experienced meanings would be reduced to the category of social attitude' (Danziger, 1996, p. 24). Operational definitions came to reduce rich concepts such as intelligence and attitude. Intelligence notoriously became defined by psychometricians as something that could be measured by intelligence tests. Likewise, attitudes were in danger of being reduced, by social psychologists using attitude scales, to what these scales could measure.

Attitude measurement technology required that aspects of human behaviour be turned into the kind of information that lends itself to counting: that is, it had to be turned into numbers. Counting can be used in a mode that has no effect on the individual who produces the information, as, for example, in the content analysis of texts. In attitude research, however, the use of measurement has an effect on the behaviour of participants. Although this arithmetisation looks ordinary to today's eyes (nowadays we are all used to ticking boxes on scaled questionnaires), it required a radical step: that a position that someone held about some aspect of their life could be reduced to a single statement and represented as a number. Imagine the possibility that a respondent has not articulated a certain attitude previously, but in needing to respond to a particular situation has simply acted out a specific value position according to his or her conscience: for example, by agreeing to help someone in trouble. Subsequently he or she could be expected to tick a box, based on someone else's statement about attitudes to helping others, representing a position on a five- or seven-point scale that quantifies that attitude.

_____ *Pause for reflection* _____

Why is this a problem?
I remember the first time I filled in a questionnaire of this kind, I kept wanting to answer 'it depends' to most of the questions, but there was no space for that. Many years later, I have developed a critical understanding of my early reaction. I was being required to generalise in order to fulfil the requirements of the method. These requirements are underpinned by a set of theoretical assumptions about the nature of attitudes: they are taken to be general (rather than partially specific to circumstance and the relationship within which they are being expressed) and stable (rather than fluid). In other words, attitude measurement assumes a stable and consistent individual who possesses 'attitudes'. The approach tends to imply that 'there are objective features out there that naturally exist in some amount,

and the investigator merely has to find the best way to capture this fact' (Danziger, 1996, p. 30). This suits prediction and control but leaves out more dynamic and situated features of people's potential responses and experiences.

This is a further example of how a method can produce a limited and distorted vision of human behaviour. A different methodology could open out the question, rather than reduce it to a number. It could be based on a different starting point about people's responses, regarding them as varying, depending on an almost infinite range of considerations specific to the situation. However, this requires that attention be paid to the uniqueness of individuals as well as to what they have in common with others. Such an approach requires case-based methodology, and this has distinct limitations for prediction and hence for control of groups and populations. Here, then, is another example of power relations: that certain applications of knowledge – for example, by government or commercial organisations – require information in particular forms. As a consequence, methods tend to be developed in some directions rather than others. Attitude measurement is a prime example.

In 1932, Rensis Likert invented a scaling method which is now ubiquitous in attitude and personality measurement. (Others preceded it – notably Thurstone's – but Likert's proved the most usable.) A Likert scale is a bipolar psychometric scale usually used in questionnaires. A bipolar scale means that the questions require respondents to specify their level of agreement to each statement in a list on a single dimension, with a negative response at one end and a positive one at the other. Sometimes the scale provides five points ('Strongly disagree', 'disagree', 'neither agree nor disagree', 'agree', 'strongly agree') but a seven- or nine-point scale can also be used. Often the middle point is not available in order to force a choice and ensure that results will not converge around the mean.

Box 2.7   A discursive critique of attitude measurement

Jonathan Potter and Margaret Wetherell (1987) (see also Chapter 1) conducted a detailed critique of attitude measurement from the perspective of their discursive psychological approach, which I summarise here. Following the work of William McGuire (1985), they argue that empirical research on attitudes necessarily assumes that when an attitude is being expressed, people are actually providing responses which 'locate "objects of thought" on "dimensions of judgement"' (McGuire, 1985, p. 239). Potter and Wetherell use an example from research (Marsh, 1976) that measured attitudes on a typical Likert scale. Marsh asked respondents to express their attitudes towards 'coloured immigrants' on a bipolar scale marked 'completely sympathetic' to 'completely unsympathetic', with a mid point of 'no feelings about them either way'. Using McGuire's terms, 'coloured immigrants' is the object of thought and the responses offered on the bipolar scale provide the dimension of judgement.

There are several problems with this, common to all attitude scales, which Potter and Wetherell detail (1987, pp. 44–6). I want to focus on the assumption – necessary to the method – that each respondent is using the same object of

> thought when provided with the cue: in this case, 'coloured immigrants'. If this cannot be assumed, the method does not work as a means of generalisation, which is deemed to be its great value. Potter and Wetherell argue that each person's object is actually different. This is part of their wider criticism that quantitative methods do not allow for variation in participants' responses. They use statements produced in interviews to show just how variable participants' attitudinal objects are – only they see these as discursive. Even a statement such as 'I'm not anti them at all, you know' (Potter and Wetherell, 1987, p. 46) defies being fixed, even though, if treated as an attitude, it could correspond to an endorsement of the 'sympathetic' end of Marsh's Likert scale. Potter and Wetherell go on to demonstrate the complexity of this statement in the context of the wider utterance, focusing on the discourse itself, rather than the mind of the respondent. They argue that it is impossible to separate the object of thought from the evaluation: rather, the speaker constructs a version of the object.

The power relations exemplified in attitude measurement can be summarised as follows. Change in the meaning of common words such as 'attitude' and 'intelligence', reduced in the service of measurement to an operational definition, has a variety of effects. People positioned by psychometric rules and procedures acquiesce in fitting their meanings onto an arithmetised scale. In order to answer at all, they comply with, and therefore contribute to, the reproduction of the assumption that attitudes are relatively fixed, unitary phenomena, rather than dynamic and conflictual. This fits with the purposes of prediction and control and reinforces the widespread use of attitude scales. It also shapes subjectivity.

5.1   Summary

Whereas the 'crisis' was based on criticisms of experimental methodology, the other quantitative methodology – psychometrics – has been subject to very little critique. In this section, I have placed the development of social psychometrics (attitude and opinion measurement) in its historical context and again documented the ways in which the methods produced a certain kind of knowledge about people's beliefs and values. I have argued that this method has a limiting and distorting effect on images of people and also that the power of the method lay not in its theoretical credentials but in its usefulness in applied contexts where generalised knowledge about human populations is sought.

6   Sampling and generalising in different approaches

There are major theoretical questions about the position and status of qualitative research in social psychology, given that 'quantitative' has been widely equated with the terms 'scientific' and 'acceptable'. In this historical context it is not surprising that the recent popularity of qualitative research in social psychology is not always matched by a clear understanding of its different starting principles. Although traditionally quantitative psychology has disavowed the central place of meaning and experience in understanding human behaviour, most experimentalists now recognise that both have some importance. My critique of quantitative social psychology has enabled me to clarify the circumstances in which such methods are – and are not – appropriate. Their dominance has meant that the scientific principles on which they are based are misapplied to methods originating in a different paradigm. The principles of qualitative research have to be conceptualised in a manner that is independent of the principles that have been dominant in quantitative psychology, and this applies in particular to sampling and generalisation. (It also applies to objectivity, but there is no space to deal with that here.)

A common example can be seen in the question of how much data to collect for a qualitative project. The question is inseparable from a methodological debate about generalisability (whether and how you can apply findings to objects outside your research group). For example, qualitative researchers at conferences often start by apologising for the small size of their sample and regret that, as a result, they cannot generalise beyond the individuals involved. Evidently their concepts of generalisability and sampling have been dictated by the idea of statistical sampling and generalisability. It is inaccurate to say that you cannot generalise from a small sample, although it is correct that you cannot generalise statistically from such a sample.

Generalisation through aggregation and statistical analysis was not always accepted as good science. Historically, when the experimental method was introduced into psychology, each participant's behavioural record of responses to a series of stimuli were analysed as a case record and not aggregated across individuals. Danziger comments that, during the twentieth century, quantitative research methods' 'reliance on this fictional creature [the "average animal"] became even more pronounced. Finally it achieved the status of a methodological fetish' (Danziger, 1990, pp. 153–4). George Yule, a British statistician, wrote in 1921: 'statistical methods ... should be regarded as ancillary, not essential. They are essential where the subject of investigation is itself an aggregate ... but [not where] the subject is the individual' (cited in Danziger, 1990, p. 225).

How else can one generalise? Many critical commentators take issue with the whole idea of generalisability in social research because, as Egon Guba and Yvonna Lincoln comment: 'What can a generalisation be except an assertion that is context free?' (1981, p. 62). Michael Patton (2002, pp. 583–4) prefers the idea of extrapolation which, rather than being based on statistics and probability, implies that attention has been paid to the conditions under which the findings could be applicable in other situations. Theoretical extrapolation from case study data requires that care is taken to specify what constraints may operate on it (depending on the idea we are hoping to transfer) as a result of location, social position and the like. The situating of knowledge in its context is a central tenet of qualitative research.

The answer to the question of how many cases are needed in a study is therefore not clear-cut. For some purposes, a single case is adequate. The number is going to depend on the research question, the method, the type of analysis, the status of the theories being used, the mode of and constraints on generalisability.

6.1 Summary

In this section, you have been encouraged to step outside one of the key principles of scientific method – generalisability – and reconsider its limits. I have argued that different principles of extrapolation from evidence are appropriate in qualitative research paradigms.

7 Conclusions

The object of social psychological knowledge – people in their social settings – is necessarily affected by the research methods used. No method is neutral. By acknowledging that social psychological methods have effects on the knowledge they produce, it becomes incumbent on researchers to consider those effects and make informed choices on the basis of what is worth knowing, and to whom. The ontological and methodological commitments behind these choices should be made explicit:

- What view of the person (ontology) in their social setting is behind the research question?

- Given this view, what methodology is appropriate?

- What methods and design follow this methodology?

Adherence to the principle of being explicit about these underpinnings should not only lead to greater openness and less dogma in social psychology, but also to better research.

References

Baumrind, D. (1964) 'Some thoughts on ethics of research: after reading Milgram's "behavioral study of obedience"', *American Psychologist*, vol. 19, pp. 42–3.

Danziger, K. (1985) 'The methodological imperative in psychology', *Philosophy of Social Science*, vol. 15, pp. 1–13.

Danziger, K. (1990) *Constructing the Subject: Historical Origins of Psychological Research*, Cambridge, Cambridge University Press.

Danziger, K. (1996) 'The practice of psychological discourse' in Graumann, C. F. and Gergen, K.J. (eds) *Historical Dimensions of Psychological Discourse*, Cambridge, Cambridge University Press, pp. 17–35.

Edwards, D. (1999) 'Emotion discourse', *Culture and Psychology*, vol. 5, no.3, pp. 271–91.

Gergen, K.J. (1973) 'Social psychology as history', *Journal of Personality and Social Psychology*, vol. 26, pp 309–20.

Gergen, K.J. (1978) 'Experimentation in social psychology: a reappraisal', *European Journal of Social Psychology*, vol. 8, pp. 507–27.

Graumann, C.F. (1988) 'Introduction to a history of social psychology' in Hewstone, M., Stroebe, W., Codol, J.P. and Stephenson, G. (eds) *Introduction to Social Psychology: A European Perspective*, Oxford, Basil Blackwell, pp. 3–19.

Guba, e.g. and Lincoln, Y.S. (1981) *Effective Evaluation: Improving the Usefulness of Evaluation Results through Responsive and Naturalistic Approaches*, San Francisco and London, Jossey-Bass.

Harré, R. (1979) *Social Being*, Oxford, Blackwell.

Hewstone, M., Manstead, A. and Stroebe, W. (eds) (1997) *The Blackwell Reader in Social Psychology*, Oxford, Blackwell.

Jones, E. (1985) 'Major developments in social psychology during the past five decades' in Lindzey, G. and Aronson, E. (eds) *The Handbook of Social Psychology*, vol. 1: *Theory and Method* (3rd edn), New York, Random House, pp. 47–107.

Marsh, A. (1976) 'Who hates the blacks?', *New Society*, 23 September, pp. 649–52.

McGuire, W.J. (1985) 'Attitudes and attitude change' in G. Lindzey and E. Aronson (eds) *Handbook of Social Psychology* (3rd edn), New York, Random House, vol. 2, pp. 136–314.

Milgram, S. (1963) 'Behavioral study of obedience', *Journal of Abnormal and Social Psychology*, vol. 67, pp. 371-8.

Milgram, S. (1965) 'Some conditions of obedience and disobedience to authority', *Human Relations*, vol. 18, pp. 57–76.

Milgram, S. (1974) *Obedience to Authority: An Experimental View*, London, Tavistock.

Milgram, S. (1977) *The Individual in a Social World: Essays and Experiments*, Reading, MA, Addison Wesley.

Mishler, e.g. (1986) *Research Interviewing: Context and Narrative*, Cambridge, MA, Harvard University Press.

Mixon, D. (1971) 'Behaviour analysis treating subjects as actors rather than organisms', *Journal for the Theory of Social Behaviour*, vol. 1, pp. 19–31.

Orne, M.T. (1962) 'On the social psychology of the psychology experiment: with particular reference to demand characteristics and their implications', *American Psychologist*, vol. 17, pp. 776–83.

Patton, M.Q. (2002) *Qualitative Research and Evaluation Methods* (3rd edn), London, Sage.

Polkinghorne, D.E. (1988) *Narrative Knowing and the Human Sciences*, Albany, NY, State University of New York Press.

Potter, J. and Wetherell, M. (1987) *Social Psychology and Discourse: Beyond Attitudes and Behaviour*, London, Sage.

Reid, S. (ed.) (1997) *Developments in Infant Observation: The Tavistock Model*, London and New York, Routledge.

Rosenthal, R. (1966) *Experimenter Effects in Behavioral Research*, New York, Appleton-Century-Crofts.

Silverman, I. (1977) 'Why social psychology fails', *Canadian Psychological Review*, vol. 18, pp. 353–8.

Spears, R., Hollway, W. and Edwards, D. (2005) 'Three views on hate', *The Psychologist*, vol. 18, no. 9, September, pp. 844–7.

Tajfel, H. (1972) 'Experiments in a vacuum' in Israel, J. and Tajfel, H. (eds) *The Context of Social Psychology: A Critical Assessment*, London, Academic Press.

Thurstone, L.L. (1928) 'Attitudes can be measured', *American Journal of Sociology*, vol. 23, pp. 529–554.

Chapter 3

Families

by Helen Lucey, The Open University

Contents

Learning outcomes

By the end of this chapter you should:

- have gained an overview of how families have traditionally been studied in psychological social psychology, especially developmental social psychology
- be able to identify aspects of family processes and relationships that are not addressed by current research and appreciate the contributions that sociological social psychology can make to the study of families
- be able to identify the key features of a discursive psychological perspective and understand how they can be applied to an analysis of identity construction in relation to singleness and the gendered division of labour
- be able to identify the key features of a social psychoanalytic perspective and understand how they have been applied to an analysis of sibling relationships through one case study of five sisters
- be aware that family forms are diverse in relationships and practices according to cultural differences, sexuality and personal preferences.

---

1 Introduction

In all cultures, it is likely that our earliest experiences of relationships will take place within some form of family or close kinship system. We have direct experience of relationships both with our own families and through the experiences of people with whom we interact, as well as those depicted in newspapers, on television and in other media. It has been argued that the family is society's most important institution because it provides the key environment in which children develop physically, emotionally and socially. It is in families that we have the most opportunities to learn what is necessary to become well-adjusted adults who can live with others in society. Families may also provide material and emotional resources, and care throughout the life course. They are therefore seen as core institutions; responsible for the development and happiness of individuals and essential for the well-being and reproduction of society as a whole.

For most of us the first group we belong to is a family group, and it is in families and family-type groups that our feelings about individuality and collectivity, belonging, connection and separation, dependence and independence take shape. Families and close personal relationships give us a vital framework through which we come to make sense of ourselves and the world in which we live.

This chapter presents the rudiments of a social psychology of families by considering relevant social psychological analyses that focus simultaneously on social and individual processes within different kinds of families. It will present social psychological work on families from discursive psychological and social psychoanalytic perspectives.

1.1 Psychology and families

There has been consistent attention in social psychology to the various dimensions of groups, including how they are formed, how they relate to other groups and their influence on the cognition, opinion and self-identity of their members (Breinlinger, 1996; Brown, 2000; Hogg, 1992; Kelly and Tajfel, 1981; Turner et al., 1987). However, although families are often mentioned as an example of a group, they have been relatively neglected by social psychologists as a topic for focused study in their own right.

It is within developmental psychology that families have been most researched. Here, concern has been directed towards families as the locations of both *causes* and *outcomes* in individuals in relation to topics such as attachment, intelligence, personality type, mental well-being, educational achievement, and emotional and occupational success. A consistent focus in this sub-discipline of psychology is on mother–child interactions (fathers are far less studied; see O'Brien, 2005), and thousands of publications explore the optimal and the most deleterious conditions for childrearing. Research in this tradition tends to focus on the *failure* of good outcomes for family members, such as eating disorders and incest (Cawson et al., 2000), and looks for causes of such failures in the family. So, for example, educational and developmental psychologists make strong links between what mothers do with their children in the early years at home, and how easily and quickly children learn the principles of reading, writing and mathematics at school (Flouri and Buchanan, 2004). There has, however, been some attention to families as a context for child development (e.g. White and Woollett, 1991).

In developmental psychology, most attention is focused on young children (Bradley, 1989). It is important to note that particular ideas about children's subjectivity and agency (or lack of it) pervade this field: children are treated as if they have no ontology, no 'being' in their own right, but rather as though they are in the process of 'becoming' (James and Prout, 1990). But there has persisted a social strand in developmental psychology that has increasingly contested the idea that childhood is merely a transitional stage to adulthood and that children are passive, naive and incompetent (e.g., Dunn, 2004).

In considering young people's transitions to adulthood and the relationship between biological and psychological development, developmental social psychologists focus on adolescents. Adolescence is viewed as a 'normal' transitional phase, characterised by struggles for separation from parents and emotional turbulence in the process of autonomous identity formation (Coleman, 1990). In this model of adolescence, with its focus on the individual, the peer group is considered, and the family, if included, tends to be analysed for its effect on adolescent outcomes (e.g. Heaven, 2001; Larson et al., 2006). It is because developmental psychologists are concerned to look specifically at what goes on 'inside' families that the 'boundaries' of the family are firmly drawn. By delineating what is and what is not a family, psychological investigation can proceed with some certainty about what is being observed and measured – that is, whether it is happening inside the family and is therefore an effect of family events, practices or processes.

Although developmental and clinical psychologists who are interested in families do emphasise that they are not static entities, it is the changes produced through the cognitive, biological, and sexual development of children and young people that are seen as most relevant (Durkin, 1995). Because the family is understood as a predominantly individual and private domain, it is mapped out as separate from the more public realms of society and culture and seen to be neither influenced by these dimensions nor as having an influence on them. Furthermore, the psychological processes that occur in families through interactions between family members tend to be viewed as 'universal', so that differences between families, although often acknowledged, are inclined to be marginalised and flattened out in the analysis of data, or to be analysed for evidence of deviance. Thus relationships between family members, the emotional and developmental tasks of families and the kinds of practices that are best suited to fulfilling these tasks are treated as if they are historically and culturally static. Feminist social psychologists, in particular, have challenged over-generalised accounts of development and childrearing that render differences of 'race', gender and class invisible (Walkerdine and Lucey, 1989; Phoenix, 1991). The notion of situated knowledges is important here. It brings to our attention the ways in which psychological ideas that are produced in particular contexts at specific times greatly influence commonsense and professional ideas about *all* mothers, fathers and children. These ideas have informed government policy in the areas of health, welfare and education.

1.2   Building a social psychology of the family

The very notion of family holds some of the tensions with which the discipline of social psychology struggles – tensions between how to conceptualise self and other, individual and society, private and public. These tensions are reflected in the divergence in social psychology between psychological social psychology (PSP) and sociological social psychology (SSP). This is why families afford fascinating possibilities for an emerging social psychology in which the individual is not studied as isolated from social, cultural and structural processes. The study of families, therefore, can shed valuable light on power relations and situated knowledges and attempt to transcend individual–social and agency–structure dualisms.

Whereas psychological social-developmental psychologists have emphasised the role of families in the socialisation and development of children, the focus for sociological social psychologists is on societal processes and the ways in which these impact on family structures and practices. Thus in SSP, the boundaries of the family are seen as fluid and more permeable. Families are characterised less by universal and unchanging features, processes and practices, and more by the effects of constant 'traffic' between them and the social, cultural, institutional and political world. Therefore an SSP focus on families conceives them as dynamic and changing; recognises the central role of language and discourse within and about families; looks at diversity between families; examines the meanings and experiences associated with particular family forms for those within and outside them, and the interrelationship between societal policy and practices and family forms and practices. For example, a sociological social psychologist will explore the contradictions between demographic data that show that families are a key site of change in many societies, and qualitative research that reveals the extent to which people are committed to 'the family' as a site of unchanging tradition.

I will keep families in focus in precisely these ways and refer to work that contributes towards a social psychology that is concerned not to split the individual from the social, nor to reduce the social to interpersonal relations within families, but to pay attention to the social, cultural and historical context of families and what goes on in them. Therefore I will concentrate on two social psychological perspectives – namely, discursive psychological and social psychoanalytic – to explore topics such as transnational families, gay and lesbian parenthood, singleness, gender, the domestic division of labour and the place of sibling relationships in personal and group identity construction.

ACTIVITY 3.1

Take a moment to think about what a family is. How do we define who are family members and who are not? Is biology or legal status the only basis for membership? Can families be child free? Can a single person living alone constitute a family? Do pets count as family members? Consider, for example, the following two headlines:

'We'd rather be with friends'

Qualitative research by the Cava Research Group (for the study of care, values and the future of welfare) at the University of Leeds, finds that increasingly it is friendship that really matters in people's lives. In or outside heterosexual couples, the people they interviewed were turning to friends for emotional support.

(*New Statesman*, 15–30 December 2003, p. 80)

'Friends are the new family'

One in three people now live alone, but as romantic partnerships decline, new forms of intimate relationships appear to be taking their place.

(*The Guardian*, 12 December 2003)

The notion that friendships are more or just as valuable as family relationships has entered popular discourses about contemporary subjectivity. The headlines from the articles in Activity 3.1, about changing practices and expectations in contemporary family relationships, express ideas about the need for equality in personal relationships, freedom from fixed 'roles' and family obligations, and constancy in the face of temporary romantic partnerships. These ideas may also be a response to more fragmented lives in which family members live far apart and have less day-to-day contact.

1.3   Summary

This section pointed to the importance of families as contexts of socialisation and of individual and group identity formation. It outlined the ways in which families have been studied by psychological social-developmental psychologists and noted that much of this work has focused on families as sites of causes and outcomes in terms of the emotional and mental development of individuals. Most attention has been paid to mother–child interactions and far less to fathers or adolescents. Psychological social psychology (PSP) tends to treat the individual and the social as two distinct entities which are studied separately. In contrast, I propose a sociological social psychology (SSP) of the family that emphasises the mutual constitution of individuals and groups.

2   Families and change

As well as including parents, partners, children, siblings, aunts, uncles and cousins, family networks may also include close friends, step-parents and step-children, ex-partners and ex-sons- and daughters-in-law. The idea of an identifiable and clearly 'bounded' family (McKie et al., 2005) is clearly up for debate.

Studies that have explored how children define who and what constitutes 'family' raise questions about the boundaries of family, and challenge assumed links between social and biological ties. In her study of 8–14 year-olds, Virginia Morrow (1998) concluded that children consider the *quality* of relationships between family members as well as the roles performed by individuals to be more important than marriage or biological relatedness. Rosalind Edwards et al. (2006) found that children frequently include as family members peers, parents' friends, neighbours and teachers who they feel particularly close to. There is evidence that the boundaries that people set around families vary according to ethnic, class, cultural, religious and political contexts (Cicirelli, 1994). For example, in African Caribbean families children may include a wide range of biologically and non-biologically related people as relatives (Chamberlain, 1999).

2.1   Transnational families and identities

'Networks of affection', as Fiona Williams (2004, p. 17) calls families and close relationships, are influenced by many forces, including economic changes and patterns of employment. The history and shape of present-day Europe is steeped in the movement of people through slavery, colonial regimes, economic necessity and war, political unrest and persecution. As a consequence of globalisation, a more recent twist to this is the proliferation of transnational families in which, although family members are dispersed across several nation states, modern modes of communication and possibilities for international travel mean that affiliations and bonds may be maintained in ways that were previously much harder.

Figure 3.1   A family group

_____ *Pause for reflection* _____

For many of us, where we come from is tied up with our identity. My parents were both born in southern Ireland and came to the UK during the Second World War as part of the Irish diaspora. Despite being born and brought up in London, where I've always lived, I still think of myself as 'London-Irish' rather than British. This identity was forged through religious and cultural practices, regular family get-togethers and through the constant telling and retelling of stories about 'home'. Does your family history of being located in one place and/or migration or relocation have meaning for you and your identity?

_____

Constance Sutton (2004) explored the role of family reunion rituals of three African Caribbean transnational families by carrying out in-depth interviews with people who had taken part in them. These took place 'back home' in Barbados, Grenada and Trinidad. She found that the concept of family was highly 'elastic' on these islands, with a broad definition of who counted as 'kin' – something that reinforced the inclusiveness of the concept of family that was being celebrated. A key function of the activities was to bring children together in order for them to 'get to know their family', where the connection between family and identity was made explicit: one woman summed this up when she said 'knowing your family is knowing yourself'. Family reunions and the rituals within them were a way of creating 'the knowledge that "family" is your most basic (collective) identity' (Sutton, 2004, p. 245).

Sutton illuminates the complexities of contemporary processes of migration and the significance of family practices in constructing individual and family identities. She shows how demarcations between individuals and groups regarding questions of identity are often blurred as well as subject to change. The tensions and contradictions between individual agency and the constraints of structural forces are also highlighted: economic necessity is the force that drives most people to migrate from the Caribbean Islands to Canada, the USA and the UK, and yet other structural processes (i.e. availability of international travel) allow for the exercise of personal agency in choosing to return 'home', at least for a holiday.

2.2　Changing family forms

Large-scale surveys such as the ten-yearly UK Census show that there have been significant changes in the composition of households over the last thirty years, with steep increases in lone-parent and single-person households. They point to huge changes in women's full-time participation in the labour market, even when they have dependent children, and reveal shifts in patterns of fertility and child bearing. For some, such social shifts are viewed as undermining the values and bonds that underpin families (Putnam, 2000). With the de-traditionalisation of family forms comes the weakening of family ties (Beck and Beck-Gernsheim, 2002). Some argue that this results in the individualisation of close relationships, with love and intimacy becoming more central, but more difficult to secure and maintain (Giddens, 1992). Others cast a more optimistic light on such changes, arguing that they have resulted in more egalitarian relationships, as well as in the emergence of families of 'choice' and the growing importance of non-kin relationships, such as friendships (Roseneil and Budgeon, 2004).

In 2005 the Civil Partnership Act in the UK provided same-sex couples with similar rights to married couples. Although changes in the law help legitimate the idea that families can be made up of same-sex couples, there is evidence that heteronormativity, the everyday construction of heterosexual relations as the normal and natural order of things, still holds sway. Normative ideas about family life are reproduced both at the level of mundane conversations and practices, as well as at institutional and governmental levels. Darren Langdridge and Eric Blyth (2001) found that access to assisted conception services appears to rely on a 'traditional' notion of the family with the consequence that large numbers of potential service users are excluded, in particular, single women and lesbian couples. Others argue that gay and lesbian parenting continues to provoke strong anxieties within a heteronormative society, and one of the most prominent of contemporary responses is to focus on the supposed 'differences' that such families and their children exhibit, whether those differences are interpreted positively or negatively (Hicks, 2005).

Figure 3.2   Elaine and Debbie Gaston were one of the first lesbian couples in the UK to get 'married' in a civil partnership ceremony. Debbie is a minister at Brighton Metropolitan Community Church. They performed their ceremony in Brighton Town Hall.

2.3   Summary

This section has considered diversity and difference between families including some of the economic and social changes over the last thirty years that have influenced families. Quantitative and qualitative research suggest that diversity rather than homogeneity characterises living arrangements and family forms, with the boundaries of families becoming more fluid. Sutton's study of 'transnational' families illuminated how processes of globalisation can add to this fluidity. This alerted us to the intertwining of individual identity with membership of a family group, and drew our attention to the tensions between individual agency and structural forces. Whether the changes taking place in families are positive or negative is strongly debated. Whereas some celebrate the de-traditionalisation of family forms and the possibilities this offers for the emergence of new family forms, normative ideologies about 'traditional', heterosexual families dominate institutional and everyday thinking on families.

The ideological aspect of everyday discourse and social practices is a central thread that runs through the following discussion of 'singleness', family life and domestic practices.

3   A discursive psychological perspective on families

3.1   Principles of a discursive psychological perspective

Chapters 1 and 2 have shown that discursive psychology is a diverse disciplinary domain, both theoretically and in terms of methodologies. The examples of research in this section illustrate the kind of approach that 'critical' discursive psychology (CDP) takes to the study of families (Wetherell, 1998). This approach is concerned with both the study of discourse resources and the analysis of discursive processes and social practices. The social and performative aspects of language use are studied within a cultural and historical context.

A CDP perspective:

■   focuses on the part that language and discourse play in constructing social reality. This is a concern with discourse processes as a form of social action and talk as a means of constructing social reality rather than simply a way of communicating ideas and experiences (as Austin (1962) put it: 'people do things with words');

■   assumes that speakers draw on already existing cultural ideas in their discourse (discourse resources);

■   focuses on the analysis of spoken or written 'texts', such as conversations, interview transcripts, diaries;

■   identifies how people use commonsense but contradictory explanations (interpretative repertoires); how they take up or attribute identities (subject positions); how their talk is situated in the context of giving an account and thus rhetorically constructed to perform justifications and blamings;

■   through its analysis of the above, aims to highlight the ideological features of discourse and examine how social inequalities are constructed and reconstructed in and through the everyday use of language.

In the following sections, discourses of 'singleness' and 'domestic housework' are used as examples that show how issues of family membership and domestic labour are related to unequal and gendered power relations. Both examples emphasise that these social relations help to make us who we are.

3.2   Singleness

I have included a piece of research on singleness in this chapter because the notion of singleness is constructed against the notion of family, as its opposite. Singleness, along with other non-conventional family forms, provides an opportunity to look at how the limits of family are constructed in discourse and to explore the meanings of family and the impact of families on an individual's identity. Sasha Roseneil and Shelley Budgeon (2004) found that far from being isolated solitary individuals, single people are often woven into rich and complex networks of intimacy, friendship, care and support. Despite this, the discourse resources available to single women are wholly inadequate in capturing their experience, as the following discussion highlights.

Although the number of single-person households has increased significantly in the last fifteen years, singleness is not viewed as a normative or a psychologically healthy condition for men or women (Adams, 1976). It is not understood as an individual preference or choice, but rather as a personal failure, 'a deficit identity, defined by lack and by the shared conception of single women as outside normal family life and intimate relationships' (Reynolds and Taylor, 2004). In response to this situation, Jill Reynolds and Margaret Wetherell argue for a feminist psychology of singleness based on critical discursive psychology, with the focus on the patterning of ideology rather than the supposed dysfunction of single women (2003, p. 489). First, they maintain that the single state and the status of singleness are *socially constructed* in that they must be understood as historically and culturally variable. Second, they argue that singleness is a *social category* which, like the use of all categories, is constructed in an attempt to provide a neat framework for social life. Third, they claim singleness is a discourse; a set of complex meanings and practices that produces knowledge and forms of truth about single people. Connected to this is the notion that singleness is constructed in relation to power as an 'ideological field'. Finally, Reynolds and Wetherell propose that singleness should be studied as a set of *personal narratives* and *subject positions*.

> Social history, social practices and the ideological field around singleness construct a cultural slot and a set of identity possibilities. The process, however, of living in this slot and living with these possibilities (working with them, complying, resisting and transforming them) becomes a personal identity project for the individual single woman. In developing narratives and accounts of themselves, and in making sense of their lives and life choices, people work up the discursive resources available as identity. Indeed, narratives are a way of managing identity in a shifting, fragmented and complex ideological field.
>
> (Reynolds and Wetherell, 2003, p. 493)

In interviews with thirty women, Reynolds and Wetherell explored the ways in which women who define themselves as single draw on interpretative repertoires that are available in the public arena. These interpretative repertoires are the 'building blocks' through which people develop accounts and versions of significant events and through which they perform social life. They consist of 'what everyone knows' about a topic, but they are often contradictory (Reynolds and Wetherell, 2003, p. 496). Reynolds and Wetherell have shown that singleness for women is an uneasy subject position replete with idealised and pathologised repertoires of singleness as:

- personal deficit
- social exclusion

- independence and choice
- self-actualisation and achievement.

Box 3.1   Single women's repertoires of choice

In both of the following extracts, Annie and Lyn are responding to a question about what they find it easy or difficult to do as single women, and they draw on contrasting repertoires to describe and make sense of their experience. In the first extract, Annie constructs singleness as a positive condition, through the repertoires of independence and choice. However, while singleness is idealised here, it also holds the danger of being thought 'selfish'. In the second extract, the repertoire of social exclusion is drawn through a stark contrast between singleness and coupledom. Here, the world of couples is constructed as a privileged space, whereas singleness is perceived as being excluded, lacking and disadvantaged.

> Annie: Um, well, it's silly little things really. I suppose like being able to decorate the house exactly as you like there's no compromise in anything, you can do anything you want. I mean people can moan and say that's stupid and say well there's not a lot I wanted, you know, whereas when I was married you are forever sort of um toning down what you like, or what you want. I know that's a very selfish attitude but I do enjoy being able to have exactly my own way. Bad things, I don't think there's anything particularly bad about it, it's hard put to find any down side you know.
>
> (Reynolds and Wetherell, 2003, p. 500)

> Lyn: [...] And I think that you don't get locked into a sort of social network if you're single, or I haven't, it hasn't been my experience. And when I was in my 30s a single friend said to me 'oh well couples won't invite us because they're scared of us; they think we're going to walk off with their men'. And I don't think of it the same way now but I think there are, there are, there is this sort of couple network thing. And they'll invite each other round to dinner and you'll sort of share it and swap it and make it equal and as a single person I have never felt included in that.
>
> (Reynolds and Wetherell, 2003, p. 499)

These polarised and inconsistent repertoires present single women with ideological dilemmas that must somehow be resolved when they talk about themselves and their identities. They may distance themselves from the denigrating evaluations of singleness and instead construct it positively through repertoires of choice, independence, self-development and achievement. However, taking up this position presents a dilemma because it then becomes difficult to express a desire to change things. Alternatively, women who talk freely and without shame about wanting a relationship are in jeopardy of being constructed as lacking, dysfunctional and 'desperate'. The most positive strategy used by a small number of women in Reynolds's and Wetherell's study 'was to develop a reflexive account and talk about the dilemmas per se rather than alternating between each side of them as experiential truths' (Reynolds and Wetherell, 2003, p. 507).

_____ *Pause for reflection* _____

Think of some of the ways that single men and women are positively and/or negatively represented in the media. Are these representations different for older and younger single men and women? Can you identify any dilemmas?

3.3   Gender: the domestic division of labour and power

One area that interests feminist social psychologists is the unequal division of domestic labour within households.

Research finds that women do far more childcare and housework than men (Baxter, 2000), even when they are also in paid employment (Dempsey, 1997). However, this situation does not persist simply because men are unwilling to share domestic work equally: although most heterosexual couples support the principle of parity in taking responsibility for household tasks, those same couples may also look upon the unequal division of their own family and house work as fair (Coltrane, 2000). This paradox has led researchers to probe into the feelings and attitudes that people have towards the distribution of housework and childcare and to build a social psychology of the domestic division of labour (Hawkins et al., 1998).

Box 3.2   The Distributive Justice Framework

The Distributive Justice Framework (DJF) is based on questionnaire methodology and has become an influential perspective in the social psychology of domestic labour (Thompson, 1991). It states women's sense of entitlement in order to understand and explain gender inequalities in domestic work and identifies three factors that form this sense of entitlement:

- outcome values (housework and childcare can be important in creating and maintaining loving relationships)
- comparison referents (women who compare their relationship favourably with that of other people feel more satisfied with the allocation of housework in their own partnership)
- justifications (include beliefs that men have less time for housework, are less able to multi-task, and do not have the same standards as women; additionally, women are more likely to evaluate the division of housework as reasonable if they feel that it has been discussed openly).

Much DJF research is based on questionnaire surveys, the advantage of which is that it allows for a comparative analysis across large populations. Such surveys are less helpful when it comes to looking at people's sense of fairness with regard to the allocation of housework and childcare in families.

ACTIVITY 3.2

Read the following extract from Caroline Dryden's (1999) qualitative study of gender relationships in marriage. Think about the ways in which Rachael makes sense of the division of housework in her marriage.

CAROLINE: What about in your own marriage?

RACHAEL: Mm.

CAROLINE: Do you think that gender roles are an issue for you in any way, or not?

RACHAEL: [pause] Um [pause], well, getting back to the tangible things, yes I mean there are certain things I mean it would be – I mean Gordon would never clean the loo. I mean he would say that he would, I mean I s'pose he'd pour some bleach down it occasionally you know but, with the sort of bad aim our sons have got, you know, he wouldn't, he wouldn't even think of it. And – I know I'm at home and he's at work so in fact that sort of scotches your question but I mean I don't think he would even think of it, even if I were working full-time. Um [pause] I don't know though, I mean on the other h– on the other hand I mean he might put the hoover attachment on and go round all the sort of plasterwork or something which is a thing that ...

CAROLINE: You wouldn't do it?

RACHAEL: I would never do so [pause]. I s'pose he's fairly sort of enlightened, he just hates housework. [Both laugh].

(Dryden, 1999, pp. 39–40)

We do not know from this short extract whether or not Rachael thinks that the division of tasks is fair, but we do know that she sees housework as her responsibility. She justifies this by saying that her husband works full-time and therefore makes a greater economic contribution to the household and that he 'just hates housework'. Nevertheless, Rachael can present him as 'enlightened' by referring to a task that he takes on that she would 'never do'.

Discursive psychologists do not use questionnaires, but they would analyse extracts such as the interview with Rachael (above) to show how she constructs gender roles and how she evaluates her own and her partner's input to domestic work. John Dixon and Margaret Wetherell point out that 'Principles such as "fair shares" or "equity", for example, are moral evaluations that are quite literally *brought to meaning* within day-to-day discourse' rather than pre-given meanings that are simply 'expressed' through language (2004, p. 175, italics in original). For example, Nigel Edley and Margaret Wetherell (1999) point out some of the contradictory repertoires and dilemmas that arise when young men draw on available commonsense ideas to talk about parenting responsibilities and gender equality.

Dixon and Wetherell (2004) note that most research on family life takes judgements of fairness out of the contexts in which they usually arise and tends to hide the *situated* discursive practices that make up everyday family life. Questionnaire methodology takes no account of the wider ideological context that influences family negotiations to the advantage of some and disadvantage of others. It gives little idea of how domestic practices are implicated in the construction of identities, nor of the variety of domestic tasks that women engage in during the course of a day. These may include an argument with a partner about doing the laundry, trying to get children to clean their bedrooms and asking a boss for some annual leave during the school holidays. 'Each of these moments evokes different identities, constructs a different psychology, evolves through different routines of social interaction, and involves different power relations' (Dixon and Wetherell, 2004, p. 174).

Unequal gender relations are deeply embedded in the way that domestic life is organised. In *The Second Shift*, Arlie Hochschild (1989) notes that 'economies of gratitude' are discernible in interactional sequences in which men's participation in household tasks is typically understood as 'gifts' or 'favours'. We might read Rachael's comments in the extract above in this light: there is an implicit gratitude expressed in the way she frames her husband's minimal involvement in housework through the unusual, infrequent and, arguably, non-essential task of vacuuming the plasterwork. In contrast, women's contributions to domestic work are more or less taken for granted. For Dixon and Wetherell, the notion of economies of gratitude illustrates well the kinds of *dialogic* practices that provide the foundations for couples' shared definitions of justice and equality in the domestic realm. It reveals that, although constructions of fairness may be jointly accomplished, they do not always represent a fair compromise. This is because they are strongly influenced by cultural ideologies that define gender inequalities as normative.

3.4   Summary

This section has concentrated on critical discursive psychological (CDP) work on questions of singleness and of the gendered division of labour in heterosexual families. This perspective focuses closely on the part that language and discourse play in constructing identities and looks at people's use of dominant discourses that construct and reconstruct inequality in their everyday lives. It assumes that language is action-orientated and that people make use of the discursive resources that are available to them. These resources are not fixed, but are produced in dynamic relation with social, historical and cultural conditions.

This perspective allows an exploration of the ways in which ideology and power work within family negotiations about domestic labour to the benefit of some and detriment of others. It has also shown how contradictory discourses of singleness place single women outside 'family', and omit their desires and preferences as well as the complexity of their personal relationships and connections.

In the next section I change direction in terms of perspective to look at the insights that a social psychoanalytic perspective on family and identity might give us, with a particular focus on the part that siblings play in the formation of individual and family-group identities.

4   A social psychoanalytic perspective on family life

Being and having a sibling is an experience that is familiar to many of us – although it is becoming less common in many affluent countries. In 2001, nearly 60 per cent of children in the UK lived in households containing more than one child and 20 per cent of these contained three or more children (Office for National Statistics, 2001). These figures do not account for the number of siblings, half-siblings and step-siblings who live in separate households.

In this section I will take a social psychoanalytic perspective to look at the relationships of children and young people with their siblings. This work moves away from the strictly developmental focus of traditional psychology and psychoanalysis. It explores the place that sisters and brothers have in the emotional life of children and young people and the ways in which they enter into processes of personal and group identity formation.

_____ *Pause for reflection* _____

Are you a brother or a sister or are you an only child? If you do have siblings, what were your feelings about them when you were growing up? Have those feelings changed as you've grown older? If you did not have siblings, did this seem an advantage or disadvantage when you were growing up? Did you think about what it would be like to have a sister or brother, or did you wish for one?

_____

Studying siblings brings us to one of the tensions at the core of social psychology as a discipline, for siblings are at one and the same time individual *and* social, same *and* different. How can a social psychoanalytic approach address this central problematic without falling into the trap of either prioritising the individual, essential subject who is separate from sociality, or the over-socialised subject, entirely determined by structure and with no agency?

4.1   Principles of a social psychoanalytic perspective

The basic principles of the social psychoanalytic approach frame this section. Some of the principles overlap with those of other approaches, such as discursive and phenomenological, but they are differentiated from all other variations of psychology and other branches of the social sciences by the underpinning concept of a dynamic, conflictual unconscious. A social psychoanalytic approach:

■   emphasises the dynamic, relational and *inseparable* nature of psychological and social life to look at how subjectivity emerges in the social domain (Frosh, 2003)

- theorises and analyses unconscious as well as conscious processes

- maintains that anxiety and the strategies developed to defend against the difficult feelings that anxiety provokes play an important part in the construction of individual, social, cultural and institutional lives

- is theoretically plural in that it brings concepts together that can take account of the *interior* processes of the human mind (individual and group emotions) with those that relate to arenas of the social world (structure and power)

- emphasises interpretative, qualitative methods.

The starting point for a social psychoanalytic perspective is the idea that unconscious as well as conscious processes (the latter being thoughts of which we are aware and which we can recall to consciousness at will) are mutually formative of subjectivity. Sigmund Freud began to formulate his ideas about unconscious mechanisms and dynamics after observing that, under hypnosis, patients often recalled memories, stories and wishes which they could not remember when they were awake, even though these had a powerful effect on the person's mood and behaviour. The idea that our behaviour and interactions are partly the product of irrational and unconscious processes challenges strongly-held psychological beliefs about human nature and human relationships. Much psychological research on families, as well as the social policy and socialwork practices it informs, assumes that people are guided by reasonable and rational motives, that they generally know what they are doing and why they are doing it, and are in control of their lives. In contrast, psychoanalysis (and following that a social psychoanalytic perspective) suggests that conscious thought is only the superficial tip of the iceberg, and that it is within the realm of vast although submerged unconscious processes that most of the material of our inner worlds – ideas, emotions, desires and motives – resides. In this view, unconscious anxiety is managed through unconscious mechanisms such as splitting, projection and projective identification.

Box 3.3   Unconscious defence mechanisms

Splitting is a primitive psychic mechanism in which the self and others are perceived as either all good or all bad. There is an inability to integrate the positive and negative qualities of self and others into a more psychologically realistic and coherent picture.

Projection is a psychic defence mechanism that is helpful in protecting the subject from painful or unacceptable knowledge about the self. Thoughts, feelings and attributes considered 'bad' (e.g. weakness, anger, loneliness, homosexual desire, incompetence – the list could go on!) are projected out of the self and onto an object 'over there' where they can be condemned and maybe even punished, as may happen in the process of scapegoating. Valued or esteemed ideas may also be expelled in this way, as a means to protect against the destructive tendencies of the self or others. The object of these projections may then be idealised.

Projective identification is closely linked to projection. Although there is debate about the meaning of projective identification, most agree that it involves action

> that goes further than projection. The object of the projection is altered by it and begins to behave as though s/he is actually characterised by the feelings, thoughts, beliefs or attributes that have been projected. Thomas Ogden (1982) describes it as simultaneously a type of psychological defence, communication and human relationship.

In a social psychoanalytic framework, unconscious anxiety is understood as inevitable, 'normal' and central to the development of the personality (Freud, 1936). We are also motivated by unconscious desires, some of which may be in conflict with conscious thoughts and feelings and may provoke anxiety. Contradictory wishes, and the strategies employed to defend against unconscious anxiety that this conflict stirs up, have a powerful effect on the constitution of 'reality', to the extent that they create distortions of perception. 'If ... the unconscious pervades all thinking – then there can be no unbiased realistic perception, no simple distinction between what we are "imagining" and what we know to be real' (Frosh, 2002, p. 51).

Discursive psychologists and those applying a social psychoanalytic approach share the principle that reality and our experience of any external reality is a co-construction, created through social and interpersonal interactions. They would also agree on the importance of discourse in the production of subjectivity as well as the emphasis on the place of history, location and culture in examining why certain subject positions are taken up and not others. Wendy Hollway (1984) and others working within a social psychoanalytic perspective (e.g. Walkerdine et al., 2001; Frosh et al., 2002) have suggested that the notion of 'investment' rather than 'choice' is useful in understanding the contradictions and complexities involved in the take-up and refusal of particular subject positions, and that these investments are simultaneously psychic and social. Here, the notion that we can 'choose' from an array of available discourses does not take account of some of the less rational and unconscious forces at play in human subjectivity. A psychoanalytically informed idea of investment moves us away from assumptions about rational intentionality and allows for the idea that unconscious conflicts also influence the take-up of subject positions.

4.2   Psychoanalysis and the family

Psychoanalysis offers a dramatic analysis of the interior of family life and focuses on mothers and fathers, the psychological needs and desires of children, the structure and development of the personality, and the growth of sexual and gender identity. Generally, psychoanalysts view the family as a place that is governed by repressed and contradictory emotions that are aggressive and loving, destructive and reparative. In this view, families are highly charged and intense emotional environments, within which children engage with other people as social human beings from infancy onwards.

Like psychological social-developmental psychology, psychoanalysis has focused closely on the developmental significance of children's relationships in families and has paid most attention to relationships between children and their parents/care givers.

4.3   Psychoanalysis and siblings

Freud posited the notion of the Oedipus complex to explain the gendered psycho-sexual development of children. Briefly, this stated that a child's attachment to the parent of the opposite sex goes alongside envious and aggressive feelings towards the parent of the same sex, which because of fear of punishment from the same-sex parent are largely repressed. Freud argued that this is a universal emotional process that establishes the foundations of all other relationships.

This assertion has had particular consequences for how sibling relationships are understood within psychoanalytic thought. Because it regards the parent–child relationship as *the* most important one in creating an emotional environment in which children might grow into psychological health, siblings are rather sidelined (Bank and Kahn, 1982). The feminist psychoanalyst Juliet Mitchell (2000) notes that intense sibling bonds and other 'lateral' relationships, such as those with peers, are not viewed as having their own intrinsic value but are instead seen to be a response to unsatisfactory parenting, as a substitute for 'good enough' mothering. Prophecy Coles (2003) argues that this reduces them to 'bit-part' actors in the Oedipal theatre and renders them irrelevant in discussions of mental health. Furthermore, sibling attachment is marginalised; rivalry is posited as the norm with sibling experience extrapolated from that of the eldest (i.e. as characterised by feelings of envy and rivalry towards the new baby) and meanings of birth order and status for siblings ignored.

Siblings are therefore put in a contradictory position in psychoanalytic thought: on the one hand, they are treated as marginal figures in the child's psychic life, but on the other, when they do appear they are understood as significant enough to provoke 'primal hatred' and 'unfathomably deep hostility' (Coles, 2003, p. 29). The concentration on sibling rivalry means that the bonds of affection and love that can exist between siblings are often overlooked, except in literature.

Mitchell points to another contradiction between the theory and clinical practice of psychoanalysis: 'Siblings are everywhere in psychoanalytic accounts – even though they are absent from the theory and the clinical practice' (Mitchell, 2000, p. xi). She argues that, when considering sibling relationships from a group psychology perspective, we need to think about the construction of the ego.

> The ego is thought of as the centre of the person, its function being to maintain equilibrium between the desires of the id, the realities of the external world and the demands of society and its culture which are eventually internalised in the form of the superego.
>
> (Thomas, 1996, p. 298)

This is the internal faculty that symbolises ethical and moral restrictions on the pleasure-seeking id. Its role is to put boundaries around desires that are deemed to be unacceptable and to advocate a constant 'striving towards perfection' (Freud, 1953–74, vol. 22, p. 67). Ego-ideals are important in the strengthening of the superego and can be internalisations of parts of people to whom the ego (subject) aspires. An ego-ideal can also be in the guise of a scrutinising, pestering and critical internal 'voice'. In the Freudian classical model, this ego-ideal is viewed as being modelled on the father, whose approval or censorship the child takes in as a dimension of her/his own personality. But need this symbolic figure be based on a parent? Mitchell asks:

> But isn't it also likely that the original model may be another child, a heroic or critical older (or other) sibling? For most of us when our conscience is putting us down, making us feel inferior, the voice we hear is reminiscent of the tauntings not of adults but of other children.
>
> (Mitchell, 2003, p. 12)

As siblings often form the major object-elements of a child's early life, the notion that siblings are introjected to become parts of the self is conducive to the idea that siblings are central to the development of the self.

4.4 Five sisters

The following extract comes from research carried out by myself and Ros Edwards on sibling relationships in different kinds of families (Edwards et al., 2006). It is taken from an interview with two sisters, Habiba and Shabnur. They are two of five Bangladeshi sisters: Azra, aged 24, Habiba, aged 21, Sabina, aged 20, Shabnur, aged 15 and Misha, aged 11. The eldest sister is married and lives with her husband's family. The other four sisters live with their mother and father. The family are practising Muslims and live in an inner-city neighbourhood that has a diverse population in terms of type of housing, class, ethnicity and length of residency.

ACTIVITY 3.3

As you read the extract, think about the place that the oldest sister, Azra, held in the minds and hearts of this group of sisters. Keep in mind what Mitchell says about siblings and the construction of ego-ideals.

HABIBA: I would go out of my way to do something for Azra. And I would not say no. I would not refuse.

SHABNUR: I don't think that's just you with Azra. That's for any of us.

HABIBA: Any of us.

SHABNUR: Any of us.

HABIBA: Because she's the eldest.

SHABNUR: I think because we have respect for her and in our eyes she's never done anything bad, and she's so pure and good inside that we all respect her so much. Any of us would be willing to do anything, but she rarely, very rarely asks us to do anything, does she?

HELEN: What's special about her, that you all feel like that?

SHABNUR: There's something special about her, that's so warm, that all of us really admire her.

HABIBA: She's a very genuine person. And if you went to her for advice, you'd know that it's from the heart and it's never meant to be bad. Because sometimes people will hold back, and never tell the truth or be honest. Even when she, Helen, even when she pressures you to just say study, or do something that you can slack in, you don't think ... I was so scared of like, getting a 2:2, I was like, how am I going to face her? It was very much that I didn't want to let her down. I didn't want her to think Habiba only got a 2:2. Not that she would, because only the day before I got my results she was saying – Habiba, it doesn't matter if you get a 2:2, don't stress, it's OK.

SHABNUR: And the thing is, if somebody shouts at you it's over and done with. But because you see her, like when you've done something bad, she doesn't shout at you, but her expression makes you feel even more guilty. So that keeps me out of trouble.

HABIBA: Because she's so nice to us you feel bad for letting her down, because she's never let us down.

SHABNUR: Yeah.

Mitchell's point that siblings can be internalised as ego-ideals would seem to be illustrated by these sisters' identifications with Azra, the eldest sister who had recently married and moved away. Azra was idealised by all but the youngest of her siblings as someone who embodied purity, goodness, kindness and good sense. This made the sisters dread the very thought of being judged negatively by her in any way. Azra thus represents a potent moral authority among her sisters and has been taken in (introjected) as an 'internal policeman' so that the thought of disappointing her or incurring her disapproval in any way exerts a powerful influence on their behaviour.

4.5   Subjectivity and interdependence: family, culture and community

In developing a social psychoanalytic perspective on the family it is not enough to consider only the psychodynamics of sibling relationships; we also need to consider how social and structural forces and processes are interwoven with individual and group psychic processes. For instance, common themes emerged across the narratives of the sisters, which highlighted how their relationships with one another were influenced by ethical and moral codes within the family and in the wider Muslim community with which they identified. These included being helpful to their parents and one another, showing respect for their parents and other elders, and understanding the self as part of a family and community collective rather than as an autonomous individual.

Throughout their narratives, the sisters emphasised the importance of the family, and stressed an active, dynamic sense of belonging. This kind of involvement and investment in the immediate and wider family inevitably leads to a scaling down of similar investments in non-family friendships and the development of an extensive social life with people outside the family.

SHABNUR: I'm a very homely girl, as it is. I do prefer to stay at home and doing stuff at home. I think I've grown out of the stage of going out with friends and having to go to the cinema, blah blah blah ... Because I've grown to a stage where friends really aren't that important anymore.

Monique Hennink and her colleagues (1999) found that Asian teenage girls and young women are more influenced than British white girls and young women of the same age by cultural traditions, religious obligations, family loyalties and community expectations. For the Asian sisters and brothers in our study, respectability and personal and family reputation were key themes in how they felt about themselves and one another. Sabina imagines the consequences of herself or one of her sisters transgressing cultural rules on marriage:

SABINA: The stigma that it would bring. The rumours. My reputation as a family. Our status. It would just go down straight away. And the way our culture works, is say if Habiba was to get married now, and my big sister liked a boy, my parents refused, and she ended up running away. My second sister's got a very good proposal, the guy's a doctor, you know, very religious, well mannered, everything, and they will research the background and see whether the elder sister has got married, did she marry into a good family? And all this will be taken into account.

The psychoanalytic view of the subject as unconsciously defended challenges the extent to which we can ever be entirely autonomous individuals. The social psychoanalytic perspective takes the tensions that arise between the desire for unique individuality with our wish to be part of a group further by considering the possibilities and limits of individual agency alongside the effect of structural forces outside our direct control, such as 'race' and ethnicity, class and culture. The idea that one should put the needs of the collective before one's own needs seems to be the antithesis of the model of the 'ideal' self in Western societies, where dependence is viewed as weakness and desirable adult status is achieved by its rejection.

The five sisters presented a strong challenge to the denial of dependency, and instead put *interdependency* at the heart of their ideas about what it means to be a sister, a daughter, a Muslim, and an adult woman. What may look like a slip of the tongue when Sabina refers to 'My reputation as a family' is actually an expression of this interdependency. It wasn't that this was absent from the narratives of sisters and brothers from white European and African Caribbean families in our study; far from it (see Edwards et al., 2006). But it was a pattern that was most pronounced in the Asian sibling groups. In this model of subjectivity, growing into maturity is synonymous with active and responsible membership of intimate (familial), social (local and global communities) and sometimes religious groups. These themes were present in the narratives of all the sisters, but it is important to remember that although these represented model practices that should be aimed for, they were not necessarily achieved by all of the sisters, or all of the time. At points when a sister 'failed' to live up to these codes, the monitoring and regulative role of siblings, especially the older ones towards the younger, was evident. For these sisters, the authority automatically invested in older siblings was closely linked to the importance of maintaining the family's good reputation in the local community.

4.6   Summary

This section has explored the contribution that a social psychoanalytic perspective can make to a social psychology of families. Underpinned by the notion of a dynamic unconscious and an anxiously defended subject, this perspective holds that psychological and social lives are inseparable. Because siblings are *simultaneously* unique and have some shared social and genetic inheritance, they epitomise tensions in social psychology between individual and social processes, and are ideal subjects for investigating the porosity of individual/social boundaries. However, traditional psychoanalytic theories place siblings in a tricky position: as unimportant in terms of psychological development at the same time as provoking terrible rivalry in development.

In the light of Mitchell's idea that not only parents but siblings can become ego-ideals, whose approval or censorship the child internalises in the construction of the super-ego, we considered a study of children and young people's sibling relationships and focused on a group of five Asian Muslim sisters. Through this case study I argued that in order to move from a psychoanalytic to a social psychoanalytic analysis, we must go beyond the psychodynamics of this particular sibling group to consider the influence of social and cultural forces. Azra had become internalised by her younger sisters as both an idealised figure that was a source of inspiration as well as a moral authority. This psychic process was in constant dynamic interplay with expectations, codes of behaviour and practices that circulated within the family and in the wider Muslim community. At the heart of these ideas lay an understanding of the self as profoundly social; as inextricably bound up with parents, sisters, extended family and communities of identification. With the demarcation between self and others blurred and permeable, *inter*subjectivity and *inter*dependency become more visible and less obscured by an insistence on autonomous individuality. Siblings *do* become part of the self and, for this particular group of sisters, their introjection as ego-ideals is supported through both psychic processes *and* social practices. Thus a social psychoanalytic analysis illuminates the way that social meanings and unconscious intersubjective processes are mutually reproductive of certain cultural practices and subjectivities.

5   Summary and conclusion

I opened this chapter by asserting the importance of families in the construction of individual and group subjectivities and went on to outline the ways in which social psychologists have studied them. In doing so, it became clear that although families have been major objects of study in psychological social psychology (PSP), the developmental focus of much of this work has neglected many aspects of families. The rest of the chapter has been dedicated to thinking about and analysing families from two particularly *sociological* social psychological perspectives – discursive psychological and social psychoanalytic.

Although you will now be aware of some of the differences between the perspectives, you will also have got a sense of their common ground through the research examples given here. Both perspectives lend themselves to an exploration of the place of families in the construction of identities. In contrast with much PSP work on families, neither perspective draws clear boundaries between what goes on inside families and what goes on outside them. They do not isolate individuals from broader social, cultural and structural processes. Instead, they attempt to transcend individual–social and agency–structure dualisms by conceptualising family forms, relationships, processes and practices as diverse, dynamic and subject to influences from within and without.

Both perspectives are concerned with:

- the indissoluble links between *individuals and society*
- the complex connections between *agency* and *structure*
- the historical and cultural *situatedness* of families
- the importance of *power relations* among family members and in wider social relations
- diversity and difference between families
- the meanings and experiences of those within families
- negotiations between family members
- everyday discourse and practices in families
- the influence of ideology on family processes and practices.

This chapter has demonstrated how viewing families through sociological social psychological theoretical lenses can open up what is a well-researched developmental social psychological area in valuable ways, and in doing so it can raise important social psychological questions about the place of family relationships, practices and discourses in our internal and external lives.

References

Adams, M. (1976) *Single Blessedness: Observations on the Single Status in Married Society*, New York, Basic Books.

Austin, J.L. (1962) *How to Do Things with Words*, Cambridge, MA, Harvard University Press.

Bank, S. and Kahn, M. (1982) *The Sibling Bond*, New York, Basic Books.

Baxter, J. (2000) 'The joys and justice of housework', *Sociology*, vol. 34, pp. 609–31.

Beck, U. and Beck-Gernsheim, E. (2002) *Individualization*, London, Sage.

Bradley, B.S. (1989) *Visions of Infancy: A Critical Introduction to Child Psychology*, Cambridge, Polity Press.

Brown, R. (2000) *Group Processes: Dynamics Within and Between Groups*, Oxford, Blackwell.

Cawson, P., Walters, C., Booker, S. and Kelly, G. (2000) *Child Maltreatment in the United Kingdom: A Study of the Prevalence of Child Abuse and Neglect*, London, National Society for the Protection and Care of Children.

Chamberlain, M. (1999) 'Brothers and sisters, uncles and aunts: a lateral perspective on Caribbean families' in Silva, E. and Smart, C. (eds) *The New Family?*, London, Sage.

Cicirelli, V. (1994) 'Sibling relationships in cross-cultural perspective', *Journal of Marriage and the Family*, vol. 56, pp. 7–20.

Coleman, J. (1990) *The Nature of Adolescence*, London, Routledge.

Coles, P. (2003) *The Importance of Sibling Relationships in Psychoanalysis*, London, Karnac Books.

Coltrane, S. (2000) 'Research on household labor: modelling and measuring the social embeddedness of routine family work', *Journal of Marriage and the Family*, vol. 62, pp. 1208–33.

Dempsey, K.C. (1997) 'Attempting to explain women's perceptions of the fairness of the division of housework', *Journal of Family Studies*, vol. 5, pp. 2–24.

Dixon, J. and Wetherell, M. (2004) 'On discourse and dirty nappies: gender, the division of household labour and the social psychology of distributive justice', *Theory and Psychology*, vol. 14, no. 2, pp. 167–89.

Dryden, C. (1999) *Being Married, Doing Gender: A Critical Analysis of Gender Relationships in Marriage*, London, Routledge.

Dunn, J. (2004) *Children's Friendships: The Beginnings of Intimacy*, Oxford, Blackwell.

Durkin, K. (1995) *Developmental Social Psychology: From Infancy to Old Age*, Oxford, Blackwell.

Edley, N. and Wetherell, M. (1999) 'Imagined futures: young men's talk about fatherhood and domestic life', *British Journal of Social Psychology*, vol. 38, pp. 181–94.

Edwards, R., Hadfield, L., Lucey, H. and Mauthner, M. (2006) *Sisters and Brothers: Sibling Identities and Relationships*, London, Routledge, Taylor and Francis.

Flouri, E. and Buchanan, A. (2004) 'Early father's and mother's involvement and child's later educational outcomes', *British Journal of Educational Psychology*, vol. 74, pp. 141–53.

Freud, S. (1936) *Inhibitions, Symptoms and Anxiety*, London, Hogarth Press.

Freud, S. (1953–74) *The Standard Edition of the Complete Psychological Works of Sigmund Freud* (ed. J. Strachey), 24 vols, London, Hogarth and Institute of Psycho-Analysis.

Frosh, S. (2002) *Key Concepts in Psychoanalysis*, London, The British Library.

Frosh, S. (2003) 'Psychosocial studies and psychology: is a critical approach emerging?', *Human Relations*, vol. 56, no. 2, pp. 1545–67.

Frosh, S., Phoenix, A. and Pattman, R. (2002) *Young Masculinities*, Basingstoke, Palgrave.

Giddens, A. (1992) *The Transformation of Intimacy: Sexuality, Love and Eroticism in Modern Societies*, Cambridge, Polity Press.

Hawkins, A.J., Marshall, C.M. and Allen, S.M. (1998) 'The orientation toward domestic labor questionnaire: exploring dual-earner wives' sense of fairness about family work', *Journal of Family Psychology*, vol. 12, pp. 244–58.

Heaven, P. (2001) *The Social Psychology of Adolescence*, New York, Palgrave Macmillan.

Hennink, M., Diamond, I. and Cooper, P. (1999) 'Young Asian women and relationships: traditional or transitional?', *Ethnic and Racial Studies*, vol. 22, no. 5, pp. 867–89.

Hicks, S. (2005) 'Is gay parenting bad for kids? Responding to the "very idea of difference" in research on lesbian and gay parents', *Sexualities*, vol. 8, no. 2, pp. 153–68.

Hochschild, A. (1989) *The Second Shift: Working Parents and the Revolution at Home*, New York, Viking.

Hogg, M.A. (1992) *The Social Psychology of Group Cohesiveness*, New York, Harvester.

Hollway, W. (1984) 'Gender difference and the production of subjectivity' in Henriques, J., Hollway, W., Urwin, C., Venn, C. and Walkerdine, V. (eds) *Changing the Subject: Psychology, Social Regulation and Subjectivity*, London, Routledge.

James, A. and Prout, A. (eds) (1990) *Constructing and Reconstructing Childhood: Contemporary Issues in the Sociological Study of Childhood*, London, Falmer Press.

Kelly, C. and Breinlinger, S. (1996) *The Social Psychology of Collective Action*, London, Falmer Press.

Langdridge, D. and Blyth, E. (2001) 'Regulation of assisted conception services in Europe: implications of the new reproductive technologies for "the family"', *Journal of Social Welfare and Family Law*, vol. 23, no. 1, pp. 45–64.

Larson, R., Wiley, A. and Branscomb, K. (eds) (2006) 'Family mealtime as a context of development and socialization', *New Directions for Child and Adolescent Development*, San Francisco, Jossey-Bass, no. 111.

McKie, L., Cunningham-Burley, S. and McKendrick, J. (2005) *Families in Society: Boundaries and Relationships*, Bristol, Policy Press.

Mitchell, J. (2000) *Mad Men and Medusas: Reclaiming Hysteria and the Effects of Sibling Relationships on the Human Condition*, Harmondsworth, Penguin.

Mitchell, J. (2003) *Siblings, Sex and Violence*, Cambridge, Polity Press.

Morrow, V. (1998) *Understanding Families: Children's Perspectives*, London, National Children's Bureau.

O'Brien, M. (2005) *Shared Caring: Bringing Fathers into the Frame*, Working Paper Series No. 18, Equal Opportunities Commission.

Office for National Statistics (2001) *Census 2001* [online], National Statistics, www.statistics.gov.uk (Accessed 11 October 2006).

Ogden, T.H. (1982) *Projective Identification and Psychotherapeutic Technique*, London, Karnac.

Phoenix, A. (1991) *Young Mothers?*, Cambridge, Polity Press.

Putnam, R. (2000) *Bowling Alone – the Collapse and Revival of American Community*, New York, Simon and Schuster.

Reynolds, J. and Taylor, S. (2004) 'Narrating singleness: life stories and deficit identities', *Narrative Inquiry*, vol. 15, no. 2, pp. 197–215.

Reynolds, J. and Wetherell, M. (2003) 'The discursive climate of singleness: the consequences for women's negotiation of a single identity', *Feminism and Psychology*, vol. 13, no. 4, pp. 489–510.

Roseneil, S. and Budgeon, S. (2004) 'Cultures of intimacy and care beyond "the family": personal life and social change in the early 21st century', *Current Sociology*, vol. 52, no. 2, pp. 135–59.

Sutton, C.R. (2004) 'Celebrating ourselves: the family reunion rituals of African-Caribbean transnational families', *Global Networks*, vol. 4, no. 3, pp. 243–57.

Tajfel, H. (1981) *Human Groups and Social Categories: Studies in Social Psychology*, Cambridge, Cambridge University Press.

Thomas, K. (1996) 'The defensive self: a psychodynamic perspective' in Stevens, R. (ed.) *Understanding the Self*, London and Milton Keynes, Sage with The Open University Press.

Thompson, L. (1991) 'Family work: women's sense of fairness', *Journal of Family Issues*, vol. 12, pp. 181–96.

Turner, J.C., Hogg, M.A., Oakes, P.J., Reicher, S.D. and Wetherell, M.S. (1987) *Rediscovering the Social Group: A Self-categorization Theory*, Oxford, Blackwell.

Walkerdine, V. and Lucey, H. (1989) *Democracy in the Kitchen: Regulating Mothers and Socialising Daughters*, London, Virago.

Walkerdine V., Lucey, H. and Melody, J. (2001) *Growing Up Girl: Psychosocial Explorations of Gender and Class*, London, Palgrave.

Wetherell, M. (1998) 'Positioning and interpretative repertoires: conversation analysis and post-structuralism in dialogue', *Discourse and Society*, vol. 8, no. 3, pp. 387–412.

White, D. and Woollett, A. (1991) *Families: A Context for Development*, London, Routledge.

Williams, F. (2004) *Rethinking Families*, London, Calouste Gulbenkian Foundation.

Chapter 4

Emotion

by Brian Parkinson, University of Oxford

Contents

Learning outcomes

By the end of this chapter, you should have gained:

■ an understanding of the range of contemporary social psychological approaches to emotion

■ familiarity with the cognitive social and discursive psychological perspectives on emotion

■ awareness of contemporary debates in social psychology relating to the role of social and cultural factors in emotion, and the meaning of facial expressions

■ a systematic, critical and sophisticated understanding of key ideas, theoretical debates and epistemology within the social psychology of emotion.

1   Introduction

The last time I got angry was while trying to arrange this year's summer holiday. It had to be during the school vacation, somewhere not too hot, too busy, or too expensive. Apart from that, I was told, anywhere would be fine. After another two-hour stint on the internet, checking the availability of various rental properties over a painfully slow connection, I found something that looked pretty good. Not perfect, maybe, but positively luxurious in comparison with most of the places that had come up. Near the sea, scenic location – the lot. At last something that would do. I didn't want to oversell what I'd found so I went back into the living room and said, perhaps a little too casually, 'Come and have a look at this!' Reluctantly Gillian followed me into the bedroom where my laptop was wired up. It was now after 10 p.m. We were both tired and didn't really want to be bothered with any more arranging, or any more agonising about where to go. 'Hmm, looks nice,' she said, after reading the details and inspecting the photos in minute detail 'but do we really want to go that far north? It's almost Scotland.' I didn't lose my temper. I didn't even raise my voice, but it must have been clear that this was not the response I'd hoped for. 'Maybe we just shouldn't bother then,' was all that I said.

Emotional episodes even as trivial as this tend to stick in our memories. When we tell stories about them, they often follow a particular pattern: something happens; we get excited or upset about it; the end. Often our aim in recounting these events is precisely to explain how things looked from our perspective, what it was in particular that caused the emotional effect. Re-reading my narrative, I don't think that I come out of it too well. It sounds as though I'm playing the role of martyr, sulkily demanding credit for something I hadn't been obliged to do in the first place. But it's still an attempt to justify what might seem from the outside to be unwarranted pique. Does my anecdote really explain why I got angry, then, or is it just a story told to make my conduct seem more reasonable? Can emotional narratives ever simply describe psychological facts, or must they always present things selectively for particular purposes? And in either case, should the story really end with the emotion, instead of following through its consequences (for other people and ourselves)?

For some people, the obvious place to look if we want to understand emotions is inside our brains or bodies. The undeniable, subjective aspect of emotional experience is treated as an indication of a literally internal location. If this is so, the topic of emotion can be left largely to biologists and neurophysiologists. From the opposite angle, some theorists see emotions as purely cultural artefacts wholly constituted by societal rules and representations. Thus, emotion is reserved for sociology and anthropology rather than psychology. In fact, emotion resists dualistic positioning on the individual–society axis in either of these ways. Despite their subjective aspects and their susceptibility to cultural influence, emotional processes have a distinctively social psychological flavour because they play out in the course of interpersonal episodes operating within a broader relational, institutional, and cultural context (Parkinson et al., 2005). As my personal story illustrates, emotions often happen in the course of interactions with other people, and shape the course of those interactions. Something someone does or says makes you cross, upset or pleased, and your emotional reaction in turn affects what they do or say afterwards. Further, these emotions are interpreted and regulated in accordance with rules laid down by society. Why, then, do we so often think of our emotions as intensely personal and private states? Resolving the tension between these apparently conflicting aspects of our emotional lives is one of the most difficult tasks facing emotion research. By the end of this chapter, you will be in a better position to decide just how far social psychological research can get into the heart of emotion and go beyond its particular version of individual–society dualism.

Pause for reflection

How do you think emotions should be characterised? Are they simply private experiences that are easily pinned down in words, or do they only make sense when related to the context in which they occur? Is there an inner core to emotion around which its other characteristics cluster, or does emotion reside in the pattern of responses, the inner twinges, impulses, facial movements and so on, that are often associated with it? In the former case, as Jim Averill and Elma Nunley (1992) suggest, emotion can be seen as rather like an artichoke, where picking away at the surface ultimately reveals its heart. In the latter case, emotion is more like an onion, only consisting of layers without any real core. But by asking yourself which of these alternative views is true, are you addressing something already out there (or in here) in the psychological world, or simply trying to draw lines around processes and events with no intrinsic interconnections? Perhaps the words we use when presenting ourselves or others in emotional terms permit no precise definition in the first place. Possibly what we take to be vagueness or indeterminacy is actually flexibility that can be deployed to achieve certain conversational goals. These issues are worth thinking about now because different answers have been proposed by the different theorists and researchers considered in the rest of this chapter.

I will begin with a brief history of psychological theories of emotion. Early psychologists tried to explain the subjective aspects of emotion, but with the development of the experimental approach, attention shifted increasingly to objectively measurable components such as facial expressions and physiological responses (which may or may not be directly related to the essence of emotion, if there is one – see above). The role of emotions in social life is now beginning to attract more attention, and to test the limits of purely experimental approaches.

Then I will turn to the question of what links together the different components or aspects of emotion, such as cognitive appraisals, bodily responses, facial expressions and so on. Many biologically orientated theorists believe that a small set of 'basic' emotions is pre-programmed in the brain at birth, and each represents a packaged set of components designed to solve adaptive problems. According to this view, more complex, socially articulated emotions emerge later in development, when these basic emotions combine with each other or with cognitions of various kinds. An alternative view is that the different elements of all emotions (even the supposedly 'basic' ones) come together over the course of development as a consequence of learning rather than any biological imperative. Finally, some theorists believe that emotions do not exist as distinct psychological objects in the first place, and their apparent structure reflects the imposition of imperfect cultural concepts onto experience.

Problems in resolving these disputes may be sidestepped by changing the focus of investigation from emotions or their cognitive representations to the way that we formulate events in emotional terms in ongoing discourse. What makes an event count as 'emotional' or as an instance of 'anger' may be a matter that is contested or affirmed over the course of conversations and arguments between two or more people. I will end the chapter by considering how such a discursive psychological approach might be reconciled with conclusions derived from the more traditional experimental approach.

2   What makes emotion emotional?

2.1   James's feedback theory

Although philosophers had already discussed emotions for centuries, William James's (1884) theory is often considered the first genuinely psychological theory of how emotions happen. James asked himself an apparently simple question: What adds the distinctively emotional quality to experience – its characteristic heat, colour or piquancy? His answer was that we feel emotion only when we sense changes taking place inside our bodies in response to our perception of an event. For example, when something frightens us, our heart may begin to race, we may feel an uncomfortable sensation in the pit of our stomach, break out in a cold sweat and so on. According to James, our usual assumption is that these bodily changes are the consequences of a separate emotion that has already happened. By contrast, his theory states that the body reacts automatically before emotion occurs and that the emotion is precisely the perception of this reaction (i.e. feedback from the body, see Figure 4.1):

> Our natural way of thinking ... is that the mental perception of some fact excites the mental affection called the emotion, and that this latter state of mind gives rise to the bodily expression. My thesis, on the contrary, is that *the bodily changes follow directly the perception of the exciting fact, and that our feeling of the same changes as they occur IS the emotion.*
>
> (James, 1884, p. 449, emphasis in original)

According to James, each distinct emotion was caused by a unique pattern of bodily changes. Thus, anger is produced by a different set of internal perceptions from fear, embarrassment or joy.

Box 4.1   James's thought experiment

James's theory is based partly on an introspective 'thought experiment'. First he thought of an emotion, then he tried to remove from that emotion all of the symptoms of bodily activity (sensations from muscles, skin, guts, etc). Try this out for yourself. James concluded that there was nothing left of the emotion after the bodily sensations were subtracted, but maybe that depends on what he imagined that emotion consisted of in the first place. Indeed, his background assumption seems to be that the place to look for the essence of emotion is inside an individual's brain or body. But does introspection automatically lead us to a correct interpretation of our experience? Perhaps our socially learned presuppositions shape our perceptions of what we are feeling from the outset.

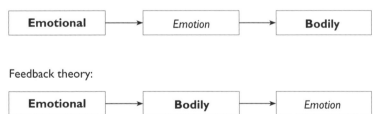

Common sense:

| Emotional | → | Emotion | → | Bodily |

Feedback theory:

| Emotional | → | Bodily | → | Emotion |

Figure 4.1   James's reversal of common sense

One problem with this theory is that it doesn't say how the perception of an emotional event leads to a particular profile of bodily change in the first place. For example, how does the body know that a fear-producing response pattern needs to be produced when a frightening object (a bear or an examination paper) is confronted? In effect, events must be perceived as frightening before appropriate bodily reactions can be initiated, so in what sense does the specific emotion depend on the bodily sensations rather than the initial interpretation of what is happening? Later in this chapter, this alternative appraisal-based explanation of emotion will be reviewed (e.g. Ellsworth, 1994).

2.2   Cannon's theory

A second problem was that James's conclusion that different emotions were caused by distinctive patterns of bodily change was based on introspection, and as a consequence of increasing pressure to make psychology an objectively grounded science, such evidence was soon superseded by quantitative measurement of bodily changes. For example, Walter Cannon, one of James's ex-students, concluded that the measured physiological patterns associated with contrasting emotional states such as anger and fear were actually rather similar (Cannon, 1927). If emotion differences were really based on perceiving these patterns, anger and fear should not feel different from one another.

Cannon believed that a common pattern of 'activation' of the autonomic nervous system was associated with a wide range of different emotions. This activation served to release metabolic energy in order to cope with emergencies rather than to provide internal signals that an emotion was happening. In fact, Cannon thought that the experience of emotion was produced in the brain rather than in the lower body.

Neither James's nor Cannon's theory presents a specifically social psychological account of emotion. In both cases, the events triggering emotion might be social, but the emotional process itself is primarily physiological. Both theories look inwards rather than outwards to pinpoint emotion's direct causes. However, a theory inspired by the ideas of James and Cannon, and developed by the American experimental social psychologist Stanley Schachter, implied that social factors may play a more crucial role.

2.3   Schachter's theory

Schachter's interest in emotion derived from earlier research into the psychology of affiliation (Schachter, 1959). In one of his experiments, he found that participants who were expecting to receive electric shocks preferred to wait with another participant awaiting the same fate rather than someone who was not expecting shocks. Schachter's explanation was that people try to make sense of their emotions by comparing them with those of others facing comparable situations. But why would people need to calibrate their own emotions against other people's if they already knew exactly what they were feeling, as the theories of James and Cannon imply?

Schachter believed that James was correct that the heat behind emotion comes from bodily perception, but Cannon was correct that the bodily changes associated with different emotions are quite similar. If so, autonomic activation can tell us that an emotion of some kind may be occurring, but not what emotion it is. How, then, do we work out whether we are feeling anger or fear? According to Schachter, we infer emotional quality from the current situation and from how other people are reacting to it (see Figure 4.2).

In Schachter's view, emotion depends on two factors: autonomic activation in the body (the physiological factor) which determines the intensity of the experienced emotion, and cognitions about the situation (the cognitive factor) which determine the quality of the experienced emotion. We experience anger when we believe that our autonomic activation is caused by an irritating situation, and joy when we believe that activation is caused by something pleasant.

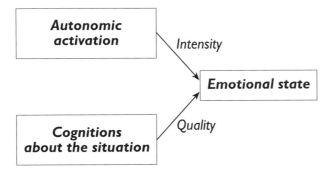

Figure 4.2   Schachter's two-factor theory of emotion

To test this theory, Schachter and Singer (1962) devised an experiment in which autonomic activation was artificially induced in situations with contrasting emotional implications. Participants believed that the research was intended to assess the effects of a newly formulated vitamin compound ('Suproxin') on perception, and the study began with all participants being injected with what they thought was Suproxin, but was actually either adrenaline (causing autonomic activation) or a placebo (causing no physiological symptoms).

Some adrenaline-injected participants were correctly warned about the injection's effects on their bodies (increased heart-rate, clammy hands, etc) and could therefore interpret their symptoms as entirely due to the injection. However, others were misinformed about the injection's effects and therefore had no obvious non-emotional explanation for their internal state.

The experimenters stage-managed the situation to facilitate specific emotional interpretations for the unexplained activation experienced by these participants. In the euphoria condition, participants were left in a waiting room with an experimental accomplice posing as another participant. This accomplice improvised a basketball game using screwed-up paper and a waste-bin, and played with some hula hoops that happened to be lying around to create an atmosphere of 'fun and games'. In the anger condition, both participant and accomplice filled out a questionnaire which asked increasingly personal and insulting questions. The accomplice grew progressively more irritated and eventually stormed out of the room.

According to Schachter's theory, participants should have experienced emotion only if both of the two factors were present; that is, if they were experiencing autonomic activation and also believed that this activation was caused by an emotional situation. Any emotion experienced under these conditions should have corresponded to the apparent implications of the accomplice's behaviour (i.e. participants should have experienced anger when experiencing previously unexplained arousal while with the angry accomplice, and euphoria when experiencing unexplained arousal with the euphoric accomplice).

In fact, results were less clear-cut. For example, participants experiencing 'unexplained arousal' did not consistently report more emotion than placebo participants. One reason may be that the situations were powerful enough to induce emotion even without the addition of artificial arousal. Another problem was that participants experiencing unexplained arousal in the 'anger' condition actually reported themselves to be mildly happy!

Box 4.2   Schachter's and Singer's methodology

Schachter's approach to emotion is an experimental one. Instead of assuming that causal processes can be directly apprehended using introspection, he tried to manipulate independent variables that might interact to produce emotion as an effect. Unusually for a social psychologist, one of these 'factors' was physiological. The other, however, was interpersonally manipulated. Apart from the obvious issues arising from the use of an artificial situation to investigate a phenomenon that is usually contextualised in established socio-cultural settings, Schachter also faced the recurrent issue of how 'emotion' should be operationalised. In Schachter's and Singer's experiment, one measure was based on participants' responses to questions about their emotional experiences during the experiment (e.g. 'How happy were you feeling?'). This makes sense given Schachter's view of emotions as personal interpretations of bodily experience. However, would your report of happiness or anger on a questionnaire that you know the experimenter will read always correspond to experienced emotion itself? Schachter argued that anger self-reports underestimated actual anger because participants did not want to admit to the experimenter that the study had made them angry, so even he did not believe that these measures are infallible.

Another obvious issue with Schachter's and Singer's methodology concerns ethics. Participants were unwittingly drugged, misled about the purpose of the experiment, and, in one condition, asked insulting questions (e.g. 'With how many men (other than your father) has your mother had extra-marital relationships?'). Indeed, when Marshall and Zimbardo (1979) sought to replicate Schachter's and Singer's study in the late 1970s, the University's Ethics Committee only permitted the 'euphoria' and not the 'anger' condition. It is debatable whether even this should have been permitted.

Although experimental evidence for Schachter's theory remains inconclusive (see Reisenzein, 1983), the idea that people's emotional reactions are shaped by interpretation of the situation, and calibrated against the emotional reactions of others who are present, had a lasting impact. Most subsequent emotion theorists (including Schachter himself, 1964) have argued that emotions are usually initiated not by perceptions of autonomic activity, but by appraisals of emotional events. Thus, physiological and cognitive responses usually emerge in parallel, and are not literally independent variables that can be manipulated separately in experiments like those of Schachter and Singer.

2.4 Summary

The theories reviewed in this section tried to specify what it is that adds the distinctive emotional quality to emotional experience (What makes emotion feel emotional? What makes anger feel like anger?). James believed that changes sensed in our bodies are at the heart of emotional experience, whereas Cannon believed that emotional experience is generated inside the brain. By contrast, Schachter claimed that emotion is a consequence of combining information from our bodies with perceptions of what is going on around us. Although each of these theories captures a partial truth about what happens when we become emotional, looking for the essence of emotion in subjective experience may be over-restrictive.

3 Appraisal theory

Magda Arnold (1960), who coined the term appraisal theory, arrived at her conclusions about emotion by posing a similar question to the one from James's earlier thought experiment. But instead of asking how we can tell that our internal state is emotional, Arnold considered what it is that makes our perception of *what is happening in the external world* an emotional rather than a non-emotional perception.

Her answer was that emotion specifically requires that we perceive events as relevant to things that we want or don't want. Appraising something as desirable automatically leads to us being attracted towards it: the impulse to get nearer. For Arnold, this kind of action tendency rather than a subjective feeling is at the heart of emotion. Indeed, having a certain action tendency also implies that your body needs to be prepared to react in a certain way (autonomic activity) and may also be associated with characteristic facial 'expressions' (see below).

Box 4.3   What makes emotion emotional?

Why did James's and Arnold's intuitions about the distinction between emotion and non-emotion lead them to such different conclusions? One explanation is that they started with subtly different ideas about what emotion is, and asked themselves subtly different questions as a consequence. For James, whose main evidence came from introspection, explaining emotion meant explaining the distinctive flavour of subjective experience. The questions addressed by his theory were: 'How can we tell that we are experiencing an emotion?' and 'How can we tell what emotion we are experiencing?' (These are the same questions later addressed by Schachter, but his experimental rather than introspective perspective led him to doubt that participants could access the processes underlying their subjective experience.)

Arnold, by contrast, adopted a functional perspective, and conceptualised emotion not in terms of its introspective qualities but its consequences for behaviour. Rather than attempting to explain how emotion feels inside, she developed an account of how being emotional changes our orientation to the external situation. From this perspective, it is even possible that a person might be emotional without subjectively recognising the fact. For example, when engaged in an argument, I sometimes get so carried away that I end up shouting and gesticulating. At this point, the person I am arguing with may say something like: 'Calm down. It's not worth getting angry about it.' When I was younger, I recall that I occasionally reacted to this accusation by bashing my fist on the table and shouting back 'I'm not getting angry!' Not surprisingly, my accuser rarely took my word for this. Nico Frijda (1986) argues that what we are aware of while angry is often not the anger itself but rather the irritating quality of the other person's behaviour. Our emotional consciousness is directed outwards rather than inwards. Indeed, during the incident described at the beginning of this chapter, I only noticed that I was angry when I observed Gillian's reaction.

Appraisals, like bodily changes in James's account, are thought to determine not only the difference between emotion and non-emotion, but also the differences between various emotions (e.g. anger and euphoria). Figure 4.3 sets out some specific relationships between appraisals and emotions as proposed by Craig Smith and Richard Lazarus in their (1993) version of appraisal theory. Their model argues that, in order to experience any emotion, you need to appraise what is happening as affecting your current goals ('motivational relevance'). In other words, we don't get emotional about things that don't affect our lives in some way. Whether the resulting emotion is pleasant or unpleasant depends on an appraisal of 'motivational congruence' (does what is happening help or hinder my concerns?).

The specific nature of the pleasant or unpleasant emotion depends on 'secondary' appraisals, which assess how the event is to be explained (*accountability*) and what options are available for dealing with it (*coping potential*). For example, the kind of unpleasant emotion we experience when insulted depends on who is perceived as responsible. We will experience anger if we perceive the person doing the insulting as accountable, but guilt if we blame ourselves for doing something that warranted the insult. In short, whether emotion occurs, and what form it takes, depends on our appraisal of what is going on.

Of course, appraisal theorists don't think that we always need to go through a series of conscious decisions before getting emotional. Sometimes we might get angry because we have painstakingly worked out that someone else's comment was intended as an insult, but at other times we may have registered their aggressive expression more directly. According to appraisal theory, as long as we somehow perceive (consciously or otherwise) that the other is blameworthy, anger will come. But if the process leading to the emotion is unconscious, how can we tell that 'other-blame' has been registered except by noting that anger is present? Inferring other-blame from the very state that it is supposed to explain makes the argument seem circular. In practice, appraisal and emotion seem so tightly intertwined that it is difficult to tease them apart. One interpretation of the apparent connections between specific emotions and appraisal patterns might even be that people understand emotion concepts in terms of their implied appraisals, rather than experiencing independently verifiable emotions in response to those appraisals.

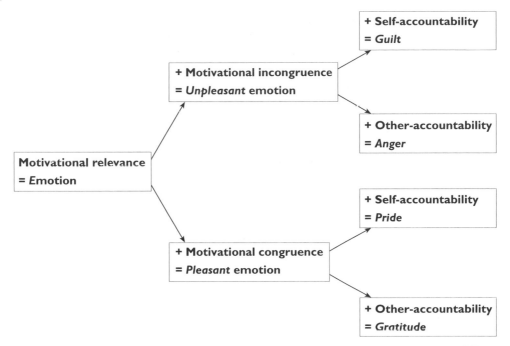

Figure 4.3   Appraisals associated with different emotions in Smith and Lazarus's (1993) model

3.1   Summary

Appraisal theory explains emotion in terms of perception and interpretation of external situations rather than internal symptoms. Its main contribution has been its attempt to specify the relational meanings corresponding to English-language emotion names such as anger, guilt and so on. However, how consistently the proposed relational meanings are related to any given emotion, and whether they capture genuine causal processes, remain in doubt.

4   Emotion and social identity

4.1   Group identification in appraisal theory

Appraisal theory is an example of the social cognitive approach. It argues that emotion cannot occur unless the situation has been perceived as *personally* significant. But don't we also feel excited, frightened or delighted about things that happen to our friends or family (or even about events occurring in a film or book)? The answer is that other people matter to us too, and what happens to them also affects us personally (even if our identification with their experiences is temporary or contrived).

In the 1990s, researchers began to investigate emotions induced by events appraised as relevant to groups we belong to rather than relevant to us personally. For example, Bertjan Doosje and his colleagues (1998) presented evidence that people can feel guilty about acts in which they have played no personal role if they believe that other members of their group have committed them. This would explain why many German people continue to feel guilty about Nazi atrocities that took place during the Second World War, even though they were not alive when these events occurred.

According to Eliot Smith (1993), social identification makes group-relevant events self-relevant and hence emotionally provocative. However, high identification may also lead people to reject ambiguous evidence of wrong-doing by their group because accepting in-group responsibility would be threatening to a valued social identity. For example, Dutch participants identifying strongly with their national identity reported *lower* collective guilt about the colonial history of the Netherlands than low national-identifying participants when informed about both good and bad aspects of that history. By contrast, they reported relatively higher levels of collective guilt when given unambiguous evidence of historic exploitation (Doosje et al., 1998).

4.2   Emotional labour

Experimenters researching collective guilt manipulate participants' appraisals to produce specified emotional effects. Similar forms of manipulation are also found in more realistic organisational situations when other people attempt to influence our appraisals in order to encourage desired emotional responses. Indeed, we may try to make *ourselves* feel differently about what is happening to us using similar techniques. Social structures may certainly constrain our appraisals and emotions but need not completely remove agency.

One example of such processes is emotional labour, which involves people actively working on their own (or others') emotions in order to meet employers' needs rather than their own. Arlie Hochschild (1983) conducted an in-depth qualitative study of flight attendants to investigate this phenomenon. She observed that these emotional labourers were sometimes trained to immerse themselves so deeply in their work role that their pleasant reactions even to obstreperous passengers became unforced and sincere. Ultimately, they learned to appraise interpersonal encounters in ways that their employers required in order to enhance customer relations. For example, one interviewee described dealing with rudeness from drunken passengers as follows:

> I try to remember if he's drinking too much, he's probably scared of flying. I think to myself, 'He's like a little child'. Really, that's what he is. And when I see him that way, I don't get mad that he's yelling at me. He's like a child yelling at me then.

> (Quoted in Hochschild, 1983, p. 55)

4.3   Summary

Emotions are affected by the groups and organisations to which we belong. One reason is that our personal appraisal is shaped by how those around us view what is happening, and by how others have taught us to appraise things. However, the social world can also influence the course of our emotions more directly by giving (temporal and spatial) structure to the events we respond to in real time.

5   Basic emotions

Research presented in the previous sections suggests that emotions depend on what is happening in the social world. For example, our emotional reactions are different when someone insults us (or our group) from when someone congratulates us. Also, our emotions have effects on others and we may regulate our emotion presentations to modulate these effects, which then in turn affect us back. But showing that the causes and consequences of emotion have a social dimension does not prove that emotions themselves are social. Indeed, most psychologists agree that at least some of their aspects are biological. How far, then, do social processes penetrate into emotional life? Does every emotion have a biological core?

Paul Ekman (1972, 2003) sets out distinctive roles for biology and socialisation in his neurocultural theory of emotion (see Figure 4.4). He argues that emotions evolved as adaptive responses to certain recurrent challenges to survival or reproduction. Biology has therefore equipped humans with 'autoappraisers' – sensors designed to detect adaptively relevant situations and to output an appropriate pre-programmed pattern of emotional response. This pattern includes autonomic changes, subjective feelings and facial expressions, each of which is distinctive to the particular emotion. For example, because those of our hunter-gatherer ancestors who were better equipped to escape predators were more likely to survive, genes specifying predator-detection and predator-avoidance were more likely to be passed down the generations. When a fast-moving object loomed, blood was pumped to muscles in preparation for flight and a characteristic threat-related face was activated to communicate peril to conspecifics.

However, this biologically-determined fear process does not remain unaffected by learning. Children learn to appraise as frightening some events that are not direct threats to survival and these too acquire the ability to activate fear. Because emotion socialisation varies from one society to the next, certain elicitors are not universal.

As well as shaping the appropriate occasions for activation of any given basic emotion, society tells us when and where we should control its expression according to 'display rules'. For example, people from the UK often learn to temper their enthusiasm about other people's successes, whereas North Americans appear more inclined to exaggerate their congratulatory expressions. Thus, the spontaneous expression of a biologically-shaped emotion may be regulated in accordance with societal expectations and norms.

Ekman's theory implies that at least some emotions are pre-wired at birth as coherent response modules, which are then subjected to some superficial cultural influence. But what is the evidence for this idea of biologically basic emotions? For many, the most decisive data come from cross-cultural studies of judgements of facial expression.

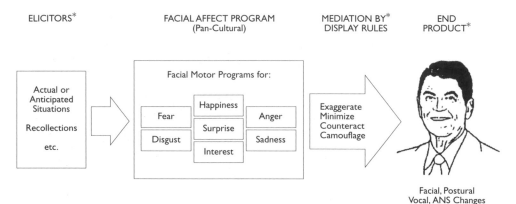

*Partly Culture-Specific

Figure 4.4   Ekman's neurocultural theory (Fridlund, 1994)

5.1   Facial expression of basic emotions

A famous set of cross-cultural studies conducted by Ekman and his colleagues (e.g. Ekman et al., 1969) demonstrated that people from several different societies matched photographed North American facial expressions (many of them posed, see Figure 4.5) to corresponding basic categories of emotion. They succeeded at this task at levels significantly above chance. This finding was replicated in New Guinea and Borneo, where participants had previously had only limited contact with Westerners, and therefore had few opportunities to learn what Western facial expressions were supposed to mean. Ekman believes that this confirms a universal connection between basic emotions and their characteristic facial expressions. Regardless of how the emotions are elicited, happiness, sadness, anger, fear, disgust and surprise are expressed in identical ways by all humans.

However, closer examination of the evidence calls this interpretation into question (Russell, 1994). Although the matching of faces to emotion words was non-random among members of remote cultures, showing that they were not simply guessing what the faces meant, overall agreement about the correct emotional label for each category of facial expression was much lower than 100 per cent (except for smiles, which were consistently associated with 'happiness' in all societies; see Figure 4.6). If each basic emotion is directly connected with a diagnostic facial expression, why don't non-Westerners do better when performing such a simple multiple-choice task? And why are smiles interpreted more consistently than expressions of other basic emotions?

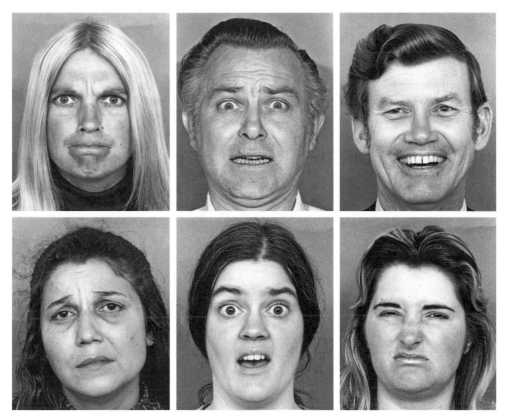

Figure 4.5   Six photographs used as expressions of basic emotions in Ekman's cross-
cultural research. Clockwise from top left these are anger, fear, happiness,
sadness, surprise and disgust

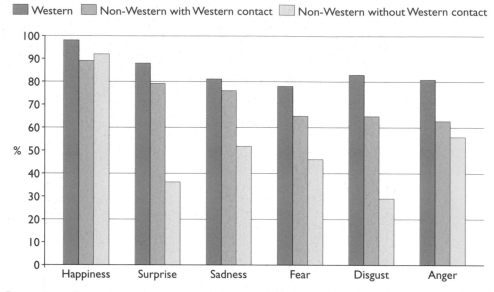

Figure 4.6   Percentage of faces allocated to predicted emotion categories in cross-cultural studies (adapted from Russell, 1994)

ACTIVITY 4.1
READING FACES

Study the photograph in Figure 4.7. It shows a boy who has not been asked to put on any particular expression of emotion. What do you think he was feeling when the picture was taken? Does his face match any of the categories identified by Ekman as illustrated in Figure 4.5? If not, does that mean that the boy is not experiencing any emotion? Perhaps there is a blend of different emotions, or perhaps the boy is trying to present a certain expression for the sake of the camera (perhaps without entirely succeeding). Or maybe his emotional experience does not easily fall into our English-language categories. Perhaps even he has no words to express what he is feeling.

Jim Russell's (1994) answer is that faces tell us something about another person's emotional experience, but don't directly reveal what kind of emotion is being experienced. Participants unfamiliar with the conventional meaning of expressions may have worked out roughly the 'correct' answer by piecing together evidence from faces rather than by immediately recognising any particular emotional meaning. For example, if upturned lips imply pleasure, then the smiling faces must indicate 'happiness', which is the only pleasant response option available. Similarly, the fixed stare and down-turned mouth of the 'anger' photograph may suggest that the person disapproved of something and is therefore possibly angry. Russell's account thus acknowledges that some aspects of facial expression are universal, but not that specific facial patterns reveal basic emotion categories.

Some theorists doubt that the central function of apparently emotional facial movements is to express emotion in the first place. For example, Alan Fridlund (1994) argues that these displays evolved to transmit information about social

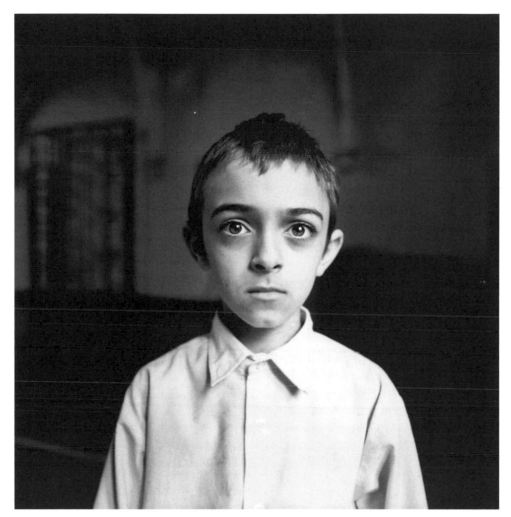

Figure 4.7

motives or behavioural intentions to others. Thus, the so-called anger face is in fact a nonverbal threat, meaning something like 'Back off or I'll attack!' According to Fridlund, such threats may be associated with anger on many occasions, but not always. Thus facial expressions may be correlated with emotion categories without having any direct connection with emotions themselves.

5.2 The nature of emotion categories

A limitation of the cross-cultural research into facial expressions is that participants did not match faces to emotions but to words describing emotions. Further, some English-language emotion words used in these studies could not be directly translated into other languages. Why, then, should our starting point for a psychological theory of emotion and its expression be concepts such as anger, fear and disgust, when other societies classify their experience in different terms (see Wierzbicka, 1999)?

Russell (2003) argues that emotion concepts are specific cultural meanings imposed on experience rather than direct reflections of psychological reality. When we gaze at the night-time stars, we may be able to trace outlines of animals, ancient deities or mythical heroes. However, few of us believe that these constellations are 'real' objects worthy of astronomical attention. Perhaps our conventional perception of emotions as separable categories is equally mistaken. Perhaps their apparent structure lies mainly in the eye of the beholder.

In contrast to appraisal theory's assumption that emotions such as anger and fear are patterned states of action readiness activated by specific appraisals, Russell proposes that we interpret an observed event in terms of 'anger' or 'fear' to the extent that its features match those that we believe characterise these emotions. For example, if I am feeling aroused and unhappy while waiting for an uncertain, potentially threatening situation to be resolved (an interview or exam, perhaps), then I am very likely to label myself as 'fearful' or 'afraid'. But this does not mean that there is an independently detectable condition of fear separate from these features, or that some underlying fear process links together the various aspects of the episode. Like Schachter, then, Russell believes that emotions are interpretations of internal experience shaped by perceptions about what is going on outside.

Consider the phenomenon of *Schadenfreude*, a malicious pleasure about someone else's misfortune. The English language had to borrow a word from German to describe this supposed emotion. But does having a name for something necessarily mean that there is a genuine something described by this name? Not in the case of 'bathwater', which is just what we call water when it is in a bath rather than somewhere else. In a similar way, perhaps *Schadenfreude* is just a word we use when our feeling of pleasure (*freude*) happens to be related to someone else's suffering (*Schaden*).

Unlike many theorists, Russell does not make the mistake of confusing the application of emotion concepts with emotions themselves. Given the cross-cultural differences in ways of describing and conceptualising emotions, for English-language speakers to assume that their categories represent the last word in carving up the emotion domain begins to seem like arrogance.

5.3   Summary

The idea of a 'basic emotion' is that the responses corresponding to words such as 'anger', 'fear' and 'happiness' hang together as coherent patterns because of their evolutionary origins. However, these linguistic categories are not perfectly correlated with supposedly diagnostic facial expressions, and do not even have precise translations in all human languages. In fact, little evidence exists that distinct emotions can be specified in terms of response patterns in the first place. Russell concludes that basic emotions cohere in perception more than in reality. But how easily and cleanly can the distinction between emotional phenomena and their representation be made in practice? Perhaps we can never access emotions themselves, only our ways of presenting and representing them.

6   Emotion discourse

One possible limitation of many psychological experiments arises from their use of so-called 'self-reports' to index emotion. In their (1998) study of collective guilt, for example, Doosje and his colleagues asked participants to rate their agreement with statements such as 'I feel guilty about the negative things done by my group.' As Russell's analysis implies, answers to such questions may tell us more about people's interpretations of their emotional experience than about emotions themselves (whatever they might be). But do these interpretations operate in a social vacuum? More specifically, do we somehow stand back from our experience and try to attach the most accurate concept to it?

Russell (2003) implies that the main problem with self-reports is that they use imperfect concepts. But imperfect against what criterion? For Russell, a valid scientific concept needs to match up with intrinsic features of the phenomenon it describes, and emotion concepts fail to do this. But are people's emotion representations designed to provide a neutral, scientific description of their internal state in the first place? Perhaps their self-reports are not direct manifestations of cognitive representations, but answers to specific questions asked in a particular context. Participants in emotion experiments are given the task of formulating their experience in prescribed terms for a definite reason, and not of providing a description that would be applicable regardless of who is asking the question and why. In short, people's representations are usually representations made to certain other people for certain purposes, and their ratings are communications rather than simple descriptions.

According to Russell, the issue that is ducked by most emotion researchers is how well emotion representations match up with actual emotional phenomena (much like early astronomers had to assess how well apparent constellations mapped onto real galaxies). By contrast, Derek Edwards's (1999) discursive psychological approach to emotion makes no assumptions about what emotions themselves might be (if they exist, there is no direct way of accessing them). Instead, he focuses directly on how emotion talk functions in everyday interactions between people. Emotion is treated not as a psychological phenomenon that needs to be pinned down and classified, but rather as a conceptual resource deployed for conversational purposes.

For Russell, a problem with cognitive representations of emotions is the fuzziness of the implied categories. There seem to be no defining features of anger, for example, only varying degrees of resemblance to a set of assumptions about how anger episodes typically unfold (a cognitive script). For Edwards, discursive (rather than cognitive) emotion formulations are flexible rather than fuzzy, allowing them to be deployed for a variety of rhetorical purposes.

For example, saying that someone has acted out of jealousy or anger may be used either to undermine the rationality of their response (they were acting out of emotion rather than reason) or to demonstrate how serious the provocation was. This point is illustrated in Edwards's (1999) analysis of excerpts from a relationship counselling session in which both members of a couple present alternative versions of events to their counsellor.

Here is Connie's description of what happened when she and Jimmy were out at a pub:

1   *Connie*: At <u>that</u> poi:nt, (0.6) Jimmy ha- (.) my-
2   Jimmy is extre<u>mely</u> jealous. Ex- extre<u>mely</u>
3   jealous <u>per:son</u>. Has a:lways been, from
4   the da:y we <u>met</u>. Y'know? An' at <u>that</u> point
5   in time, there was an episo:de, with (.) a
6   <u>bloke</u>, (.) in a pub, y'know? And <u>me:</u> having
7   a few drinks and <u>messin'</u>. (0.8) <u>That</u> was <u>it</u>.
8   (0.4) Right? And this (0.4) got all out of
9   hand to Jimmy according to <u>Jimmy</u> I was
10 a:lways doin' it and .hhh y'know a:lways
11 <u>aggravating</u> <u>him</u>. <u>He</u> was a <u>jealous</u> <u>person</u>
12 I: <u>aggra</u>vated the situation. .h And <u>he</u>
13 walked <u>out</u> that ti:me. To <u>me</u> it was (.)
14 totally <u>ridi</u>culous the <u>way</u> he (0.8) <u>goes</u> o:n
15 (0.4) <u>through</u> this <u>pro</u>blem that he ha:s.

───────────────── *Pause for reflection* ─────────────────

You may not be familiar with the transcription conventions used in these extracts. They are typical of the method known as Conversation Analysis which includes many features in addition to words and standard punctuation in order to record every detail of speech that might carry meaning.

Note how Jimmy's jealous reaction is presented as a manifestation of something about him as a person rather than as a response to any particular provocation by Connie. The implied attribution is to internal dispositional factors in Jimmy rather than to any external cause. Correspondingly, her own behaviour is treated as unexceptional so that Jimmy's response seems disproportionate. To reinforce this point, she explicitly undermines Jimmy's account of her as 'aggravating him' by claiming that he misrepresents her. But Jimmy's own account of events later the same evening emphasises how specific events caused him to enter an intense state of anger:

1   *Jimmy*: Uh: I was (.) <u>boiling</u> at this stage and
2   I was real angry with Connie ( ). And
3   uh went up to <u>bed</u> 'n (.) I lay on the bed.
4   (0.7) °got <u>into</u> bed.° (0.6) I- uh (.) could
5   hear <u>giggling</u> ('n all that) downstairs and

6   then (0.5) the <u>mu</u>sic changed (0.5) <u>slow</u>
7   records. (1.2) And um: (1.2) >and then they
8   <u>chang</u>ed to slow <u>records</u>< (0.8) I could
9   <u>hea</u>::r (1.0) that <u>Con</u>nie was <u>danc</u>ing with
10   (0.2) this <u>blo</u>:ke downstairs. (1.0) And
11   Caroline turned round and said (.) something
12   (.) about it (it was wha-) it was <u>oh</u> Connie
13   look out I'm going to tell (.) <u>Jimm</u>y on you.
14   (1.0) And (.) next thing I hear is (.) °what
15   he doesn't know (doesn't) hurt him.°
16   (0.2)
17   *Counsellor*. °I'm sorry?°
18   *Jimmy*: What he: doesn't <u>kno</u>w: doesn't <u>hurt</u> him.
19   (0.8) Soon as I heard <u>that</u> I went- (1.6)
20   <u>straight</u> down the stairs. (0.8) 'n uh (0.6)
21   threw them out. (1.2) Took <u>Con</u>nie up the
22   <u>stairs</u> and <u>threw</u> her on the <u>bed</u>. (1.6) I <u>kept</u>
23   trying to <u>ru</u>:n to <u>jump</u> out the <u>window</u>. (1.6)
24   <u>But</u> y'know: I I <u>couldn't</u>. (.) I <u>couldn't</u> (.)
25   get myself (0.4) to go <u>out</u>. (.) I <u>couldn't</u>
26   (.) <u>do</u> it.
27   *Counsellor*. So that's what you <u>felt</u> like.
28   *Jimmy*: Oh ye:h.

Although the anger reported during this episode is presented as
uncontrollable, it still has a rational cause. It is not something about Jimmy,
but something about what happened that brings about an excessive response,
much in the same way as it would in anyone whose valued relationship was
threatened. His anger is based on a justifiable appraisal of other-blame.
Furthermore, the reference to internally directed aggression seems designed to
neutralise any negative implication of the violence directed at Connie. Jimmy
was 'boiling' with anger because of what Connie did, and this led him to be
indiscriminately destructive.

Some readers may be left wondering which version of events is more accurate,
but Edwards's point is that this is indeterminate. Even the counsellor's expert
knowledge would not allow access to an independent emotional reality
separate from the opposing formulations. Maybe then it doesn't make sense to
ask whether Jimmy was really acting out of jealousy or anger, or whether his
supposed emotions were justified or not.

The difference in focus between Edwards's discursive psychological approach
and social cognitive approaches to emotion (usually based on experiments)
should be apparent. Discursive psychologists investigate how emotion talk is

deployed in conversation (or other forms of text) rather than the subjective feelings, physiological responses or facial expressions that are supposedly indexed by the associated concepts. They make no attempt at a comprehensive causal account of emotional phenomena themselves (whatever they might be), often preferring to remain agnostic about their status as psychological processes.

For some readers, this approach may seem incomplete. When I describe myself as angry, it may well be that I am responding to a particular counter-formulation and trying to direct blame externally. But might there not also be a real emotional condition imperfectly describable as anger that grounds my self-presentation? And isn't it possible to be angry in some sense before that label is attached to experience?

One answer is that psychological processes do not come with labels already attached, and it is impossible to allay all possible scepticism about the separate existence of something that should be called 'emotion'. Indeed, Edwards seems correct to conclude that calling something an 'emotion' is always a specific formulation produced for particular purposes (even when professional psychologists do it). But this need not prevent us from considering the causes and effects of non-linguistic psychological phenomena (e.g. facial expressions) that are more or less related to what laypeople present in emotional terms. Indeed, it may be possible to use similar techniques to those used by discursive psychologists to clarify how these phenomena function.

6.1 Summary

The discursive psychological approach treats 'emotion talk' not as a window through which underlying mental processes may be (imperfectly) viewed, but as part of the business of formulating meaning in conversation. According to Edwards, we need to focus on what emotion talk achieves when used in dialogue rather than what it might appear to describe.

7   Prelinguistic 'emotion'?

How would a discursive psychologist deal with the emotions of infants who have not yet learned to speak? One possibility is to explore how their conduct is formulated in emotional terms by caregivers or by developmental psychologists; another is to treat their facial movements and gestures as conversational moves performed in a nonverbal rather than a verbal medium (e.g. Selby and Bradley, 2003). The latter strategy may provide insights into the subsequent development of emotion discourse.

Vasu Reddy (2000) videotaped five infants aged between two and three months while they interacted with an adult or with their own reflection in a mirror. It was observed that the infants often turned away their eyes or head ('gaze withdrawal') while beginning to smile (see Figure 4.8) in response to another person's sustained visual attention.

As always, an element of interpretation has already crept into this superficially objective description of the behaviour sequence. For example, what actually counts as a 'smile' or 'gaze withdrawal'? One answer is that any version of events may be checked by reference to the visual record provided on the videotape (just as discursive interpretations are checked against a transcript or recording). In fact, when observers generated their own descriptions of the videotaped movements, they used words such as 'shy', 'coy' or 'embarrassed' (Draghi-Lorenz et al., 2005). Thus, the infants' presentations clearly bear similarities to what people often refer to in terms of 'embarrassment'. Indeed, Dacher Keltner (1995) has developed criteria for detecting this emotion in adults based on similar nonverbal patterns.

But are coy smiles direct expressions of internally experienced emotions? Part of the facial movement may serve the direct purpose of shutting off unwanted interpersonal stimulation rather than expressing any embarrassment. If Fridlund (1994) is correct about the functions of facial displays, a secondary function might be to inform the other person that attentional contact is no longer desired (indeed, the associated smile suggests a social signal of some kind). This patterned movement may therefore perform a relational function rather than be a symptom of a separable emotion, but this relational function itself may still be seen in emotional terms (Parkinson, 2005). Even if there can be no definitive answer to the question of whether this alignment pattern reflects genuine embarrassment, we might still agree that the form of this interaction tells us something about the role of emotions in regulating relations with others.

Figure 4.8   Coy smiles in response to sustained visual attention (Reddy, 2000)

8   Emotion as relation alignment

The discursive approach shows how emotion-related talk can serve various functions (justifying conduct, undermining another's version of events, drawing attention to your own perspective, etc). Like Russell's theory, it also raises the possibility that no simple psychological object called 'emotion', about which a causal theory can be constructed, exists. If these points are accepted, where does this leave the social psychology of emotion?

One answer is that some of the conversational consequences of formulating something in emotional terms are also achievable using nonverbal rather than verbal means. For example, instead of presenting myself as happy, I may simply smile. What's more, the function of this signal may be discerned using a form of nonverbal conversation analysis, showing that some of the supposed symptoms of emotion exert direct effects during dialogue that are read by interactants in emotional terms. A stronger claim would be that emotion discourse is partly an elaboration of the interplay of nonverbal communications, and that it is preceded developmentally by a more basic 'conversation of gestures' (e.g. Mead, 1934). Perhaps this exertion of interpersonal influence to align relations between people is at least one of the things that is meant by the phrase 'to get emotional'.

What I am calling 'emotion' in this account could never match up with all the possible usages of this word in everyday discourse, but there might still be a point in making the connection between this relational mode and some of these usages. Discourse operates in the ways it does at least partly because relations between people take certain forms prior to the onset of language.

How does the relation-alignment perspective relate to appraisal theory? One of the reasons for aligning relations with others may be because we have appraised things in a certain way. For example, I may want you to apologise because I believe you are to blame for something that has happened to me, and so I get angry with you. However, I may also enter this same blaming relational mode without actually thinking that you are to blame. For example, some children get angry whenever something goes wrong, perhaps because this kind of self-presentation has been rewarded by parents or peers in the past. Perhaps, then, people learn to use anger to achieve social effects and to communicate appraisals to others even when they have not appraised the situation in a corresponding way.

Going back to the last time I got angry, I guess I did think that Gillian should have made more effort to be positive about the holiday apartment I'd struggled to find. But what fuelled my anger may also have been partly a need to justify my efforts, or the fact that my energy levels were so low that it was difficult to resolve things by other means. Neither of us said anything about anger at the time, but the way I presented myself still achieved similar effects to describing myself as angry. Although this revised story may well be just another formulation constructed for a specific communicative purpose, that doesn't necessarily undermine its usefulness as a social psychological account of emotion.

9   Conclusion

Most psychologists agree that subjective experiences, cognitive appraisals, autonomic changes and facial expressions all relate to emotions in some way. However, beyond that, agreement is often hard to find. Theorists argue about whether connections between these processes is pre-programmed by evolution or socially learned, and about whether they are interconnected in reality rather than perception in the first place. These problems in specifying the nature of emotions are understandable if we accept that emotion concepts are part of a flexible interpretive repertoire for accusing, accounting, excusing and so on in conversation. However, social psychology can also make a contribution to the understanding of emotion by exploring the social functions and effects of processes often coordinated with emotion discourse such as nonverbal communication. The future of emotion research may lie in specifying more fully the nature of the integrated verbal and nonverbal presentations made in connection with emotion discourse.

References

Arnold, M.B. (1960) 'Emotion and personality', *Psychological Aspects*, vol. 1, New York, Columbia University Press.

Averill, J.R. and Nunley, E.P. (1992) *Voyages of the Heart: Living an Emotionally Creative Life*, New York, Free Press.

Cannon, W.B. (1927) 'The James-Lange theory of emotions: a critical examination and an alternative theory', *American Journal of Psychology*, vol. 39, pp. 106–24.

Doosje B., Branscombe, N.R., Spears, R. and Manstead, A.S.R. (1998) 'Guilty by association: when one's group has a negative history', *Journal of Personality and Social Psychology*, vol. 75, pp. 872–86.

Draghi-Lorenz, R., Reddy, V. and Morris, P. (2005) 'Young infants can be perceived as shy, coy, bashful, embarrassed', *Infant and Child Development*, vol. 14, pp. 63–83.

Edwards, D. (1999) 'Emotion discourse', *Cultural Psychology*, vol. 5, pp. 271–91.

Ekman, P. (1972) 'Universals and cultural differences in facial expressions of emotion' in J. Cole (ed.) *Nebraska Symposium on Motivation*, Lincoln, NE, University of Nebraska Press.

Ekman, P. (2003) *Emotions Revealed: Understanding Faces and Feelings*, London, Weidenfeld & Nicolson.

Ekman, P., Sorenson, E.R. and Friesen, W.V. (1969) 'Pan-cultural elements in facial displays of emotion', *Science*, vol. 164, pp. 86–8.

Ellsworth, P.C. (1994) 'William James and emotion: is a century of fame worth a century of misunderstanding?', *Psychological Review*, vol. 101, pp. 222–9.

Fridlund, A.J. (1994) *Human Facial Expression: An Evolutionary View*, San Diego, CA, Academic Press.

Frijda, N.H. (1986) *The Emotions*, Cambridge, Cambridge University Press.

Hochschild, A.R. (1983) *The Managed Heart: Commercialization of Human Feeling*, Berkeley, CA, University of California Press.

James, W. (1884) 'What is an emotion?', *Mind*, vol. 9, pp. 188–205.

Keltner, D. (1995) 'Signs of appeasement: evidence for the distinct displays of embarrassment, amusement, and shame', *Journal of Personality and Social Psychology*, vol. 68, pp. 441–54.

Marshall, G. and Zimbardo, P.G. (1979) 'Affective consequences of inadequately explained physiological arousal', *Journal of Personality and Social Psychology*, vol. 37, pp. 970–88.

Mead, G.H. (1934) *Mind, Self and Society from the Standpoint of a Social Behaviorist*, Chicago, Chicago University Press.

Parkinson, B. (2005) 'Do facial movements express emotions or communicate motives?', *Personality and Social Psychology Review*, vol. 9, pp. 278–311.

Parkinson, B., Fischer, A.H. and Manstead, A.S.R. (2005) *Emotion in Social Relations*, New York, Psychology Press.

Reddy, V. (2000) 'Coyness in early infancy', *Developmental Science*, vol. 3, pp. 186–92.

Reisenzein, R. (1983) 'The Schachter theory of emotion: two decades later', *Psychological Bulletin*, vol. 94, pp. 239–64.

Russell, J.A. (1994) 'Is there universal recognition of emotion from facial expressions? A review of the cross-cultural studies', *Psychological Bulletin*, vol. 115, pp. 102–41.

Russell, J.A. (2003) 'Core affect and the psychological construction of emotion', *Psychological Review*, vol. 110, pp. 145–72.

Schachter, S. (1959) *The Psychology of Affiliation*, Stanford, CA, Stanford University Press.

Schachter, S. (1964) 'The interaction of cognitive and physiological determinants of emotional state' in Festinger, L. (ed.) *Advances in Experimental Social Psychology*, vol. 1, New York, Academic Press, pp. 49–80.

Schachter, S. and Singer, J.E. (1962) 'Cognitive, social, and physiological determinants of emotional state', *Psychological Review*, vol. 69, pp. 379–99.

Selby, J.M. and Bradley, B.S. (2003) 'Infants in groups: a paradigm for the study of early social experience', *Human Development*, vol. 46, pp. 197–221.

Smith, C.A. and Lazarus, R.S. (1993) 'Appraisal components, core relational themes, and the emotions', *Cognition and Emotion*, vol. 7, pp. 233–69.

Smith, E.R. (1993) 'Social identity and social emotions: toward new conceptualizations of prejudice' in Mackie, D.M. and Hamilton, D.L. (eds) *Affect, Cognition, and Stereotyping: Interactive Processes in Group Perception*, San Diego, CA, Academic Press, pp. 297–315.

Wierzbicka, A. (1999) *Emotions Across Languages and Cultures: Diversity and Universals*, New York, Cambridge University Press.

Chapter 5

Self

by Wendy Hollway, The Open University

Contents

Learning outcomes

By the end of this chapter you should:

■ understand the idea that concepts of the self are situated: that is, they emerge in different historical periods and geographical locations
■ be familiar with some of the influential ideas in historical developments of concepts of the self
■ be able to distinguish between concepts of the self and experience of the self, and see ways in which these may exert mutual influence
■ understand and critique the many binary terms that characterise theories of the self
■ recognise phenomenological and social psychoanalytic approaches to the self and the empirical methods that characterise them
■ understand the idea that different methods produce specific and partial accounts of the self.

1 Introduction

One of the oddest events in the history of modern psychology is the manner in which the ego (or self) became sidetracked and lost to view. I say it is odd, because the existence of one's own self is the one fact of which every mortal person – every psychologist included – is perfectly convinced.

(Allport, 1943, p. 451)

In these days when everybody's mistaking

celebrity for talent,

self pity for humility,

style for content and

loathing for love,

they spend a lot of time getting in touch with themselves.

And then they find

self justification,

self righteousness,

self obsession,

self pity,

self loathing,

self concern,

self centredness,

self reliance

and self-serving gratification.

('Pastoral Angst', from John Cale and Bob Neuwirth's album *Last Day on Earth*, 1994)

It is remarkably difficult to define 'self'. Even the *Oxford English Dictionary* seems to circle around some core definition in the multitude of uses that it instances. Perhaps of all terms it is one that should escape being pinned down by definition. After all, each one of us uses the term on a daily basis to refer to that entity which is most 'me' (who I am); its meaning is therefore taken for granted in many crucial ways. The discussion is further complicated by the use of different words to mean more or less the same thing (self, identity, ego) and the same word – self – to mean subtly different things!

First, therefore, I will place the many terms that refer to self in the historical context of the changes in understanding of self that have influenced social psychology. The purpose of this section is to illustrate how disparate the many concepts of the self are, and how these derive from different theoretical traditions. It concludes with a summary of all the binary terms that have characterised arguments about how the self is made up. In the following two sections, I move from broad theoretical accounts of self to give some examples of how the self has been researched empirically as a social psychological topic. This reflects the principle of situated knowledges (see Chapter 1, Section 4.2): that is, the idea that the context in which knowledge is produced makes a difference to the product. In the case of research into the self, I emphasise the effect that the method has on the resultant knowledge. Section 2 is about a phenomenological approach. I illustrate how its method of eliciting rich description and its ontological focus on experience and embodiment avoid some of the binaries previously described. Section 3 demonstrates two social psychoanalytic methods, one interview-based and the other observation-based. These illustrate how methods can be consistent with a particular ontology, and how therefore they produce knowledge of the self that reflects the ontology with which they started. The final section returns to the binaries. It also restates the theme of how knowledges about the self are situated with regard to time, place and methodology.

The self is not just a social psychological concept. On the contrary, theories about the self have emanated from philosophy, sociology, psychiatry and psychoanalysis:

[The self] is a term that has long been in vogue, not only in neighboring disciplines, but in fields such as philosophy, literary studies, and history. Moreover, psychologists are the latecomers here. For several decades, while the self was virtually a taboo topic in psychology, other disciplines were producing a stream of intellectually challenging, and often conceptually subtle, studies of this topic. The chances of 'self' becoming essentially a technical psychological term in the way that 'intelligence' has do not seem high.

(Danziger, 1997, p. 137)

ACTIVITY 5.1

Why do you think that 'the self was virtually a taboo topic in psychology' during the middle decades of the twentieth century? Think back to Chapter 1 about what was happening to the discipline in the USA.

1.1   Self-consciousness

In the history of British philosophy, a decisive moment occurred when John Locke added a new chapter to his second edition of a work entitled *Essay Concerning Human Understanding*. The year was 1694. Locke's new chapter discussed the idea of personal identity 'in entirely secular terms' (Danziger, 1997, p. 141), which caused uproar because he had separated a notion of self ('personal identity') from the religious idea of 'soul'. He treated personal identity as if it were a natural, observable phenomenon. This struck a chord in a society which, embarking on a transition from agriculture to industry, found kinship ties and other markers of social identity weakening: 'Where neither social identity by descent nor the immortality of the soul provided a sufficient guarantee of permanence and stability, personal identity had to come into question' (Danziger, 1997, p. 141). Locke brought together the terms 'self' and 'consciousness' in a new way: he 'had invented a way of describing what was then a new way of experiencing the world by separating the sense of self from one's inner and outer actions' (Danziger, 1997, pp. 141–2). His emphasis on self-consciousness reflected 'modern' thought and is characteristic of ideas that are a product of the Enlightenment period of Western thought (in the eighteenth century; see Chapter 1). These ideas are changing as a result of 'postmodern' influences.

Postmodernists have criticised the way that modern concepts of the self make universal claims, and are usually careful to situate their own claims about postmodern selves in Western culture. In many third-world cultures, the family and other collective entities remain salient in positioning people. This contrasts with what sociologists of Western culture call 'individualisation'. The concept of individualisation refers to the complex processes of social transformation that, it is argued, increasingly produce individuals with a capacity for autonomy, freedom of choice and self-reflection, and these processes are assumed to run counter to the affiliations and care obligations that are traditionally rooted in kinship and unequal gender relations in which women put the care of others before their own freedom of choice (Beck and Beck-Gernsheim, 2002 [1983]).

One of the central preoccupations of postmodernism is to take account of recent changes in Western culture and theorise their effects on identities (a term, when used in the plural, that postmodernists prefer to 'self'). The ephemeral nature of the world, the illusions that accost us through media and advertising, the huge scope that people have to modify their image of self (through consumption, body modification and performance), challenge the central principle of an integrated self which was dear to modernism but is no longer viable:

> In particular, the [modernist] approach encompasses a vision of personal integrity through self-development which can survive the monstrous aggression of the world – which can 'keep on keeping on'. The self [...] is a central component of the mode of modernist reasoning [...] it is also precisely this image of the self and its potential for development which is called into question by the advent of what has come to be termed 'postmodernism'.
>
> (Frosh, 1991, p. 21)

In the place of the self-conscious, integrated, purposive and generalised self of modernism comes a situated, fragmented, ephemeral set of performances and positions that incorporates social differences such as race, class and gender. However, this is not entirely new, as we shall see. By the end of the twentieth century, postmodernism had taken further early twentieth-century sociological social psychology (SSP), with its emphasis on social influences, plurality, relationship and language, by challenging consistent and purposive self-development and the principle of integration. From this period on, you will often find self referred to as 'identity' or 'identities' (the latter to remind us that an individual has more than one).

_____ *Pause for reflection* _____

Is there a difference in meaning between 'self' and 'identity'? Think about how you use the two terms. Try out a few sentences containing both terms and work out the different connotations of each of them. You may find that you use them in clearly separable ways to mean different things, and some theorists do make clear distinctions. However, many people are less clear about how they should be distinguished, and theorists define the terms in somewhat different ways.

_____

1.2   Plural social selves

The second moment I want to pick out in the history of thought about the self is at the turn of the nineteenth and twentieth centuries. Locke's proclamation that the self resided in self-consciousness (as opposed to unselfconscious being and action) suggested a division of self into the monitoring self and the monitored self, observer and observed. The observer need not be oneself; rather, the idea grew of a self observed by others, from whom one's self-evaluation derived. This idea of the self was behind William James's 'social self' (1890), the sociologist Charles Horton Cooley's 'looking-glass self' (1902) and George Herbert Mead's (1934) distinction between 'I' and 'me'. North American sociologists took over this version of the self from philosophy and it characterised sociological social psychology for most of the twentieth century.

SSP was founded on the idea of a social self and evolved out of the philosophical distinction between the knower and the known, the subject and object of consciousness. In other words, the idea of self was based on the principle of the reflexiveness of mind: the ability to see oneself from the perspective of another person, or to become an object to oneself in much the same way that one is an object to someone else. Cooley drew on the idea that the reactions of others are like a mirror that is held up to someone, that reflects an image of the self that one can appraise like one would someone else:

> A self-idea of this sort seems to have three principal elements: the imagination of our appearance to the other person; the imagination of his judgement of that appearance; and some sort of self-feeling, such as pride or mortification. The comparison with a looking glass hardly suggests the second element, the imagined judgement, which is quite essential. The thing that moves us to pride and shame is not the mere mechanical reflection of ourselves, but an imputed sentiment, the imagined effect of this imagination upon another's mind ... We always imagine, and in imagining share, the judgements of the other mind.
>
> (Cooley, 1902, pp. 184–5)

Mead took this distinction further by linking it to the difference, in language usage, between 'I' and 'me', based on the grammar of pronouns: I am the active observer who monitors me, the observed. By this means, he paved the way for a social self that was not just social in the sense that it was sensitive to the judgements of others, but was positioned by and in the language that surrounds us all. This made 'the self' reflexive.

Once the self was no longer an indivisible unit, as the soul had been, it was a short step from seeing it as divided into two to seeing it as multiple. William James had been of the opinion that people have multiple selves: 'a man has as many social selves as there are individuals who recognize him and carry an image of him in their mind' (James, 1890, cited in Danziger, 1997, p. 148).

> **Box 5.1   Borges and his 'selves'**
>
> In this extract, the Argentinian writer Jorge Luis Borges explores two different selves. How well do these fit the ideas of Cooley and Mead about the duality of self?
>
>> The other one, the one called Borges, is the one things happen to. ... I know of Borges from the mail and see his name on a list of professors or in a biographical dictionary. I like hourglasses, maps, eighteenth-century typography, the taste of coffee and the prose of Stevenson; he shares these preferences, but in a vain way that turns them into the attributes of an actor. It would be an exaggeration to say that ours is a hostile relationship; I live, let myself go on living, so that Borges may contrive his literature, and this literature justifies me. It is no effort for me to confess that he has achieved some valid pages, but those pages cannot save me, perhaps because what is good belongs to no one, not even to him, but rather to the language and to tradition. Besides, I am destined to perish, definitively, and only some instant of myself can survive in him. Little by little, I am giving over everything to him, though I am quite aware of his perverse custom of falsifying and magnifying things. ... I shall remain in Borges, not in myself (if it is true that I am someone), but I recognize myself less in his books than in many others or in the laborious strumming of a guitar. ...I do not know which of us has written this page.
>>
>> (Borges, 1970, pp. 282–3)
>
> We can use this extract to shed light on the issue of coherence, integration, multiplicity and fragmentation. Borges is exploring the relationship between the publicly recognised writer ('he', 'the other one', 'the one called Borges') and 'I', a person that appears to be more about private tastes and pleasures. Despite his final claim not to know which one has written the page, the 'I' – the authorial voice in this extract – is not the writer of books ('I recognize myself less in his books'). Reflecting on the relationship between the two selves (or aspects of self), Borges finds that it does not feel comfortable, although they are not hostile. '... his perverse custom of falsifying and magnifying things' suggests that the 'I' feels more authentic than the 'other one'. I am reminded of Donald W. Winnicott's (1971) distinction between the true and false self, the authentic being more 'true' and the one performing for the public gaze being experienced by the former as more false (see Section 1.5). None the less, Borges's final comment suggests that the flow of his experience can move between these two selves, so that the 'I' sometimes inhabits the writer. What comes across is less a 'looking-glass self' and more multiples of 'me'.

Erving Goffman, an American sociological social psychologist (or 'microsociologist'), argued that the self in social relations behaved as if performing in a play. Goffman (1959) distinguishes between three aspects: self as performer, self as audience and self as the character performed. As part of this analogy, people were said to engage in 'face' work; that is, to put on a face for particular public purposes. When my mother applied makeup, she used the phrase 'putting on my face', which had connotations of the public front she put on to go out. The distinction between the private and public selves gained a hold through this idea. Goffman's analogy with drama is based on Mead's distinction between the 'I' and 'me' and his emphasis on people's distinctive capacity to 'take the role of the other'. Like Mead, Goffman stresses that self-consciousness renders people aware of the judgements of others and thus exerts pressure towards acting within social conventions. For many, it is self-consciousness that distinguishes humans from non-human animals. The dramaturgical analogy has been influential in training people for a wide variety of service jobs; training that involves asking people to take the role of the other (customer, patient) so as to become more sensitive to their effect on others.

1.3   The 'individual' self

Psychological social psychology (PSP), in contrast, avoided the concept of self because it was so intractable to scientific study. This meant that in the first half of the twentieth century, the philosophical and sociological ideas about the social and multiple self prevailed. Disagreeing with this state of affairs, Gordon Allport made it the subject of his presidential address, in 1943, to the 14th Annual Meeting of the Eastern Psychological Association. Thus, the concept of the self was reintroduced into North American psychology.

Allport had a serious purpose in wanting to readmit the self (or ego, as he chose to call it most of the time) into psychology. He discussed several experimental studies, arguing that they led to the conclusion 'that ego involvement or its absence, makes a critical difference in human behaviour' (1943, p. 459). In other words, the self should be a central concept in any psychology that purported to understand human behaviour. Without a concept of the ego or self, he argued, it was impossible to do justice to the unity and coherence that characterise people's behaviour and experience of themselves.

1.4   The self constituted in language and discourses

I have shown briefly how the idea of the social self emerged out of the proposition that there exists an observing self, as well as an observed self, and that the observing self takes on the views of others. Since the 'social' is such a broad category, there is room for a great deal of theoretical detail to specify the precise sense in which the self is social and this was the basis for a major paradigm shift that produced discursive psychology (see Chapter 1, Section 3.5). By demonstrating how discourses position people and thus constitute selves, this perspective goes beyond the earlier formulations about the grammar of 'I' and 'me' and the relational origins of the self.

In recent social psychology, the emphasis on how the self is constituted in discourses represents a radical challenge to a PSP based on the idea of an individual who has already developed a self and uses it as a position from which to interact. Discourses – the talk and texts of social life – are not just seen as external influences on an already existing individual that existed prior to that individual; rather, they constitute the self. In others words, the self is formed by – made up of – the meaning systems that are exchanged in the ongoing relations of social life. Theorists have pointed out that language and discourse pre-exist individuals. From the time of Mead onwards, it was possible (though not common) to think of language and thought as something that takes place intersubjectively; that is, in the space between people, with effects on them.

ACTIVITY 5.2

By midway through the twentieth century, then, the stage was set for a disagreement about the self which has contemporary reverberations throughout the social sciences and into popular beliefs about the self: is it multiple, perhaps fragmented, or is it unitary and coherent?

Think about yourself for a minute or two. Do you tend one way or the other on the question of whether selves are unitary and coherent or multiple and fragmented? Make a brief list of ways in which your self feels multiple and then another consisting of ways in which you feel unitary. What gives your self coherence? In what ways does it feel fragmented? Perhaps you – and others – are coherent and multiple, or neither unitary nor fragmented.

1.5   The real me and the true or false self

Social or individual selves, integrated or fragmented, are not the only binaries at issue in the social psychology of self. Between modern and postmodern images, the questions are raised: is the self false or true, spontaneous or self-consciously performed, authentic or inauthentic?

The idea of the 'real me' is common in the popular language of the UK in the twenty-first century. For example, participants in the Channel 4 reality TV programme *Big Brother* spend time trying to work out what is authentic about the other housemates, as opposed to what is performance. Likewise, they often protest that they are showing the real me (despite living in front of the cameras).

> The public don't like me and if I was, if I was being someone else then I wouldn't care because I could be somebody else ... But I am being the real me and it hurts to know that there are a lot of people out there who don't like the real me.
>
> (Jade Goody, 'Day 8', *Big Brother 3*, Channel 4, 2002)

Carl Rogers, usually regarded as a key figure in humanistic psychology, advanced a notion of the true self. Humanistic psychology grew stronger in North American psychology in the 1950s and 1960s as a reaction to the objectification of the self through experiment and psychometrics. According to Allport, Rogers (1942) demonstrated that 'the ego [or self] is coming into its own': 'Rogers in effect asks counsellors to [...] encourage the patient himself to restructure and re-plan his life. The patient's ego takes command. It's about time it should' (Allport, 1943, p. 473). Rogers was dedicated to strengthening this self in the face of the influences of social life, which he regarded as distorting the singular, true or real self. For humanistic psychology, feelings were the gold standard of personhood. Cale and Neuwirth's song (see the introduction to this chapter) bitingly reflects the continuing narcissistic Western preoccupation with self.

This movement in psychology was also part of a wider critique of positivism that emphasised experience as the central principle for psychology, a basic phenomenological concept. Experience provided both an epistemological principle (only through experience can we know about people in a meaningful way) and an ontological claim (we are who we are because of the sum total of our experiences). Humanistic and phenomenological psychology had this in common, but only in the USA did humanism and phenomenology become fused together. The US approach radically transformed existentialism to a focus on the self-actualising individual as agent. In Europe, phenomenology remained closely allied to philosophy and was both concerned with method and with therapeutic self-discovery. European phenomenology takes a bleaker view of humanity and is more concerned with the psychosocial in that it is concerned with the person in relation to the social.

Winnicott, a paediatrician and psychoanalyst, took the existence of a true self as a question for enquiry and explanation rather than accepting it as a starting assumption, as was often the case in psychology. For him it boiled down to the experience of 'aliveness' and this could not be taken for granted. Some children had experienced such failure in their early caring environments that they were robbed of this vitality: 'feeling real is more than existing; it is finding a way to exist as oneself, and to relate to objects as oneself and to have a self into which to retreat for relaxation' (Winnicott, 1971, p. 138). He distinguished between a true and false self on the basis of how a baby's self is formed in relation to its primary carer. If the primary carer recognises the baby's spontaneous gestures and feelings and responds accurately to them, the baby develops a true sense of itself. If babies are constantly misrecognised, in line with the mother's or father's own preferences or projections, they will only see what the parent feels. '[The baby] can only discover what he feels by seeing it reflected back. If the infant is seen in a way that makes him feel he exists, in a way that confirms him, he is free to go on looking' (Phillips, 1988, p. 128). Such relationships have effects on the adult self too, although subsequent experiences modify the earlier ones.

1.6   The unconscious intersubjective self

Intersubjectivity is a word that is used in various traditions (phenomenology, psychoanalysis, developmental and social psychology) where attempts are being made to go beyond a model of the self that assumes a self-contained and essentially asocial individual. In psychoanalytic versions of intersubjectivity, each person is made up, psychologically speaking, of introjected (unconsciously internalised) parts of others that flow dynamically between people. Psychoanalysis is famous for the concept of the unconscious. It unsettled the dominant idea that people could know themselves completely. It dethroned the idea of consciousness as the locus of self and claimed that many of the sources of motivation and action derived from 'another place' –

the unconscious. But how social is this idea? The social psychoanalytic perspective has borrowed from the 'object relations' tradition, originating in the work of Melanie Klein, because it emphasises the intersubjective dynamics of unconscious conflict. In her notion of unconscious defences against anxiety, Klein (1988a and 1988b) departed radically from the assumption that the self is a single unit, with unproblematic boundaries separating it from the external world of objects (both people and things).

Klein's proposition (based on clinical work) was that the most primitive defences against anxiety are intersubjective: that is, they move between people. The unconscious processes of projection (putting out) and introjection (taking in) of mental objects result in splitting, separating good from bad. The concept of splitting originated in Freud's view of the mind as characterised by conflict and capable of producing inconsistent thoughts and beliefs. Klein's work on the splitting of the object developed this, pointing out how objects are often given unrealistically good and bad characteristics. Later Klein emphasised the splitting of the ego, where parts of the self that are feared as bad are split off through projection and usually identified as belonging to an outside object (or person) (Hinshelwood, 1991, pp. 433–4). This splitting of objects into good and bad is the basis for what Klein termed the 'paranoid-schizoid' position; a position to which we may all resort in the face of self-threatening occurrences, because it permits us to believe in a good object, on which we can rely, uncontaminated by 'bad' threats which have been split off and located elsewhere. However, it leads to a distortion of actual circumstances in which usually there is a mixture of good and bad. With emotional maturity, Klein saw people as more often able to maintain the 'depressive' position; namely, a position in which good and bad can be acknowledged to be part of the same object. The depressive position enables the self to be more integrated.

This account avoids the common dualism of a fragmented or integrated self by conceptualising the self as in constant dynamic tension between forces that tend towards splitting (prompted by otherwise unbearable anxiety) and forces tending towards integration (recognising, where realistic, good and bad in the same object). Depressive forces act in an integrating direction because good and bad can be held within the self without the depletions that are a consequence of projection. Introjection can enlarge the ego – or self – because it involves internalising an object or a relationship with an object and identifying with it, thus enriching the ego. These processes continue throughout life, with the self remaining dynamic and more or less integrated depending on a person's past life experiences and the anxiety-provoking or security-enabling conditions of their present situation.

1.7   Summary

This brief history of changes in the treatment of self illustrates how the concept is always situated, historically, geographically and within different traditions of thought. Of course, irrespective of these changes, people go about their daily business. But the way that selves are conceptualised does not just affect ideas; through the availability of different understandings it will mediate people's self experience as well. Locke's introduction of the idea of self-consciousness was both effect (of dramatic socioeconomic changes) and cause (as the belief in a thinking, purposive self-conscious subject further permeated action). Perhaps postmodern ideas will work similarly, although it is important to recognise that these social influences do not impose themselves on a blank screen.

This section has shown how ideas about the self are disparate. Diversity can be a good thing, but the disparity that we find here is a problem because the different approaches to the self tend to boil down to a series of binaries which sets up the self as either one thing or its opposite. Before we proceed, then, let me summarise the binaries that have occurred in this brief history.

The early idea of self-consciousness emphasised both thought and conscious awareness as being central to self. The emphasis on *thought* is in contrast to humanistic psychology's belief in *feelings* as the core of the real self. The emphasis on conscious awareness has been countered by the idea of *unconscious motivations* being the source of self, or at any rate of personality, character and action. The idea of self-awareness, influenced by a consideration of the role of language in constructing selves, led to the idea of a double self, the 'I' and the 'me', as in grammar. These easily become split in ways that reflect the two major dualisms that characterise social science thinking: individual–social and agency–structure. Individual–social dualism is reproduced in the split between I and me. 'I' is the *singular individual,* whereas 'me' is the *self produced by the social influences of others' gazes.* 'I' is also the active pronoun, the subject where change is located and so represents the agent in agency–structure dualism. In contrast, the 'me' is the object of a verb in a given sentence – done to, *passive,* positioned by social influences, rather than choosing to act.

Individual–social dualism is also expressed centrally in the tension between the psychological and sociological perspective. The first concentrates on the *intrapsychic;* what happens within the individual (whether this is thought/ cognition or feeling/emotion, conscious awareness or unconscious motivation). The second sees the self as constituted in the *intersubjective* social space between people and in the social meanings available to them. Two further issues complete my list of binaries. Do parts of the self *cohere* or are they *fragmented?* Finally, introducing the time dimension, is self something experienced in the vanishing moment or something realised only over time?

Social psychology is occasionally caught on the horns of all these binaries: an uncomfortable place to sit. Attempts to understand the self, it seems, are vulnerable to all the binaries at once. Binaries are based in 'either/or' thinking. In what follows, we shall see if 'both/and' thinking helps us to understand the complexity of the self.

The purpose of reviewing the history and different theoretical approaches of self is not only to aid understanding of this topic but also to inform readers, as social psychologists and potentially as researchers on the self, of the strengths and weaknesses, possibilities and dangers involved in this field. So what lessons can be learned from it?

For me, there is something exciting, although unnerving, about this field, because the implications of seeing selves one way or another are fairly momentous. It is as if self is a core issue, quintessentially social psychological, that is wide open and yet we all have access to it through our own experience. It makes me aware that self is such a huge, elusive concept, with myriad connotations, that it feels unmanageable as a research topic. My response to these impressions is to plot two courses through the subsequent discussion. One is to focus on something more manageable than this rather amorphous idea, which is what empirical researchers have done. The second is to emphasise methodology: if self can mean this disparate variety of things, it must be a result of how it has been approached, and with what methodological choices, theoretical commitments and cultural blind spots.

2   The phenomenological self

Phenomenology studies 'phenomena' (the appearance of things) in depth in order to understand how human beings experience the world of objects which they inhabit. Broaden out this idea and you can see that phenomenology is about investigating the human condition as it manifests in people's lived experience. In this way phenomenology avoids seeing individual selves as isolated from their worlds. Two core concepts emphasise this idea. The first is 'being-in-the-world' (or, as Edmund Husserl originally captured the idea in German, 'Dasein'). The second is 'lifeworld' (written as one word), which captures the idea of the inseparability between the world which forms the setting for one's life and the subjective experience of that life. The self of phenomenology is constantly and actively making meaning out of experience. Husserl argued that a person can only know what he or she can experience. This leads to phenomenology's methodological focus on conscious lived experiences. It also means that, like the other two qualitative methods represented in this book, phenomenological psychology is comfortable with the idea of investigating subjective experience, rather than objective reality.

Husserl outlined three steps, or rules, involved in a phenomenological method. By method, he meant something rather different from what is meant by the term in social psychology: more rules that function as a guide to ways of thinking about and experiencing another person than a series of practical steps to elicit concrete responses from a participant.

The first step is the rule of 'epoché', which involves trying to *bracket* (suspend or withhold) our expectations and assumptions so as to focus on the primary data of experience (see Chapter 2, Section 2.1). Husserl asks us to focus solely on our immediate and present experiencing of objects, rather than to place them in time and space. This helps us to consider other possibilities and develop a deeper understanding of how people actually experience their lifeworlds. The second rule in the phenomenological method is to focus on description as a way of resisting explanation. It encourages us to avoid hypotheses and theories and to stay with lived experiences. The third rule is 'horizontalisation', which is simply a way of saying avoid prioritising some items of description over others but treat things as having equal significance – at least to start with.

Box 5.2   Market shopping in burkas

This example from a journalist's book-length account of an Afghan family living in war-torn Kabul illustrates the phenomenological approach as used outside an academic tradition. Åsne Seierstad is a female Norwegian journalist who spent several months in 2002 living in the household of Sultan Khan, an Afghan bookseller. Speaking of her method in the Foreword to her book *The Bookseller of Kabul* (2004), she says '[the book] is based on real events or what was told me by people who took part in those events. When I describe thoughts and feelings, the point of departure is what people told me they thought or felt in any given situation'. On this basis, she writes a strikingly detailed description of her visit with three sisters from Sultan Khan's family to buy goods at a market, dressed in burkas.

> She loses sight of her all the time. The billowing burka merges with every other billowing burka. [...] She glances at the ground. In the mud she can distinguish the dirty shoes from other dirty shoes. [...] She walks round the bazaar, looking down, following the fluttering burka. [...]
>
> The lead burka has stopped near the bed-linen counter. She feels the material and tries to gauge the colour through the grille. She bargains through the grille, whilst dark eyes can only just be seen, dimly through the lattice. The burka haggles, arms waving in the air. The nose pokes through the folds like a beak. At last she makes up her mind, gropes for her bag and reaches out a hand with some blue banknotes. The bed-linen seller measures up. [...] The material disappears into the bag under the burka.
>
> The smell of saffron, garlic, dried pepper and fresh pakora penetrates the stiff material and mingles with sweat, breath and the smell of strong soap. The nylon material is so dense that one can smell one's own breathing.
>
> [...]
>
> They walk on, and weave around with their heads in all directions to see better. Burka-women are like horses with blinkers, they can only look in one direction. Where the eye narrows the grille stops and thick material takes its place; impossible to glance sideways. The whole head must turn; another trick by the burka-inventor: a man must know what his wife is looking at.
>
> After a bit of head rotating the other two find the lead burka in the narrow alleyways of the bazaar's interior. She is assessing lace edging. [...] This purchase is so important that she flips the front piece over her head in order to see better. [...] It is difficult to assess lace from behind a gauze grille. Only the stall vendor sees her face. Even in Kabul's cool mountain air it is covered in beads of sweat. Shakila rocks her head to and fro, smiles roguishly and laughs, she haggles, yes, she even flirts. [...] She has been doing it all along, and the vendor can decipher the moods of a waving, nodding, billowing burka with ease. She can flirt with her little finger, with a foot, with the movement of a hand.

(Seierstad, 2004, pp. 88–90)

Seierstad succeeds largely in conveying the burka experience through rich and detailed description. This is the basis of the phenomenological method and consistent with the principle of epoché. She avoids interpretation and concentrates on the embodied aspect of experiencing. In the book's Foreword, she writes of how she wore the burka 'to discover for myself what it is like to be an Afghan woman' (Seierstad, 2004, p. 6). She also accompanied the sisters on market visits. She conjures up the experience of wearing a burka in a specific cultural and physical setting. The description emphasises the body and the senses to convey the experience: the way that sight is compromised with the consequence that bodily movements are affected and it is difficult to judge items for purchase; the market smells mixing with body smells because of how the breath is trapped inside the thick material; the build up of heat, so that sweat breaks out on the head.

The purpose of the burka is that women are not exposed to men outside their own families, and the extract conveys how individuality is lost as a result of this clothing. As a literary device, the identity of Shakila is not revealed by name until she uncovers her face briefly in order to see the lace better; the rest of the time she is referred to as 'the burka', with the intention no doubt of pointing out that her individual identity is not accessible under the burka. However, it also illustrates how social constraints are not wholly successful in positioning Shakila, whose individuality – and even sexuality – can be expressed through body movements despite the almost all-encompassing cover of the burka.

ACTIVITY 5.3

How successfully has Seierstad helped you to get a feeling for the experience of going to the market wearing a burka? Do you think she always follows the rules of epoché by avoiding interpretation? In order to work this out, see whether she ever moves from description to interpretation.

Phenomenology and existential philosophy are nearly synonymous. Most of the well-known names, such as Kierkegaard, Heidegger, Buber, Sartre and Merleau-Ponty, are regarded as both (see Langdridge, 2006). Existential philosophy took up the method of phenomenology and, in turn, informed phenomenology (which is both a method and a philosophy). What this means for the self is that it is approached through the concept of 'existence'. The main characteristics of existence in this tradition are that it is:

- unique (because each person makes their own meanings out of their experiences)
- actively doing (as in Sartre's claim 'to be is to do')
- freely choosing (and therefore anxious and guilty – responsible for one's actions and whether they are authentic or inauthentic)
- situated within time and in-the-world ('Dasein').

These are all ways of describing the self.

2.1 Respecting the lifeworld of an Alzheimer's sufferer

It is quite a challenge to translate these ideas into a research method. Ann and Peter Ashworth (2003) provide an example based on the experience of caring for a relative suffering from Alzheimer's disease. They base their approach on the phenomenological idea of the lifeworld and make the case that this has useful implications for care because, rather than treat the sufferer as beyond understanding, it can help carers to act respectfully through 'the discovery that the sufferer continues to be a person with a unique lifeworld' (Ashworth and Ashworth, 2003, p. 179). They identify three intersubjective characteristics of the self, viewed phenomenologically, that enable the understanding of another person:

- The other is a subject in the world, a minded being like myself [...]
- The world is, for both of us, an intersubjective one – there for everyone. So, for example, we can share the same object of attention.
- There is reciprocity of perspectives such that, standing in my position [...] you can take my mental perspective – and vice versa.

(Ashworth and Ashworth, 2003, p. 183)

Using the rules outlined above, Ashworth and Ashworth advocate that:

At each point, reflecting on a piece of talk or an action, the carer will both attempt to discover what that must say about the nature of the lifeworld of the sufferer and – at the same time – notice their own tendencies in trying to understand, and bracket them only permitting the use of perspectives which seem accurately to reflect the world of the sufferer themselves.

(Ashworth and Ashworth, 2003, p. 186)

Ashworth and Ashworth give an example of 'bracketing the question of whether the "thing experienced" is real or not':

In attempting to understand the sufferer's claim that her deceased husband 'loved it here' (when the place did not exist during his lifetime), one must consider other meanings than inaccurate memory. Appreciation of the place together with a recognition that enjoyable places of the past were normally experienced in his company may be part of the meaning of the ostensibly inaccurate statement.

(Ashworth and Ashworth, 2003, p. 186)

ACTIVITY 5.4

You can look for this article by doing an electronic journal search. Once you have brought it up on screen, scroll down and find the section on epoché and a section on self that starts 'Self, considered as part of the lifeworld, includes the attributions of identity "I'm your mother" as well as the person's experience of her own presence, agency and voice within a situation ...' (Ashworth and Ashworth, 2003, p. 191). The Alzheimer's sufferer continues to have a self 'in the sense of being the centre – the point of view – on her physical and psychological world' (Ashworth and Ashworth, 2003, p. 191).

2.2   A phenomenology of working-class experience

Simon Charlesworth (2000, p. 22) uses a phenomenological method in conjunction with the sociological theory of Pierre Bourdieu to conduct research into working-class experience. He is himself a working-class man, living in Rotherham, an ex-mining town in the north of England where unemployment is high. He wanted an approach that could convey not just the history of Rotherham but 'the impact of these phenomena on what people think or feel' (2000, p. 63). He was particularly interested in how experience can be 'inscribed in their comportment and motility, the ways they have unconsciously learned to be in the world' (p. 64). This is what Merleau-Ponty (1962) called 'incarnate subjectivity'. Charlesworth interviewed individuals in order to describe these experiences:

> S: Can I ask yer abaht ahr [how] it meks [makes] yer feel?
>
> K: Ye... [sighs and pauses]... 'cos [because] yer just constantly on an edge, know what Ah [I] mean, yer constantly on an edge, unsettled, yer thinkin' all time: yer gu to bed at night an' yer laid the'er thinkin', I mean, 'What 'appens if Ah lose mi [my] job?' ... it's allous [always] on yer mind ... Yer can't 'ave a good time... yer can't relax ... it's the'er all't time.
>
> (Charlesworth, 2000, p. 77)

Charlesworth uses a form of transcription that conveys the rhythm, tone and emotion in the speech of himself and his interviewees, as opposed to just the surface meaning ('got nowt guin' fo us ... no money ... no jobs ... nothin' fo' us to do ... we've got nowt ...' (p. 172)). Through a series of interviews, he draws conclusions not about specific individuals (who are never portrayed), but about a specific kind of situated working-class experience: 'why these people suffer and how they suffer' (p. 26). Through a phenomenological approach, he constitutes class very differently from more distanced approaches which

> ... overlook the essential truth of class that experience of it is always from amidst a world-defining context experienced through the primordial realm in which selves take shape: that is, class is not a simple matter of understanding self through a role but a locating of the flesh through inhabiting a particular social realm
>
> (Charlesworth, 2000, p. 65)

2.3   Summary

In this section, I have discussed how phenomenological psychology has approached the understanding of self. The self as 'being-in-the-world' encourages an emphasis on an active, meaning-making, embodied self, produced in the process of continuous situated experiences shared with other people. This is helpful in going beyond individual–social dualism. My main focus here is on method, in particular, on the three steps outlined by Husserl. I gave examples from journalistic participant observation, an application of the concept of lifeworld to an interview study of caring in a family, and a more sociological use of interviewing to illuminate working-class experience. These three illustrations showed the varied application of phenomenology to the understanding of self, with emphasis on embodiment, intersubjectivity and the lived experience of a social identity.

3   The social psychoanalytic self

The principles on which a social psychoanalytic perspective is based have consequences for methodology. If some of the strongest influences of self on actions and relationships are unintended and hidden from us, how does the researcher get to know about them? Psychoanalysis learns about the hidden self not through research in the usual sense, but through clinical, psychotherapeutic work, an in-depth, case-based form of producing evidence. The social psychoanalytic approach and its accompanying methods are developments of psychoanalysis, which take account of the social setting and understand the hidden aspects of self.

_____ *Pause for reflection* _____

Did you remember that, in his brief account of an experimental approach to emotions in Chapter 2, Section 2.1, Russell Spears made the same claim for experimental methods, saying that they could reach the parts that other methods don't reach through setting up situations that elicit behaviour from participants of which they are unaware? As Spears points out, this is something that experimental and social psychoanalytic methods have in common.

3.1   Vince's 'choice'

In an article published in the *British Journal of Social Psychology*, Tony Jefferson and I summarised our purposes as follows:

> The aim of this article is to explore the predicament of one man in difficult circumstances, in order to produce a psychosocial analysis that could contribute to a social psychological understanding of agency. [...]
>
> Vince, a middle-aged, working-class man from the North of England, the subject of our case study, had already been faced with difficult choices in order to hold on to a job that was bad for him. Now the choice appeared to be taken out of his hands by an illness without a discernible organic base and with no prospect of improvement that, for five months, had forced him to be on sick leave.
>
> (Hollway and Jefferson, 2005, p. 147)

It is impossible to convey the complexities of a full case study in a short section, so here I will illustrate briefly two questions, one methodological (the uses of free association) and the other ontological (the understanding of agency). The analysis was based on interview data elicited through asking a small number of narrative questions (a method called the Free Association Narrative Interview (FANI)). By enabling the interviewee to structure the sequence of his own story, the connections between one idea and the next could be made through free associations, which reveal emotionally meaningful connections in their experiences of the events recounted. In this way the method was designed to go beyond self-conscious, intentional presentation of the self to gain insights into unconscious motivations.

Agency is a salient feature of modernist approaches to the self: the central assumption is of an individual self who, albeit within constraints, can self-consciously and rationally evaluate his or her position and decide, and then act, upon his or her conclusions. A social psychoanalytic approach challenges this model of self through the centrality of the unconscious and specifies the social settings, both past and present, that impact upon conflictual unconscious dynamics.

We identified three areas of Vince's working life that were highly significant for him: the daily experience of his job, having a respectable job, and his relationship with his boss. A detailed unstructured interview enabling free associations to be articulated, followed by a case-based analysis, is consistent with these principles.

At the conclusion of our analysis (based on two interviews with Vince, each lasting about 90 minutes), we concluded that:

> By becoming too sick to work, Vince achieves a resolution, not through thought but through the body. This resolution is an elegant one. On the one hand he has not chosen to quit his job. He and others can honestly say that he would be

working if he could. His intentions remain unimpeachable. On the other hand, his collapse has achieved that desired-and-feared situation: he does not have to go to work.

(Hollway and Jefferson, 2005, p. 161)

Most qualitative analyses would probably settle for Vince's conscious self-presentation as a hard-working man who, despite himself, has been stopped from working by illness.

_____ *Pause for reflection* _____

Notice where his 'self' has been located in the last sentence. What beliefs about self does this reveal?

In contrast, we do not locate Vince's 'self' exclusively in his conscious intentions:

> Vince's intentions cannot be reduced to his conscious mind. He had come to dread his job and it must follow that a part of him wished to be rid of it. It is also clear that this part was in fundamental conflict with another part (one shot through with fears of failing as a family man) that dreaded not having this job.

(Hollway and Jefferson, 2005, p. 161)

Methodologically, the central question for our purposes here is how, as researchers, we could come to this conclusion about hidden aspects of Vince's self? To detail all our evidence would take as long as the original article, but here I will give two brief examples of the way that free association points to a participant's preoccupations and provides clues for the interpretation of data.

Although the purpose of the interview was about something rather different (about crime in the neighbourhood and the fear that it might induce), Vince quickly turned to the story of the morning when the period of sick leave began, when he was unable to go to work:

> And I got up on Monday morning and er, I was sat over there like, and er ... I felt absolutely shocking like, you know, just terrible. And er I asked me wife to ring the firm and just to say, well look, you know, I won't be coming in like, I'm feeling ill like'. [His wife rang the firm and later also rang the doctor.] She rang without me knowing like, you know, 'cos I kept saying '"no, don't phone the doctor" like, I'll be OK, I'll just 'ave a bit of time off, then I'll go back to work'. And I started – you know when she told me like [that she'd phoned the doctor] – I started panicking then you know, because er I'm, what's happening. You know, me 'eart were beating and pounding away.

(Hollway and Jefferson, 2005, p. 152)

Vince can give an account of this episode five months later, at the time of the interview, but he cannot make sense of his panic attack. He continued that he found it 'hard to explain at times ... how you do feel. I mean that court case now. I mean I think about it every day and every night, you know, it's still with me'. The principle of free association derived from psychoanalysis suggests that the juxtaposition of these two sentences is highly significant: the fact that Vince's train of thought moves from his attempts to explain feeling ill directly to the court case indicates the emotional connection between these thoughts. The association leads to a long and complicated story about when his van was stolen from outside the firm's offices and the boss threatened to sack him if he didn't tell the insurance company (and the court) a falsehood about where he had left the van. The boss's insurance money depended on it. We can see from the following, that he makes the link between this and his illness:

> And er, it took 3 years to get there like [to court]. So obviously I were worrying for 3 years, at end of it all if he didn't get 'is money, I'd be out of a job like. And 'e did win 'is claim. Er, but I still wasn't too 'appy like. Obviously I'd been worrying all them years like ... (WH: And then?) Well you know, everything – that were last November – it got to court and then Christmas 'olidays like. It er, you know, we 'ad us 'olidays like. At that particular time I thought well once it's over and done with, that pressure would go like. But it didn't. (WH: Oh right.) So I'm off er, now with depression. You know, 'cos obviously it's got me down that much.
>
> (Hollway and Jefferson, 2005, p. 153)

A puzzle remains, though. Why did he go off sick once his job was secure when, as he acknowledges, the pressure should have gone? This was not a reaction of his conscious, rational, intentional self who wanted to protect his job: it must have come from a conflicting desire, suppressed in his conscious mind but expressed through his body in his symptoms. In brief, this is why we concluded that the crucial aspect of Vince's self, expressed in his going off sick, was conflictual, hidden from his conscious self and expressed through his body and emotions (through the panic attack and his consequent psychological paralysis diagnosed as depression).

This example illustrates the close link between the method used and the conclusions about the nature of self that could be reached in this piece of empirical research. The method was informed by the psychoanalytic principles of free association and unconscious conflict. It also used a narrative principle in order to go beyond the restrictions of a semi-structured interview method (which, in my view, tends to impose the agenda of the researcher and squeeze out the preoccupations of the interviewee). The narrative method can avoid the production of an overly coherent life story by eliciting free associations. This was done by asking open but concrete questions and following the train of thought of the interviewee in subsequent interjections. I have shown how the free associative links in those trains of thought can be valuable clues in interpreting the interview data and how they can reveal hidden aspects of self. The conclusions we drew about the unconscious conflicts influencing Vince's illness would not have been possible without such a method. They then formed the basis for an analysis of agency that takes into account unconscious conflict and the activity of the body to achieve an outcome for oneself without the intervention of conscious intention.

3.2 Esther's self-worth

The addition of free association to a narrative method of eliciting information about someone's experience proved valuable in providing clues to why Vince remained ill, which then required interpretation. However, we were still limited by what Vince told us, and all methods that rely on participants' self-report (and most methods do) to some extent depend on their self-knowledge. I therefore became interested in observational methods based on a social psychoanalytic perspective. The psychoanalytic method of observing infants and children emphasises unconscious intersubjectivity as a key process in the development of self.

Again the question is raised of how it is possible to research these hidden and elusive aspects of self. The method was originally developed, not for research, but for training professionals involved with parents (usually mothers) caring for their young children. It centres on learning to observe, in minute and open-minded detail, the actions and reactions of babies and their carers together (Rustin, 1989). Since babies cannot talk, the method has developed an unusual sensitivity to how babies express themselves with their bodies. In these respects it resembles the phenomenological method. However, later in the process interpretation is used to infer internalisation, a process that is theorised in psychoanalysis as involving introjection (an unconscious intersubjective dynamic).

In the following vignette from Maggie Turp (2004), I give a brief example of the intersubjective processes that produce self-worth (which means something very similar to self-esteem) in a baby. Turp uses extracts from a two-year baby observation (an hour each week in the baby's home) to explore how the responses of the parents of a baby, Esther, are internalised to provide her with good 'internal objects' that can 'serve as building blocks for her sense of self-worth' (Turp, 2004, p. 113). Turp's account is strongly developmental in that she is extrapolating a process of internalisation of self-worth during an important period of childhood when separation and differentiation are occurring. The following example occurs when Esther is eight months old. When she starts to cry, her father looks up and says 'what happened, did you bang your head?'

> In response, Esther crawls to the window and mimes bumping her head on the window ledge. Then she puts her hand to her head. Rob says to me 'Hey look at that. She showed me what happened', and then to Esther 'That was very clever you know'. He picks her up and gives her head a rub and a kiss. Esther seems to forget the bump on her head and perks up. She rubs her nose into Rob's face in a cheeky kind of way and smiles broadly.
>
> (Turp, 2004, p. 113)

Using the concept of introjection derived from psychoanalysis (see above, Section 1.6), it is possible to interpret these pleased and proud responses to infer that Esther is in the process of introjecting a good object as she feels pleasure in her father's pleasure in her. Likewise, there is an example of her father's pride in her learning to walk which is transferred as Esther experiences her self-worth in the gaze of the observer: 'Each time she passes me, she turns and gives me a huge self-satisfied smile, looking thoroughly pleased with herself' (Turp, 2004, p. 114).

In the method of psychoanalytic observation, self-report through words is bypassed. This makes it more available for noticing the non-linguistic, unselfconscious aspects of self, particularly as they are expressed through the body, like when Esther rubs her nose on her father's face and smiles. Here again we can see that the methods and the assumptions about the self, on which they are explicitly or implicitly based, produce very different accounts of the self.

3.3   Summary

In this section, I took the psychoanalytic claim that parts of the self are hidden from self-consciousness and illustrated the implications this has for methodology. The example of Vince showed an attempt to go beyond agency–structure dualism by considering how unconscious conflict could lead to a split between the bodily self and the conscious intentional self (described further in Hollway and Jefferson, 2005). It showed how the FANI method enabled knowledge about unconscious conflict to be inferred through the free associations of the interviewee. The example of Esther showed how the development of self-worth could be inferred through psychoanalytically-informed observation (Turp, 2004).

The phenomenological and psychoanalytic approaches to the self turned out to have quite a lot in common. They both provide useful resources for going beyond the two dualisms that provide us with our interrogative themes. In both cases, the self is situated and dynamically changing through making meaning out of experiences. Both methods encourage us to recognise the embodied and also the intersubjective nature of selves. Both see anxiety as being a key feature of the human condition, although in phenomenology this is seen to lead to conscious struggle against purposelessness, while social psychoanalysis emphasises the idea that unconscious defences against anxiety lead to some actions being hidden from consciousness. Both approaches problematise consciousness in different ways, however, with phenomenology accepting the idea that there are degrees of consciousness, some reflective and some non-reflective (Van Deuzen-Smith, 1997). The psychoanalytically-informed observation method shares with the phenomenological method an interest in going beyond words, paying close and descriptive attention to embodied experience and bracketing explanation in the service of understanding the minutiae of experience.

4   Conclusions

My approach in this chapter to the huge, elusive and contentious, but centrally important topic of self has been: first to situate the social psychological debate historically within wider trends of social thought; second to focus on showing how different approaches to the topic will produce different images of the self; and third to illustrate phenomenological and social psychoanalytic approaches to self. In the process, I uncovered many binaries. Does the self reside in:

- thoughts or feelings
- mind or body or language
- conscious awareness or unconscious motivations?

Is it best conceptualised as:

- existing prior to social interactions or produced by social influences
- active agency or passive, a product of outside influences
- intrapsychic (within the individual) or intersubjective (between people)
- coherent or fragmented
- produced in the moment or realised over time?

Once these binaries are exposed and put so baldly it is quite easy to say that if either/or formulations are replaced by both/and, understanding of the self will be much better placed. I agree. However, it is more of a challenge to do the detailed work of giving an account of self where all of these considerations are integrated into a consistent explanation, rather than just added together in a list. This is by way of an agenda for the future.

It is clear that empirical methods are all going to be partial in the vision of selves that they provide. I have tried to show that, whatever methods researchers deploy, they are informed, implicitly or explicitly, by ideas about the self, and that they produce an image of the self that reflects those starting points. This circularity is inevitable and should not be disputed. However, it should be made very clear, so that the limits of what one method produces become part of an ongoing debate, and a wider understanding of the self is achieved by keeping in view the many different images of the self produced by many methods. The way that theory informs the research questions, the methods, the analysis and the conclusions is equally crucial to keep in view. Again, the inevitability of the circularity should not be regretted because it is inevitable, but should be welcomed as adding to the rich diversity of accounts of the self. Theory should inform methods and be modified by the results. It is potentially a virtuous circle of understanding – just as long as researchers do not take up reductive positions and do battle as if the holy grail of the self can be the possession of just one approach.

References

Allport, G. (1943) 'The ego in contemporary psychology', *Psychological Review*, vol. 50, pp. 451–78.

Ashworth, A. and Ashworth, P. (2003) 'The lifeworld as phenomenon and as research heuristic, exemplified by a study of the lifeworld of a person suffering Alzheimer's disease', *Journal of Phenomenological Psychology*, vol. 34, no. 2. pp. 179–205.

Beck, U. and Beck-Gernsheim, E. (2002 [1983]) 'From "living for others" to "a life of one's own"' in *Individualization*, London, Sage, pp. 54–84.

Borges, J.L. (1970) *Labyrinths*, Harmondsworth, Penguin.

Charlesworth, S. (2000) *A Phenomenology of Working Class Experience*, Cambridge, Cambridge University Press.

Cooley, C.H. (1902) *Human Nature and the Social Order*, New York, Scribner.

Danziger, K. (1997) 'The historical formation of selves' in Ashmore, R.D. and Jussim, L. (eds) *Self and Identity: Fundamental Issues*, New York and Oxford, Oxford University Press.

Frosh, S. (1991) *Identity Crisis: Modernity, Psychoanalysis and the Self*, London, Macmillan.

Goffman, E. (1959) *The Presentation of Self in Everyday Life*, Garden City, NY, Doubleday.

Hinshelwood, R.D. (1991) *Dictionary of Kleinian Thought*, London, Karnac.

Hollway, W. and Jefferson, T. (2005) 'Panic and perjury: a psycho-social exploration of agency', *British Journal of Social Psychology*, vol. 44, no. 2, pp. 147–63.

James, W. (1890) *Principles of Psychology*, New York, Holt; also available online at www.ebookmall.com/ebooks/pragmatism-and-other-writings-James-gunn-gunn-ebooks.htm (Accessed 18 May 2006).

Klein, M. (1988a) *Love, Guilt and Reparation and Other Works 1921–1945*, London, Virago.

Klein, M. (1988b) *Envy and Gratitude and Other Works 1946–1963*, London, Virago.

Langdridge, D. (2006) *Phenomenological Psychology: Theory, Research and Method*, Harlow, Pearson Education.

Mead, G.H. (1934) *Mind, Self and Society*, Chicago, IL, University of Chicago Press.

Merleau-Ponty, M. (1962) *Phenomenology of Perception*, London, Routledge.

Phillips, A. (1988) *Winnicott*, London, Fontana.

Rogers, C. (1942) *Counselling and Psychotherapy*, Boston, MA, Houghton Mifflin.

Rustin, M. (1989) in Miller, L., Rustin, M. and Shuttleworth, J. (1989) *Closely Observed Infants*, London, Duckworth.

Seierstad, Å. (2004) *The Bookseller of Kabul* (trans. I. Christopherson), London, Virago.

Turp, M. (2004) 'The capacity for self care', *International Journal of Infant Observation*, vol. 7, no. 1, pp. 108–25.

Van Deuzen-Smith, E. (1997) 'Consciousness and the unknown' in *Everyday Mysteries*, London, Routledge, Chapter 26, pp. 202–17.

Winnicott, D.W. (1971) 'Playing and reality', *Collected Papers*, London, Tavistock.

Chapter 6

Prejudice, conflict and conflict reduction

by John Dixon, Lancaster University

Contents

Learning outcomes

By the end of this chapter, you should:

- be able to compare a range of perspectives on the social psychology of conflict
- be able to evaluate critically how the discipline might be used to address some of the problems that characterise divided societies
- have gained an appreciation of the social and historical contexts within which contemporary social psychology operates.

---

1   Introduction

Historians sometimes describe the twentieth century as the 'century of blood', a period characterised by a sharp escalation of conflict between groups as well as rapid advances in the technology of violence and warfare (see the Nobel Peace Commission *Conflict Map*, (Nobelprize.org, 2006)). Events in the Middle East, South Africa and Northern Ireland, for example, have been widely publicised; events in the Philippines, Haiti and East Timor are perhaps less well known. There is evidence for both a historical growth and a geographic spread of conflict over time, and it is a disturbing fact that any map of world conflict will quickly go out of date and may leave out a great many intra-state conflicts that do not constitute fully blown 'civil wars'.

Understanding conflict between groups is a complex, interdisciplinary project whose importance lies in its profound implications for human suffering, justice and fulfilment. It requires, among other factors, an intimate knowledge of the history, geography, anthropology, economics and politics of national and international relations. While acknowledging the value of other traditions of scholarship, my aim in this chapter is to explore the contribution of social psychology to the study of conflict. I do so by discussing some of the discipline's main theoretical perspectives on intergroup conflict: cognitive social accounts of prejudice; realistic conflict theory; social identity theory; and more recent work in a social constructionist tradition. Part of the promise of these perspectives lies in their potential to clarify how the structural dynamics of conflict between groups become woven into the fabric of individual motivations, emotions, cognitions and actions, and how, in turn, social psychological factors shape the broader contexts of relations between groups. Equally important, social psychological research can be evaluated in terms of its ability to inform social policies that promote positive change. Developing this theme, Section 5 assesses the discipline's most influential framework for understanding how to reduce conflict: namely, the 'contact hypothesis'. In the chapter's conclusion, I reflect on some of the tensions that complicate (and enrich) social psychological work on prejudice, conflict and conflict reduction, thereby looking towards the future development of the field.

2   Social psychological perspectives on prejudice and conflict

2.1   Early research on the 'prejudiced personality'

Social psychological knowledge never arises in a vacuum: it invariably reflects wider cultural and political processes. The events of the Second World War had a profound impact on the social psychology of group processes, making the study of prejudice and conflict a research priority. Before the war, psychologists had been largely content to root the causes of ethnic and racial tensions in ordinary people's reactions to 'real' biological and cultural differences between groups. After the war, however, there was a sea change and a new emphasis on the role of prejudice in shaping collective relations. Psychologists wanted to understand how irrational antipathies based on faulty generalisations – to adapt Gordon Allport's (1954, p. 9) famous definition of the prejudiced mind – might contribute to racial hatred, violence and even genocide.

The first wave of social psychological research treated prejudice primarily as the outcrop of abnormal psychological development. The famous study of the 'Authoritarian Personality' by Theodor Adorno et al. (1950) depicted a type of person whose conscious respect for moral convention masks a repressed resentment towards all forms of traditional authority. Drawing on psychodynamic theory, they argued that this unconscious anger tends to become irrationally displaced onto scapegoat groups, being expressed as a generalised hatred of anyone or anything 'different'. The classic work of Milton Rokeach (1960) and his colleagues on the 'Dogmatic Personality' similarly rooted prejudice in abnormal personality development. In this tradition of research, the problem of prejudice was construed as closely related to the problem of *cognitive rigidity* (see Box 6.1). Rokeach and others argued that dogmatists suffer from a deep-seated inflexibility of thought and attitude; that they tend to see the world in terms of black and white, good and bad, and they are unable to tolerate ambiguities, loose ends or uncertainties.

Box 6.1   Investigating the 'cognitive rigidity' of the prejudiced mind

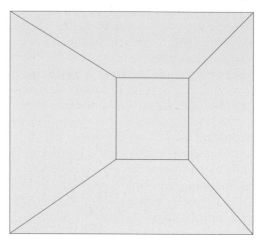

Figure 6.1   The 'truncated pyramid'

In the 1950s and 1960s, social psychologists devised a range of methods for measuring 'cognitive rigidity'. In Fisher's (1951) study, for instance, participants were shown the drawing presented in Figure 6.1, which represents a somewhat skew pyramid with its top cut off. Shortly afterwards, they were asked to draw this pyramid from memory, a task they repeated four weeks later. The results of the study are presented in Table 6.1. As you can see, after four weeks participants who scored high in prejudice were significantly more likely to remember the pyramid as symmetrical. This kind of finding has been interpreted as evidence of the inflexibility of the prejudiced mind: its tendency to see the world in clear categories that override ambiguities, exceptions and shades of grey.

Table 6.1   Percentage of high and low prejudiced participants who 'symmetricised' the pyramid

Drawers' level of prejudice	Drawn shortly after viewing	Drawn after four weeks
High prejudice	40%	62%
Low prejudice	40%	34%

2.2   'Faulty cognitions': socio-cognitive perspectives on prejudice

Theories such as the Authoritarian Personality and the Dogmatic Personality propose what might be called *aberrationist* accounts of prejudice. The authoritarian's bigotry, for example, is seen to stem from a perversion of the normal course of self-development, resulting in a maladjusted way of viewing the social world and relating to others. He or she is a 'rotten apple' who threatens to ruin the barrel (cf. Henriques, 1984). In many ways this is a comforting perspective, for it allows the majority of us to distance ourselves from problems such as racism. Authoritarians may walk among us, but they are not of us. They are the rednecks, Nazis, militarists, and other bogeymen of commonsense theories of bigotry. Since the 1970s, however, the cognitive social approach that has increasingly dominated the social psychology of prejudice has challenged this rather complacent picture.

The influence of cognitive concepts, metaphors and methods on the psychology of intergroup relations cannot be overstated. This influence is evidenced most clearly by the 'information processing' model of the person which now dominates research on prejudice. According to this model, a fruitful analogy can be drawn between the operation of computer systems and the inner workings of human cognition. In both cases, there is an active, rule-bound processing of diverse types of information, marked by sub-activities such as selection, encoding, filing, storage, retrieval, combination and so forth. Many psychologists believe that by studying the 'errors' and 'biases' inherent in such information-processing mechanisms we may uncover the cognitive origins of prejudice.

The so-called 'cognitive miser' theory of stereotyping (Fiske and Taylor, 1991) offers the best-known example of this line of argument, proposing that there are basic 'cognitive mechanisms which, in and of themselves, can lay the foundation for the development of a stereotype belief system' (Hamilton and Trolier, 1986, p. 134, cited in Augoustinos and Walker, 1998, p. 632). Its logic is simple. The world is an enormously complicated place. By classifying ourselves and others into categories (e.g. gender, race, religion, occupation) and then attributing to members of those categories certain shared characteristics (stereotypes), we are better able to store, retrieve and use information about them and to anticipate how they are likely to act in a given situation. More than this, we are able to 'free up' the mental resources we require to do the many other cognitive tasks of everyday life and prevent ourselves from becoming submerged in the messy details of unfolding events. Evidence confirms that there may be a link between stereotyping and (the strains placed upon) our cognitive capacity (e.g. see Crisp et al., 2004; McCrae et al., 1994).

From this perspective, categorisation and stereotyping are not the signs of an abnormal mind but a part of ordinary cognition. An unfortunate by-product of categorisation, for example, is that it accentuates perceived inter-category differences and minimises perceived intra-category differences (cf. Tajfel and Wilkes, 1963). In common language: categorisation exaggerates both the extent to which 'ingroup' members are perceived as similar and the extent to which 'ingroup' and 'outgroup' members are perceived as different (the Accentuation Principle). In this way, information processing may encourage precisely the kinds of 'faulty generalisations' (Allport, 1954) that define prejudiced thinking.

Because they are fundamental to our cognitive architecture, cognitive social theorists argue that categories and stereotypes are difficult to alter and may sometimes be applied in an automatic and unreflexive manner. Research on so-called *implicit prejudice* has been described as one of the most important recent developments in the social psychology of intergroup processes. As Mahzarin Banaji notes:

> In only a decade, research on the unconscious aspects of stereotyping and prejudice has produced remarkable advances in our thinking about the extent to and the manner in which beliefs (stereotypes) and attitudes (prejudice) can operate without awareness or control. Many unsettling discoveries now reveal that well-intentioned individuals can express stereotypes and prejudice previously assumed to be present only in explicitly prejudiced others.
>
> (Banaji, 1997, p. 450)

The 'unsettling discoveries' to which Banaji refers have been grounded in methodological techniques that have enabled researchers to differentiate between explicit and implicit expressions of prejudice. Traditionally, prejudice has been measured using explicit attitude and stereotype scales such as the following (adapted from the 'blatant prejudice scale' developed by Pettigrew and Meertens, 1995):

Immigrants come from less able races and this explains why they are not as well off as most British people

Strongly agree   Somewhat agree   Somewhat disagree   Strongly disagree

Using this kind of measure, surveys conducted in the USA and western Europe have seen evidence of a sharp decrease in prejudice over the past fifty years, leading some commentators to claim that prejudice is in decline. Recent research suggests, however, that this decrease in blatant prejudice is being offset by a rise in more subtle forms of prejudice. As John Dovidio and Samuel Gaertner (1998, p. 25) observe, prejudice can be likened to 'a virus that has mutated and ... evolved into different forms that are more difficult not only to recognize but also to combat'.

─────────────────── *Pause for reflection* ───────────────────

Blatant or direct measures of social attitudes are increasingly viewed as only one methodology for investigating prejudice. Can you think of more subtle or indirect ways of tapping individuals' emotional attitudes towards, or beliefs about, members of other groups?

Russell Fazio et al. (1995) conducted a classic experiment on implicit prejudice, which is useful to illustrate the kinds of methodological innovations that mark work in this area. Participants in their study (white undergraduates) were shown a random series of photos of white and black faces, each face being immediately followed by the presentation of a stimulus word. Their task was, as quickly as possible, to classify words as having either a positive or a negative meaning. Analysis of their results showed clear inhibition and facilitation effects on this task for black and white stimulus faces. That is, when the classification task was preceded by a black face, respondents' reaction times were slower for positive words but faster for negative words than when it was preceded by a white face. This finding seems to reveal an ingrained mental association between race and positive/negative values, which is activated automatically if race is primed (e.g. by showing a photo).

The fact that racial stimuli shape reaction times on relatively innocuous tasks (e.g. word classification) is certainly thought provoking. However, this kind of finding is arguably far removed from the real world patterns of conflict and discrimination that lie at the heart of this chapter, and we need to be careful not to inflate its significance. At the same time, it should be noted that several studies (e.g., Hughenberg and Bodenhausen, 2003) have indicated that people who score high on implicit prejudice measures also tend to act in ways that are connected more obviously to prejudice, somewhat increasing our confidence in their ecological validity (see Box 6.2).

Box 6.2   Facing prejudice

Kurt Hughenberg and Galen Bodenhausen (2003) studied the relationship between implicit prejudice and perceptions of facial threat. White participants watched video images of black and white faces morphing from angry to happy (see Figure 6.2). The experiment measured the time taken to detect the offset of anger (response latency). Results showed that participants high in 'implicit prejudice' viewed anger as lingering longer on black faces than participants low in implicit prejudice.

For further illustrations of implicit measures of prejudice and some revealing practical exercises visit: https://implicit.harvard.edu/implicit/uk (last accessed July 2006).

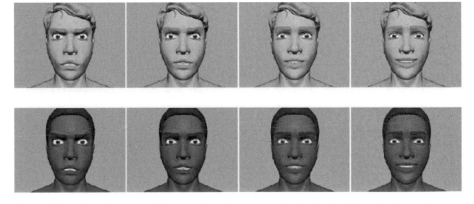

Figure 6.2   Studying implicit prejudice by measuring individuals' evaluations of facial expressions

Who exhibits implicit prejudice? Aversive racism theory is one of several perspectives that have been used to address this question, arriving at some unexpected answers. According to Dovidio and Gaertner (1998), aversive racists consciously sympathise with the victims of historical injustice and support racial equality. However, lurking beneath these explicitly tolerant attitudes is a more negative set of attitudes towards others, which tends to be expressed in 'rationalisable' ways or in situations where they are involuntarily elicited (as in the studies by Fazio et al., 1995, and Hughenberg and Bodenhausen, 2003). The interesting feature of the psychology of the aversive racist is that these two sets of attitudes are dissociated from one another. That is to say, aversive racists are not individuals who hide their 'true' attitudes from the world. Rather, they are individuals who have a *stratified response* to others, made up of a surface attitude of tolerance and a non-conscious attitude of intolerance. The figure of the aversive racist thus complicates the commonsense image of the bigot as a right-wing dogmatist or authoritarian.

2.3   Group-based approaches: the legacy of Sherif and Tajfel

The perspectives that we have sketched so far are sometimes classified as individualistic in orientation (e.g. Tajfel, 1978). This is, of course, a legitimate line of enquiry (if psychologists are not prepared to grapple with the individual level of explanation, then who is?). However, critics have argued that it cannot explain the collective dynamics of relations between groups or the nature of the psychological processes they entail.

Let us consider an example that clarifies why this is so. In March 1988, a Protestant gunman called Michael Stone attacked a Republican funeral cortege at the Milltown cemetery in West Belfast, Northern Ireland. He shot and threw grenades at Catholic mourners, killing three people and injuring more than fifty others. Pursued by an angry crowd, his life was only saved when he was arrested by members of the Royal Ulster Constabulary. A few days later, following a period of unrest in Northern Ireland, another funeral was held, this time for Kevin Brady, one of Stone's victims in the Milltown attack. As the funeral procession reached the brow of a hill in the Andersonstown area of West Belfast, mourners spotted two out-of-uniform British soldiers in an unmarked car. The soldiers tried to drive off, but were dragged from the car by a large crowd and beaten, stripped and shot dead.

We have, then, two snapshots of sectarian violence in Northern Ireland. These events are significant not only because of their brutality, but also because they were both captured live by television crews and broadcast to the world. They rapidly came to symbolise the worst excesses of the 'troubles' in Northern Ireland, lingering 'long in the public memory as a graphic example of man's inhumanity to man' (McKittrick, 1989, p. 106). My purpose in describing them is not an attempt to explain them, important though that project is. Instead, I want to consider how members of Northern Ireland's divided communities have since come to understand them – an exercise that begins to clarify the psychology of conflict.

In 1991, some three years after the Milltown and Andersonstown events, John Hunter, Maurice Stringer and Robert Watson showed groups of Catholic (n = 26) and Protestant (n = 21) respondents newsreel footage of both events and, using a free-response methodology, asked them to explain what had happened and why. Two kinds of explanations emerged from this exercise. First, respondents sometimes made *internal attributions of causality*, arguing that the violence had resulted from the personal qualities of those involved; generally these were negative qualities such as 'bloodlust' and 'psychopathic' tendencies. Second, respondents sometimes made *external attributions of causality*, arguing that violence had resulted from situational factors (e.g. 'retaliation' for previous attacks). Crucially, the tendency to offer one type of explanation or the other depended on whether the violence was being performed by members of the ingroup or the outgroup. As Tables 6.2 and 6.3 illustrate, Catholics' and Protestants' attributions for ingroup violence tended to rely heavily on situational attributions, focusing on the role of context in producing aggressive behaviour. Correspondingly, members of both communities tended to make internal, and usually negative, attributions when explaining outgroup violence: that is, they felt that the violence arose because of the personal characteristics of its perpetrators.

Table 6.2   Catholic explanations for political violence in Northern Ireland

	Internal causes	Contextual causes
Catholic violence	17.9%	78.1%
Protestant violence	79.2%	20.8%

Table 6.3   Protestant explanations for political violence in Northern Ireland

	Internal causes	Contextual causes
Catholic violence	71.5%	28.5%
Protestant violence	28.5%	71.5%

(Tables based on data presented in Hunter et al., 1991, pp. 261–6)

It is easy to see how the pattern of attributions documented in Tables 6.2 and 6.3 may sustain a cycle of distrust and mutual recrimination, with each party to a conflict blaming the other for the generation, maintenance and escalation of violence. It should be noted that this pattern is by no means specific to the Northern Ireland situation. The tendency to attribute negative outgroup behaviour to internal causes, for example, has been repeatedly documented in psychological research and seems to be normal in societies where there is a history of conflict and people have a strong sense of group identity (Pettigrew, 1979). In my view, it is not possible to understand fully these kinds of group-serving attributions by using the perspectives presented thus far in the chapter. What is striking about the findings by Hunter et al. (1991) is the consensual and intergroup nature of the pattern, with Protestant and Catholic attributions forming a mirror image of one another. It seems unlikely that this pattern is the result of the respondents possessing a similarly (sectarian) personality type. Some other psychological process must shape their readiness to respond along sectarian lines (and I shall presently suggest that the concept of 'social identity' is important in this regard). Nor is an explanation in terms of information processing entirely convincing. Although cognitive processes such as categorisation and stereotyping are clearly involved here, it is difficult to see how a theory based on cognitive economy could explain how and why this particular pattern of collectively shared and ethnocentric attributions has arisen. In order to do so, one must recognise that such attributions reflect the broader organisation and ideology of intergroup relations and are not the spontaneous product of individual psychology, a point that brings us to the work of Muzafer Sherif and Henri Tajfel.

Sherif is a leading figure in the social psychology of conflict. Explaining what first drew him to this topic, he noted that, as a boy:

> it influenced me deeply to see each group with a selfless degree of comradeship within its bounds and a corresponding degree of animosity, destructiveness and vindictiveness towards the detested outgroup – their behaviour characterized by compassion and prejudice, heights of self-sacrifice and bestial destructiveness.

> (Sherif, 1967, p. 9)

Sherif felt that attempts to root this behavioural pattern in the psychology of the individual were guilty of a 'levels of explanation' error. He argued that personal prejudice generally expresses the deeper structural conditions of relations between groups. Change those structural conditions, he argued, and you will change the psychology of the individuals they encompass.

The 'boys' camp studies' that Sherif conducted in the late 1950s and early 1960s represent the classic demonstration of this idea. He established a relationship of *negative goal interdependence* between rival groups: a type of competition in which one group's victory necessarily comes at the other group's expense. Sherif wanted to explore the effects of this group-level intervention on the boys' interpersonal relations. As he predicted, it had the effect of radically increasing the boys' sense of ingroup solidarity and loyalty. Correspondingly, it created forms of outgroup prejudice that had a genuine undercurrent of violence, frequently requiring pacification by Sherif and his team of 'camp counsellors' (mainly psychologists in disguise). The boys formed negative stereotypes of rival groups, segregated themselves from one another, created their own flags and insignia, burned the flags and insignia of the other team, stockpiled weapons, verbally and physically abused one another, and generally behaved in a manner all too reminiscent of real world conflict. It was only when Sherif altered the underlying nature of relations between the groups, establishing a relationship of *positive goal interdependence*, that this pattern began to abate. By putting the teams of boys into situations where they had to cooperate to achieve mutually desired goals he was able gradually to change their negative perceptions of one another.

Like many good ideas, the idea that prejudice reflects a material conflict of interests at a collective level is at once simple and obvious. Historically, many conflicts between groups have been waged around a struggle for resources, such as power, wealth and land, and it seems intuitive that these kinds of struggles shape intergroup attitudes. Are any of us surprised to learn, for example, that factory work teams who perceive themselves to be in most direct competition with one another also tend to express higher levels of ingroup bias when judging their mutual contributions to a company (Brown et al., 1986)? Or, more grimly, to learn that white on black murder rates in the USA are highest in cities where there is greatest economic competition between race groups (Jacobs and Wood, 1999)?

The realistic conflict model also sheds light on the data represented in Tables 6.2 and 6.3. Sherif and others working in this tradition of research would insist that, in order to understand this pattern of group serving attributions in Northern Ireland, we need to move beyond the analysis of individual psychology to consider the possibility that such attributions are a rational response to living in a society where collective 'interests' are organised along sectarian lines. The term 'rational' is used advisedly here. It points to an important distinction between the model of prejudice proposed by work in a Sherifian tradition and the model of prejudice that dominates the rest of social psychology (see also Taylor and Moghadam, 1994). Whereas most social psychological research treats prejudice as an irrational form of 'bias', the realistic conflict tradition emphasises its role in furthering the objective goals of the parties to a conflict.

However, the work of Tajfel and his colleagues has revealed that this proposition is insufficient to explain either the historical patterning or the social psychology of intergroup conflict (Tajfel, 1978; Tajfel and Turner, 1986). As its name suggests, social identity theory holds that individuals define themselves in terms of their identification with social groups and that this process has important implications for understanding intergroup relations. As well as being unique personalities, Tajfel argued, our sense of self derives from our membership of social categories such as class, community, race, ethnicity, gender, religion and nationality. When we identify with such categories, we literally 'take on board' their defining stereotypes in order to fashion a sense of who we are. Crucially, in any given context our social identities are formed not in isolation but *relationally*. In many everyday situations in Northern Ireland, for instance, the identity 'Catholic' acquires meaning via its comparative contrast with the identity 'Protestant'. Of course, this process of social comparison does not merely involve an intellectual weighing of information. Because social identities carry emotional implications for individuals' and groups' sense of worth, we are generally motivated to emphasise the qualities that positively distinguish 'us' from 'them'. Indeed, when acting in terms of our group identities, our perceptions of social reality tend to become *depersonalised* (see Cairns et al., 1995, for a discussion of the role of social identity dynamics in explaining intergroup conflict in Northern Ireland).

_____ *Pause for reflection* _____

Look again at the results presented in Tables 6.2 and 6.3. What do they reveal about the nature of 'depersonalised' perceptions of social events and realities?
_____

The social identity account suggests that objective competition for scarce resources is sufficient but not necessary for intergroup conflict to emerge within a society. As Hewstone and Greenland (2000, p. 139) observe: 'many apparently pointless conflicts become more understandable when viewed as, at least in part, attempts to establish, maintain or defend cherished social identities'. However, if the 'need' for a positive group identity is conceived as a psychological universal, rooted in the hearts and minds of individuals, do social identity theorists not ultimately reduce collective behaviour to individual psychology? This argument opens up a complex series of questions and debates that cannot be unpacked here. Suffice to say that Tajfel himself was insistent that differentiation cannot be understood outside its social context (e.g., Tajfel, 1981). Just as we do not as individuals invent, for example, what it means to be 'Irish' or 'male' or 'white', so too the contextual processes that generate, channel or stifle intergroup conflict are not reducible to individual psychology.

Tajfel was particularly interested in the role of so-called 'ideological belief systems' in shaping the likelihood that identity struggles boil over into direct confrontation between groups. It is only, he suggested, when members of a lower status group perceive the status quo as unjust and unstable that overt conflict with dominant groups becomes likely. Thus, one cannot begin to understand the emergence of political conflict in places such as Northern Ireland, Palestine and apartheid South Africa without also understanding how struggles to redefine identity have been nurtured by a growing sense of the illegitimacy and vulnerability of the social hierarchy.

2.4   Summary

Initially, social psychological research treated prejudice primarily as the result of abnormal psychological development. Later approaches, focusing on categorisation and stereotyping, suggested prejudice could not simply be dismissed in this way. However, they were still rather *individualistic* theories (e.g. Tajfel, 1978). In contrast to the treatment of prejudice as an irrational form of 'bias', the realistic conflict and social identity traditions stress its role in advancing the material gains or identity of a group. Prejudice may be morally reprehensible, but it is not sense-less.

3   'Serviceable others': the discursive construction and legitimisation of conflict

The idea that ideological or 'collective belief systems' shape relations of conflict between groups is vitally important (Eidelson and Eidelson, 2003), and it raises the question of how communities may create their own, often opposing, versions of the meaning of intergroup relations. How and with what consequences, for instance, do group members manufacture shared explanations of violent encounters such as those that occurred in the Milltown cemetery and Andersonstown in Northern Ireland (see Section 2.3)? This theme surfaces in various ways in contemporary social psychology, with some researchers referring to the role of 'socially shared cognitions', others to 'social representations', and still others to 'discourses' or 'interpretative repertoires'.

Discursive psychologists suggest that language is a precondition for much of what we call 'social psychology' (Potter and Wetherell, 1987). Our psychological lives, they argue, are profoundly shaped by the linguistic resources that our culture makes available to us and that we must use to make sense of social reality. Indeed, they hold that many of the higher-order reasoning processes that feature within psychological work on prejudice and conflict (e.g. stereotyping, the calculation of collective interests, the formation of social attitudes, the attribution of causality) are only possible because we share a common language and are able to jointly 'construct' the meanings of our social relations and identities.

A cardinal principle of discursive psychology is that our accounts of social reality are never transparent *reflections* of an already given state of affairs; rather, they actively construct the meaning of everyday relations in ways that serve varying social and political functions. As a worked example that extends our earlier discussion of the Northern Ireland situation, consider the following accounts of political violence in Extracts 6.1 and 6.2, which are taken from a book of published interviews called *Perceptions: Cultures in Conflict* (Kerr, 1996). The first account is provided by David Nicholl, a representative of the Protestant-dominated United Democratic Party. The second account is provided by Donncha MacNiallais, a former Republican prisoner.

EXTRACT 6.1

I am still angry that the troubles happened, and like most ordinary Protestants I wish to God they had never happened. We have inflicted brutality on each other over the past twenty-five years, and there have been atrocities, innumerable atrocities. One of those that spring to mind is the La Mon House bombing where bodies were shovelled off the streets, charred to a crisp. I found it most distressing to see the pictures that appeared at that particular time, and again after the Enniskillen massacre. There have also been terrible atrocities committed by Protestants, and that's regrettable, but from a personal perspective, I can only say that I think that had there not been a reaction from the Protestant community it would have been worse for us. The IRA would have slaughtered a lot more than the 3,167 who have died during the troubles. Ultimately it was the IRA who were responsible for the onset of violence.

(Nicholl in Kerr, 1996)

EXTRACT 6.2

Loyalist violence is not just a reaction to Republican violence. That is not only a myth, but also a barefaced lie. Loyalist violence is fascist and terrorist. It's right-wing. If you look at it on a psychological basis, it's linked very closely to the death squads in South America and South Africa. In any areas of conflict where you have a radical revolutionary struggle you are always going to have a right-wing fascist tendency operating as a sort of secret arm of the state, prepared to carry out what the state does not want to openly carry out, and that is what Loyalists have been doing for years. They have been going out and butchering Catholics, and they are not really interested in whether that Catholic is a member of the IRA, a member of Sinn Féin, the SDLP, a trade unionist, or even a practising Catholic. All they are interested in is that that person is a Catholic, and they are prepared to kill him or her in order to try and terrorise the entire Catholic/Nationalist community into accepting what they want us to accept, which is second-class citizenship in a state that is a gerrymander.

(MacNiallais in Kerr, 1996)

These accounts clearly formulate contrasting versions of the nature of violent conflict in Northern Ireland. That violence is occurring and is being perpetrated by members of both the Protestant and the Catholic communities is not disputed. However, the speakers offer different – indeed, rhetorically opposed (Billig, 1991) – arguments concerning its nature, origins and culprits. Notwithstanding his concession that there 'have also been terrible atrocities committed by Protestants', the speaker in Extract 6.1 attributes primary responsibility for 'the troubles' to the IRA. His account selectively emphasises acts of brutality committed by the IRA, such as the Enniskillen and La Mon bombings, whereas Protestant violence is constructed as a 'regrettable' but necessary 'reaction' on the part of the Protestant community, an essentially *defensive* step that has actually saved many lives. By contrast, the speaker in Extract 6.2 directly disputes the argument that Protestant violence is merely 'reactive'. He defines such violence instead as an active form of right-wing aggression, sponsored by the state, which terrorises and murders Catholic people indiscriminately in order to maintain the status quo. IRA activity in Northern Ireland is framed more positively as part of a 'radical revolutionary struggle' against a system that treats the 'Nationalist' community as 'second-class citizens'.

In terms of their global functions, then, one might argue that these kinds of accounts are designed to legitimate some forms of collective violence and de-legitimate others. At the very least, they establish a moral hierarchy in which

Loyalist and Republican violence becomes graded in terms of its level of acceptability.

It is not difficult to see how these kinds of accounts may help to sustain fundamentally incompatible constructions of the political realities of the Northern Ireland situation, maintaining the kind of context in which potential for ongoing conflict is heightened. To appreciate the full weight of this point, we must recognise how variations on these arguments are constantly being relayed and circulated in everyday conversations, mass media reports, and political or religious speeches in Northern Ireland, acting as an interpretive framework through which emerging events are evaluated. In this way, such accounts may form part of the 'longer conversation' (Wetherell, 1998) of sectarian ideology in Northern Ireland.

_____ *Pause for reflection* _____

What does the analysis of such discourse tell us about the *psychology* of prejudice and conflict?

_____

One objection to the discursive perspective is that it neglects the inner world of cognition and emotion on which psychologists have traditionally focused. Discursive psychology, its critics object, is literally 'all talk'. In its remorseless concern with the details of what people are saying about the world (and what they are doing when they are saying it), it appears to throw out the psychological baby with the bathwater (cf. Abrams and Hogg, 1990).

Responding to this kind of criticism, researchers such as Derek Edwards and Jonathan Potter have pointed out that discursive psychology re-specifies and enriches rather than ignores the psychological domain. Psychological processes are treated not as mysterious happenings 'in the head', but as public practices that we perform to give meaning to our social relationships within particular contexts. On the one hand, this approach necessitates attention to how members strategically employ a shared 'psychological thesaurus' (Edwards, 2004, p. 7) in making sense of everyday happenings. Consider, for example, what the speaker in Extract 6.2 is doing in defining the 'psychological basis' of loyalism in terms of its connection with fascism and the death squads in South Africa and South America.

On the other hand, discursive psychology arguably expands our understanding of the psychological processes that have traditionally been central to the psychology of prejudice and conflict. Take, for instance, the process of categorisation. As we have seen, categorisation is generally treated by psychologists as a cognitive process that enables a 'bureaucratically efficient' (Billig, 1985) organisation of information but, unfortunately, biases our perceptions of others. Discursive social psychologists develop this perspective by pointing to the flexible and varied functions that categorisation serves within ordinary accounts of group behaviour, thus opening up a new set of questions.

_____ *Pause for reflection* _____

Why, for example, is the opening rejection of political violence in Extract 6.1 framed as representative of the position held by 'most ordinary Protestants'? What is accomplished in Extract 6.2 by the mention of a wide range of sub-categories of people in the nationalist community who have been victims of Loyalist violence? What are the likely effects of the category construction of 'second-class citizens' in the closing sentence?

_____

In order to answer such questions, we need to view categories, and the stereotypes with which they are associated, as rhetorical and political as well as cognitive resources (Augoustinos and Walker, 1998; Edwards, 1991). In this way, discursive psychologists have invited us to think critically about the *politics of category construction* (Reicher and Hopkins, 2001) and to recognise how our ways of classifying others often service collective interests. This point is worth considering when you next encounter discourses about 'Islamic fundamentalists', 'asylum seekers', 'suicide bombers', 'terrorists', or the many other labels through which the boundaries between 'us' and 'them' are constantly being drawn.

ACTIVITY 6.1

Collect any recent media account of an event of political conflict or violence. Now underline the main category labels used in this account to classify the parties involved. What are the potential consequences of employing these – as opposed to other – category constructions in this particular context? What rhetorical functions might they serve within your account (e.g. in terms of attributing responsibility for violence)? Discursive psychologists believe that social psychologists need to be fundamentally concerned with this kind of functional analysis of everyday discourse.

3.1   Summary

This section considered the contribution of discursive social psychology to understanding the social construction and legitimisation of conflict. Discursive psychologists focus on language as a precondition and process for 'social psychology', actively constructing the meaning of everyday relations on all levels, as exemplified in the extracts from Northern Ireland.

4   Social psychological perspectives on conflict reduction

I introduced the chapter by contemplating the recent history and geography of intergroup conflict around the globe. The chapter's aim so far has been to outline some social psychological perspectives on the intergroup processes that have resulted in so many violent encounters in many parts of the world.

However instructive it may be, this exercise carries dangers that need to be kept in mind. Perhaps most problematic is that it is easy to misread history as a testament to the idea that conflict between groups is a universal and immutable process. After all, if it is the norm in so many parts of the world, and over such long periods of time, must we not accept conflict as a feature of all societies? Reicher (2004) argues that this kind of position is both invalid and reactionary. It is invalid because it overlooks societies that are characterised by relations of solidarity between groups (or at least where relations are changing for the better). It is reactionary because it encourages a passive acceptance of the inevitability of conflict. In this regard, Reicher is particularly critical of research that treats prejudice as a 'natural' outcrop of human cognition and motivation or that treats exploitative relations as basic to the human condition.

Reicher's commentary raises questions about social psychology's role in promoting social change. Historically, psychological work on intergroup relations has been characterised by a tension between scholarship and advocacy, a tension that fuelled heated debates in the 1960s and 1970s about the discipline's lack of practical relevance (sometimes called 'the crisis in social psychology').

_____ **Pause for reflection** _____

Is our role as social psychologists simply to discover the kinds of processes that underlie prejudice and conflict or should we be actively intervening to shape public policy in ways that transform society? Should we try to maintain our detachment and objectivity or should we take a stance and become advocates of change?

_____

These questions have shaped the tradition of psychological research on conflict reduction that has arguably had the greatest impact on public policy: namely, research on the contact hypothesis.

5   Getting to know you: the social psychology of contact and desegregation

5.1   The paradox of contact

Although it is sometimes misrepresented as such, the contact hypothesis does not propose that mere interaction between members of different groups is sufficient to improve relations between them. Its supporters have always recognised that things are more complicated than this. The paradox of contact, as Allport (1954) pointed out, is that our interactions with others may either increase or reduce our prejudice towards them. A recent survey of race attitudes in Britain, for example, found that the more multiracial the composition of a city, the more negative the inhabitants' racial attitudes tended to be (Lemos, 2005). Living in a diverse environment, it seems, does not in itself guarantee that one will embrace diversity.

5.2   When and why does contact reduce prejudice?

The paradox of contact is resolved when one recognises that the situational conditions of interaction between groups are critical. A great deal of psychological research on the contact hypothesis has attempted to identify these conditions, resulting in a lengthy set of recommendations that include the following points. Contact should

- be regular and frequent

- occur between individuals who share equality of status

- involve a balanced ratio of ingroup to outgroup members

- have genuine 'acquaintance potential'

- be free from competition

- involve interaction with a 'counter-stereotypic' member of another group

- be organised around cooperation towards the achievement of 'superordinate goals'

- be normatively and institutionally supported.

One problem with this 'laundry list' (Pettigrew, 1986) of factors is that it does not amount to a coherent explanation of *why* contact works. In early research, the positive contact effects were attributed to a somewhat vague process of education, based on the idea that interaction overcomes ignorance and allows us to discover our similarities to others. During the past two decades, the limitations of classic contact theory have inspired a number of reformulations, which have been grounded in the social identity framework that we considered earlier in the chapter. Marilynn Brewer and Norman Miller (1984), for example, have argued that contact works best when it occurs in contexts where group differences are de-emphasised (the Decategorisation Model of Contact). In such contexts, we may come to know one another as individuals rather than as representatives of social categories. Contact can become personalised, affording us the opportunity of intimacy so that gradually we can 'attend to information that replaces category identity as the most useful basis for classifying each other' (Brewer and Miller, 1984, p. 288).

However, Hewstone and Rupert Brown (1986) have argued that this perspective misinterprets the implications of social identity theory for understanding contact. They suggest that it is unrealistic to expect group members to accept passively the suppression of their collective identities and values. (Public debate in France on the rights of Muslim girls to wear the hajib – a head scarf – provides a case in point.) The whole point of social identity theory, after all, is that our sense of group distinctiveness is central to our sense of who we are and what we are worth. Thus, directly opposing the Brewer and Miller position, Hewstone and Brown argue that for contact to be successful it must be an *intergroup* process in which participants view one another not as individuals but as representatives of their social categories (the

Pluralist Model of Contact). In practice, this approach translates into a policy of multiculturalism, leading to institutional reforms that favour 'mutual differentiation' – a social climate in which group differences are celebrated as positive phenomena. The multicultural ethos that permeates many schools in the UK illustrates this kind of policy in action. When schoolchildren are invited to learn and celebrate the history, literature, religious practices or food of another culture, they are being encouraged to both recognise and celebrate their differences. The danger here, of course, is that by underlining the importance of groups, even in a sympathetic fashion, we may cue struggles over the comparative value of groups. Mutual differentiation may easily tip into plain prejudice.

If it is sometimes difficult to break down social divisions, then perhaps some form of realignment of group boundaries is possible. This idea underlies Gaertner and Dovidio's (2000) model of contact, which holds that contact has most influence when it promotes a common ingroup identity, encouraging members of different sub-groups to see one another as members of a shared ingroup (the Recategorisation Model of Contact). Instead of reducing the importance of group identification, then, re-categorisation attempts to shift category boundaries in the direction of greater inclusiveness, a technique that seems to work in some contexts. A number of experimental and field studies have confirmed that situations that generate representations of 'we' (rather than 'us' and 'them') can indeed decrease prejudice (e.g. Gaertner et al., 1990). However, in societies where intergroup conflict has a long and violent history, the unifying influence of supcrordinate identities may remain fragile. The resurgence of sub-group identities and their associated prejudices lingers as a constant threat (cf. Brewer, 1996).

5.3 Some limits of the contact hypothesis

The contact hypothesis offers a blueprint for social change that is based on the rehabilitation of prejudiced individuals. If only, the argument goes, we can experience contact under the 'right' conditions, then the negative attitudes we hold towards others might be changed. Brewer and Brown (1998) have recently described this notion as one of the most successful and long-lived ideas in the history of social psychology, and the contact hypothesis is now firmly established as 'one of psychology's most effective strategies for improving intergroup relations' (Dovidio et al., 2003, p. 5). Both implicitly and explicitly, it continues to inform public policy in many societies, including that in the UK (see Box 6.3). However, the contact hypothesis has also been subjected to several searching critiques, a few of which we shall now consider.

Box 6.3   Applying social psychology to real events of conflict

This box contains an exercise to encourage you to consider the applied implications of social psychological knowledge for understanding and transforming real world processes of conflict between groups. It is also designed to encourage an exploration of the possibilities and limits of the contact hypothesis as a framework for reducing conflict.

Background: the 'summer of violence' and the legacy of ethnic segregation in the north-west of England

In July 2001, a series of so-called 'race riots' occurred in several towns in the north-west of England, principally in Oldham, Bradford and Burnley, resulting in hundreds of serious injuries and millions of pounds' worth of damage to property. The so-called 'summer of violence' resulted in a series of high-profile government inquiries, the most important of which was the Cantle Report.

Figure 6.3   Conflict in Bradford, England 2001

The Cantle Report on the need for greater contact and 'community cohesion'

The report rooted the main cause of conflict in the 'depth of polarisation' between ethnic communities, condemning the fact that people in many British towns and cities were living 'parallel lives':

> Whilst the physical segregation of housing estates and inner city areas came as no surprise, the team was particularly struck by the depth of polarization of our towns and cities. The extent to which these physical divisions were compounded by so many other aspects of our daily lives was very evident. Separate education arrangements, community and voluntary bodies, employment, places of worship, language, social and cultural habits, means that many communities operate on the basis of a series of parallel lives. These lives do not seem to touch at any point let alone overlap and promote any meaningful interchanges.

(Cantle Report, 2001, p. 9)

The report also made a number of specific recommendations for improving intergroup relations in British society, notably: (1) it proposed interventions that encourage interaction and exchange between ethnic communities: 'This should include the promotion of cross-cultural contact between different communities at all levels, foster understanding and respect, and break down barriers' (Cantle Report, 2001, p. 11); and (2) more controversially, it made a series of recommendations regarding the creation of a common sense of national and local citizenship. According to the report's authors, too many white British residents of cities such as Bradford and Oldham are nostalgic for the 'halcyon days' of a monocultural British society, whereas too many Asian residents look back to their 'countries of origin' for a sense of identity and belonging. In order to improve community cohesion, some sense of common values and identity needs to be established.

ACTIVITY 6.2

With this general background in mind, consider the following points

- How might existing research and theory on the contact hypothesis strengthen, enrich, qualify or contradict the arguments and recommendations set out in the Cantle Report?

- What are the strengths and weaknesses of contact theory as a way of understanding and changing 'race relations' in divided communities such as those in Bradford, Burnley and Oldham?

- More generally, what problems do psychologists face when they attempt to apply psychological knowledge to 'real life' cases of intergroup conflict? How, if at all, can those problems be overcome?

Is the contact hypothesis idealistic? Much of the existing psychological literature on the nature and consequences of desegregation has involved a search for the 'optimal' conditions of intergroup contact, the circumstances under which prejudice is reduced most effectively. Since the inception of the contact hypothesis in the early years of the last century, psychologists have elaborated and tested an ever-expanding list of boundary conditions for 'good' interaction between members of different groups. As these conditions seldom exist in pure form in the real world, much research has focused either on laboratory conditions or specialised situations in which optimal contact can be easily manufactured, at least for a short period of time. The danger here is that research may ultimately produce knowledge that conceals the starker realities of everyday interactions between members of different groups and fails to explain how optimal conditions might be established in the everyday circumstances in which the majority of contact occurs (Dixon et al., 2005).

Can interpersonal contact change intergroup relations and perceptions? A second set of criticisms of contact theory has focused on its 'theoretical individualism'. For one thing, much research has suggested that the effects of contact on *interpersonal* perceptions may not generalise to shape *intergroup* perceptions, a problem that has been extensively researched in the contact literature. Contact, for example, often leads people to regard particular individuals as 'exceptions to the rule' rather than leading them to abandon their wider stereotype systems.

A related criticism has highlighted what is arguably a more fundamental limitation of the contact hypothesis. What if the processes that govern conflict between groups are relatively autonomous from interactions between individuals? What if such processes are grounded in members' collectively constructed sense of their group's 'positioning' (Blumer, 1958) in relation to other groups – a shared historical and political sense of the meaning of the relationship between 'us' and 'them' that is relatively impervious to the day-to-day contacts experienced by individual members?

5.4   Towards a discursive analysis of contact and desegregation

Consideration of a recent study in the discursive tradition may help us to develop the above point. Nick Hopkins and Vered Kahani-Hopkins (2006) have examined British Muslims' perceptions of interventions designed to promote integration with non-Muslims. They found that Muslims' constructions of the meaning of 'contact' and 'integration' must be viewed in a context of historical change. Over the past two decades, Muslims' experiences of discrimination in spheres such as employment and education have become organised along religious rather than racial lines, with communities becoming increasingly concerned about the problem of so-called 'Islamaphobia'.

This has led to the emergence of somewhat disparate constructions of the relationship between contact and social change. On the one hand, in line with the contact hypothesis, some Muslims view integration as vital to the struggle against Islamaphobia. Thus they advocate programmes to encourage dialogue, dispelling the myth that Islamic communities are somehow 'closed' to interaction with members of other faiths. On the other hand, and in opposition to this framework for understanding the meaning of contact, other Muslims define Islamaphobia as reflecting a fundamental antagonism between Islam and the West, an antagonism that expresses a timeless moral struggle between *haqq* (truth) and *batil* (falsehood). According to this theory of social relations, contact is likely to subvert Muslim identity, promote decadence and moral corruption, and, critically, undermine the potential for collective resistance to discrimination.

A central theme of the research of Hopkins and Kahani-Hopkins, then, is that communities may hold their own contradictory 'theories' of contact. These culturally-embedded theories, which are not readily translated into analytic categories of traditional contact research, have implications for the success of interventions designed to promote interaction between groups. If, for example, contact is seen as threatening the extent to which members are able to preserve valued forms of religious expression, then it is unlikely to have a beneficial impact on social relations. To the contrary, it is likely to reproduce forms of isolation that contact researchers conceive as problematic but group members themselves conceive as necessary to the maintenance of their social identity.

5.5   Summary

The dominant approach to conflict reduction has been the contact hypothesis which has attempted to identify the optimal conditions for positive contact. However, a list of factors does not amount to an explanation of *why* contact works. Dixon et al. (2005) have suggested that the growing laundry list of optimal conditions for contact is in danger of leaving the contact hypothesis irrelevant to everyday encounters between groups in politically divided societies such as South Africa, Northern Ireland and the Middle East. More recent research in the discursive tradition may offer deeper insights into how constructions of the meaning of 'contact' and 'integration' must be viewed in context.

6   Conclusions

A recurring theme of this chapter is the idea that conflict between groups is rooted in the errors and biases of the prejudiced mind, which stem either from the pathological reactions of particular types of person (e.g. authoritarians, aversive racists) or from certain universal features of human psychology (e.g. categorisation, stereotyping). In their influential book, *Mapping the Discourse of Racism*, Margaret Wetherell and Jonathan Potter (1992) have outlined some of the limitations of this so-called 'prejudice problematic' in social psychology. To begin with, this approach has entrenched a highly individualistic perspective on social change. Even if psychologists acknowledge the cultural and political determinants of our everyday relationships, their research remains overly focused on processes occurring in relative isolation 'under the skull'. Recent work on implicit prejudice has, if anything, increased this individualistic orientation. Though fascinating in their own right, studies of aversive racism and other forms of implicit prejudice are designed to delve deeper and deeper into the recesses of the isolated individual's psyche and to concentrate psychological interventions at this level of analysis.

Building on the insights of discursive psychology, I believe that it is now time for social psychologists to break with assumptions of the prejudice problematic. They need to consider how to transform not only the cognitive and emotional reactions of *individuals* but also the *collective practices* used by communities to define and treat others. These practices generate shared constructions of social reality that are more complicated, subtle and contradictory than simple measures of prejudice can possibly register, constructions that are not easily reduced to the 'faulty' thoughts or feelings of individuals. Indeed, it is revealing that violent conflict is often enacted, not in the name of irrational attitudes or stereotypes, but in the name of apparently positive moral values such as 'justice', 'rights', 'community' and even 'peace'. The question that social psychologists need to address, then, is: how do we transform the discursive frameworks that sustain collective violence and that entrench a shared sense of entitlement and positioning that lead dominant groups to defend their privileges (Blumer, 1958)?

Social psychologists' over-reliance on the concept of prejudice as a means of understanding relations between groups has had another unfortunate consequence. It has quietly entrenched the idea that conflict is necessarily a bad thing, something born out of hatred and misinformation about others. One has sympathy with this view. It is easy to look at a world enflamed by hostility and assume that conflict is an evil that must invariably be extinguished. However, this is ultimately a simplistic stance. To adapt Charles Cooley's dictum that conflict provides the 'fire' for social change, we must acknowledge how conflict acts as a progressive 'fire under the boiler' of social change as well as a destructive and consuming force. Interestingly, this two-sided nature is captured in the Chinese symbol for conflict (see Figure 6.4) which signifies both opportunity and struggle simultaneously.

Figure 6.4   The Chinese symbol for conflict

Among its other positive functions, conflict helps to disrupt inequitable social orders, a point that is central to work in the social identity tradition. This tradition represents an attempt to explain how, why and when low-status groups seek to transform the status quo (and how, why and when they are likely to acquiesce in their own exploitation). Conflict is conceived as transformative not only in the sense that it promotes a fairer distribution of resources, but also in the way that it allows people to forge a more positive sense of their collective identities and values. This insight complicates social psychologists' tendency to treat conflict as a regressive phenomenon that needs to be reduced via the rehabilitation of the prejudiced individual or the introduction of programmes of assimilation and integration. The identity politics that now impel collective struggles in so many parts of the world require a more reflexive, varied and contextualised approach.

References

Abrams, D. and Hogg, M. (1990) 'The context of discourse: let's not throw out the baby with the bath water', *Philosophical Psychology*, vol. 3, pp. 219–25.

Adorno, T.W., Frankel-Brunswik, E., Levinson, D. and Sanford, D. (1950) *The Authoritarian Personality*, New York, Harper.

Allport, G.W. (1954) *The Nature of Prejudice*, Garden City, NY, Doubleday.

Augoustinos, M. and Walker, I. (1998) 'The construction of stereotypes within psychology: from social cognition to ideology', *Theory and Psychology*, vol. 8, pp. 622–52.

Banaji, M.R. (1997) 'Introductory comments', *Journal of Experimental Social Psychology*, vol. 33, pp. 449–50.

Billig, M. (1985) 'Prejudice, categorization, and particularization: from a perceptual to a rhetorical approach', *European Journal of Social Psychology*, vol. 15, pp. 79–103.

Billig, M. (1991) *Ideology and Opinions*, London, Sage.

Blumer, H. (1958) 'Race prejudice as a sense of group position', *Pacific Sociological Review*, vol. 1, pp. 3–7.

Brewer, M.B. (1996) 'When contact is not enough: social identity and intergroup cooperation', *International Journal of Intercultural Relations*, vol. 20, pp. 291–303.

Brewer, M.B. and Brown, R. (1998) 'Intergroup relations' in Gilbert, D.T., Fiske, S. and Lindsey, G. (eds) *Handbook of Social Psychology*, Boston, MA, McGraw-Hill.

Brewer, M.B. and Miller, N. (1984) 'Beyond the contact hypothesis: theoretical perspectives on desegregation' in Miller, N. and Brewer, M.B. (eds) *Groups in Contact: A Psychology of Desegregation*, New York, Academic Press.

Brown, R., Condor, S., Matthews, A., Wade, G. and Williams, J. (1986) 'Explaining intergroup differentiation in an industrial organization', *Journal of Occupational Psychology*, vol. 59, pp. 273–86.

Cairns, E., Wilson, R., Gallagher, T. and Trew, K. (1995) 'Psychology's contribution to understanding conflict in Northern Ireland', *Peace and Conflict: Journal of Peace Psychology*, vol. 1, pp. 131–48.

Cantle Report (Home Office) (2001) *Community Cohesion: A Report of the Independent Review Team Chaired by Ted Cantle*, London, The Stationery Office.

Crisp, R.J., Perks, N., Stone, C.H. and Farr, M.J. (2004) 'Cognitive busyness and the processing of evaluative information in intergroup contexts', *Journal of Social Psychology*, vol. 144, pp. 541–4.

Dixon, J.A., Durrheim, K. and Tredoux, C. (2005) 'Beyond the optimal strategy: a "reality check" for the contact hypothesis', *American Psychologist*, vol. 60, pp. 697–711.

Dovidio, J.F. and Gaertner, S. (1998) 'On the nature of contemporary prejudice: the causes, consequences and challenges of aversive racism' in Eberhardt, J. and Fiske, S.T. (eds) *Confronting Racism: The Problem and the Response*, Newbury Park, CA, Sage.

Dovidio, J.F., Gaertner, S. and Kawamaki, K. (2003) 'Intergroup contact: the past, present and the future', *Group Processes and Intergroup Relations*, vol. 6, pp. 5–20.

Edwards, D. (1991) 'Categories are for talking: on the cognitive and discursive bases of categorization', *Theory and Psychology*, vol. 1, pp. 515–42.

Edwards, D. (2004) 'Discursive psychology' in Fitch, K.L. and Sanders, R.E. (eds) (2005) *Handbook of Language and Social Interaction*, London, Lawrence Erlbaum.

Eidelson, R.J. and Eidelson, J.I. (2003) 'Dangerous ideas: five beliefs that propel groups into conflict', *American Psychologist*, vol. 58, pp. 182–92.

Fazio, R.H., Jackson, J.R., Dunton, B.C. and Williams, C.J. (1995) 'Variability in automatic activation as an unobtrusive measure of racial attitudes: a bona fide pipeline', *Journal of Personality and Social Psychology*, vol. 69, pp. 1013–27.

Fisher, J. (1951) 'The memory process and certain psychosocial attitudes, with special reference to the law of Praganz', *Journal of Personality*, vol. 19, pp. 406–20.

Fiske, S.T. and Taylor, S.E. (1991) *Social Cognition*, New York, McGraw-Hill.

Gaertner, S.L. and Dovidio, J.F. (2000) *Reducing Intergroup Bias: The Common Identity Model*, Hove, Psychology Press.

Gaertner, S.L, Mann, J.A., Dovidio, J.F. and Murrell, A. (1990) 'How does cooperation reduce intergroup bias?', *Journal of Personality and Social Psychology*, vol. 59, pp. 692–704.

Henriques, J. (1984) 'Social psychology and the politics of racism' in Henriques, J., Hollway, W., Urwin, C., Venn. C. and Walkerdine. V. (eds) *Changing the Subject: Psychology, Social Regulation and Subjectivity*, London, Methuen.

Hewstone, M. and Brown, R. (eds) (1986) *Contact and Conflict in Intergroup Encounters*, Oxford, Basil Blackwell.

Hewstone, M. and Brown, R. (1986) 'Contact is not enough: an intergroup perspective on the "contact hypothesis"' in Hewstone and Brown (eds) (1986).

Hewstone, M. and Greenland, K. (2000) 'Intergroup conflict', *International Journal of Psychology*, vol. 35, pp. 136–44.

Hopkins, N. and Kahani-Hopkins, V. (2006) 'Minority theories of intergroup relations and intergroup contact: conceptualising "Islamaphobia" and the opportunities for social change', *British Journal of Social Psychology*, vol. 45, pp. 245–64.

Hughenberg, K. and Bodenhausen, G.V. (2003) 'Facing prejudice: implicit prejudice and the perception of facial threat', *Psychological Science*, vol. 14, pp. 640–3.

Hunter, J.A., Stringer, M. and Watson, R.P. (1991) 'Intergroup violence and intergroup attributions', *British Journal of Social Psychology*, vol. 30 pp. 261–6.

Jacobs, D. and Wood, K. (1999) 'Interracial conflict and intergroup homicide', *American Journal of Sociology*, vol. 105, pp. 157–90.

Kerr, A. (ed.) (1996) *Perceptions: Cultures in Conflict*, Derry, Guildhall Press.

Lemos, G. (2005) *The Search for Tolerance: Challenging and Changing Racist Attitudes amongst Young People*, York, Joseph Rowntree Foundation.

McCrae, C.N., Milne, A.B. and Bodenhausen, G.V. (1994) 'Stereotyping as energy-saving devices: a peek inside the cognitive toolbox', *Journal of Personality and Social Psychology*, vol. 66, pp. 37–47.

McKittrick, D. (1989) *Despatches from Belfast*, Belfast, Blackstaff.

Nobelprize.org (2006) *Conflict Map*, http://nobelprize.org/peace/educational/conflictmap/conflictmap.html (Accessed 4 August 2006).

Pettigrew, T.F. (1979) 'The ultimate attribution error: extending Allport's cognitive analysis of prejudice', *Personality and Social Psychology Bulletin*, vol. 5, pp. 461–76.

Pettigrew, T.F. (1986) 'The intergroup contact hypothesis reconsidered' in Hewstone and Brown (eds) (1986).

Pettigrew, T.F. and Meertens, R.W. (1995) 'Subtle and blatant prejudice in Western Europe', *European Journal of Social Psychology*, vol. 25, pp. 57–75.

Potter, J. and Wetherell, M. (1987) *Discourse and Social Psychology*, London, Sage.

Reicher, S. (2004) 'The context of social identity: domination, resistance and change', *Political Psychology*, vol. 25, pp. 921–45.

Reicher, S. and Hopkins, N. (2001) 'Psychology and the end of history: a critique and proposal for the psychology of categorisation', *Political Psychology*, vol. 22, pp. 383–407.

Rokeach, M. (1960) *The Open and the Closed Mind*, Basic Books, New York.

Sherif, M. (1967) *Group Conflict and Cooperation: Their Social Psychology*, London, Routledge and Kegan Paul.

Tajfel, H. (1978) 'Intergroup behaviour: individualistic perspectives' in Tajfel, H. and Fraser, C. (eds) *Introducing Social Psychology*, Harmondsworth, Penguin.

Tajfel, H. (1981) 'Social stereotypes and social groups' in Turner, J.C. and Giles, H. (eds) *Intergroup Behaviour*, Oxford, Blackwell.

Tajfel, H. and Turner, J. (1986) 'The social identity theory of intergroup behaviour' in Worchel, S. and Austin, W.G. (eds) *Psychology of Intergroup Relations*, Chicago, IL, Nelson-Hall.

Tajfel, H. and Wilkes, A. (1963) 'Classification and quantitative judgement', *British Journal of Psychology*, vol. 54, pp. 101–14.

Taylor, D.M. and Moghaddam, F.M. (1994) *Theories of Intergroup Relations: International Social Psychological Perspectives* (3rd edn), London, Praeger.

Wetherell, M. (1998) 'Positioning and interpretative repertoires: conversation analysis and post-structuralism in dialogue', *Discourse and Society*, vol. 9, pp. 387–412.

Wetherell, M. and Potter, J. (1992) *Mapping the Language of Racism: Discourse and the Legitimation of Exploitation*, London, Harvester Wheatsheaf.

Chapter 7

Embodiment

by Linda Finlay and Darren Langdridge, The Open University

Contents

> **Learning outcomes**
>
> By the end of this chapter you will be able to:
>
> - critique simplistic mind–body, individual–social and agency–structure dualisms and appreciate how the body, self and society are interconnected
> - describe how discursive and phenomenological psychologists conceptualise the body
> - compare and contrast the methodologies and findings of discursive and phenomenological researchers
> - critically evaluate discursive and phenomenological approaches to the body.

1   Introduction

> Behind your thoughts and feelings, my brother, stands a mighty commander, an unknown sage – he is called Self. He lives in your body, he is your body.
>
> (Nietzsche, 1961 [1883], p. 62)

At first glance you might be curious about why we're including a chapter on bodies, or rather *embodiment* – the process or state of living in a body – in a book on social psychology. The body has generally been treated as a biological object in psychology, crucially important with regard to brain physiology or human development but not something that has been considered a key topic in social psychology. However, when you recognise that it is through the body that we relate to other people and the world about us, then perhaps it does make sense. Our body is the vehicle for communicating with others and for carrying out our everyday lives. It is impossible to separate our bodies from who we are and what we do in the social world. At all levels – individual, relational and cultural – we can see that something as apparently 'personal' and 'natural' as the body is also intensely 'social'. Two psychological perspectives (the discursive and phenomenological) in particular highlight this strong social dimension of embodiment and will therefore form the core of this chapter.

In Section 2 of this chapter we will consider connections between an individual's body, personal identity and social world. Here we intend to pick up on the dualisms outlined in Chapters 2 and 5, but most notably that between mind and body. In particular, we will show how the body has been thought of as an object separate from the mind, and how this dualism has led to a similar separation, until relatively recently at least, in psychology. In this chapter, you will once again find yourself encouraged to challenge approaches that present the world in terms of simplistic binaries (mind–body, individual–social, agency–structure). Sections 3 and 4 turn the spotlight on discursive and phenomenological perspectives in order to illustrate their contrasting approaches to the body. Many of the examples in this chapter concern health and illness. This is for two reasons: first, because a very great deal of psychological and sociological work on the body has – perhaps unsurprisingly – focused on this topic; and second, because health and illness have formed the site of a considerable corpus of literature that is critical of the ways in which the body has been constructed/positioned as the passive recipient of legal and medical interventions (but more on this below). Throughout the chapter we encourage you to move beyond seeing the body simply as a biological object in which the mind resides and, instead, challenge you to think of the ways in which this mind–body dualism may be overcome such that we might recognise the importance of bodies in our lived experience of the world.

2   Identity and the body

2.1   Resisting a body–mind–social split

To what extent are you your body? The seventeenth-century philosopher René Descartes saw human subjective experience (including rationality, thought and spirituality) as separate and fundamentally different from the objective world of matter, that of our bodies and the physical universe. This idea of a fundamental divide between mind and matter (as two different kinds of 'stuff') set the stage for centuries of debate on what came to be known as *Cartesian dualism*. Critics of this way of understanding people point to the way that Western culture has soaked up this mind–body dualism and tends unknowingly to reproduce it.

Psychology, too, has not been free from dualist views and practices. As you know from Chapter 1, much of the last fifty years of psychology has been taken up with questions of the 'mind' and, in the process, the body has often been entirely ignored. Furthermore, where the body has appeared, although the mind–body dualism has disappeared, the psychological and social complexity of the body has also invariably been lost, as biologically-orientated psychologists have tended to reduce psychology to biology (most notably to the brain). That is, they adopt a *monist* position, where there is only one kind of 'stuff' – which, in this case, is physical biological stuff. Indeed, in recent years, there has been a strong focus on the genetic basis of human behaviour: what Joseph Schwartz (1997) rather scathingly referred to as a new 'genetic fundamentalism'.

Many contemporary social psychologists would be critical of any *reductionist* account in which a person is 'reduced' simply to their body or biology or, alternatively, to their mind. Instead, they argue that people need to be viewed in a way that recognises the biological, the psychological *and* the social. From this point of view, mind–body dualism and simple physical reductionism emerge as both simplistic and unhelpful.

> The sense of personhood we possess is at least partly based on the feel we have of our own bodies, as much as in the symbols which define our unique social

identity ... if the body is not the person, then what is the person? The body image and self-image we develop is based on the sense of being embodied and the way in which this experience is mediated by culture.

(Burkitt, 1999, p. 147)

Although bodily experience is rooted in biology, Robert Connell (1987, p. 84) argues it is also imbued with the social world – a 'life-history-in-society'. So, for instance, bodily differences between men and women, Connell says, are not just a physical given. Rather, as men and women, we are continually working with, and transforming, our natural, biological selves, intentionally and unintentionally. There is a personal dimension to this process. For example, we bring to it our own particular motivations and understandings. But larger societal influences – relationships, ideology, language, social structures – also play a part. However, there is disagreement about the extent to which our body and our biology shape who we are. If our sense of self or identity comes from our body, to what extent can we choose our identities by changing our bodies? And furthermore, what role does society play in shaping both our bodies and our identities? These questions of individual–social and agency–structure dualisms form the basis of the next sub-section in which we consider the notion of the body as an 'identity project'.

2.2   Body as 'identity project'

In Western culture, television 'makeover' shows in which individuals opt for plastic surgery or are given advice on clothes, makeup, diet and exercise have gained considerable popular appeal. It seems that large numbers of people are buying into the idea that lives can be radically changed through such makeovers. Supposedly unattractive people who are unhappy with their lives are transformed into supposedly more beautiful and happy people leading satisfying lives. In reality, however, does reshaping or redefining the body radically change people's identity and experience of the world?

Box 7.1   Michael Jackson's body project

The pop singer Michael Jackson is an interesting example of someone who has focused on changing his body. In his autobiography *Moonwalk* (Jackson, 1988), he tells how he was deeply unhappy with his appearance, in particular his wide nose and dark skin. Although he denies he has deliberately lightened his skin and had all the surgery attributed to him, his body has radically altered. Jackson has turned his body into an active project, seemingly designed to blur his identity in terms of sex, race/ethnicity and age. Increasingly, medical and technological advances offer the means for more extreme reconstructions of the body. Jackson's apparently personal body project is both socially rooted and produces social effects. His choice, to become white skinned and narrow nosed, is not, therefore, only due to personal eccentricity, but is linked with the racialised power relations current in Western societies.

The fact that we can 'do' things with our body and present or display ourselves in different ways suggests that our identity is not entirely fixed or determined by our bodies. In the West, at least, people can make a conscious decision to change their bodies through surgery, dieting, drugs, exercise and the clothes they wear. As people change their bodies in these ways, you could say that they also change how they feel about themselves and their roles in society, and how they're perceived by others (all of which are aspects of identity). In Western societies, people appear to have some measure of freedom or opportunity to choose an identity:

> Questions of identity, individual and collective, confront us at every turn ... We are interpellated and interrogated by a multiplicity of voices to consider and reconsider our identities. How we think of ourselves ... is up for grabs, open to negotiation, subject to choice to an unprecedented extent.
>
> (Roseneil and Seymour, 1999, p. 1)

The sociologist Anthony Giddens (1991) has noted how people 'use' their bodies – for example, through fashion and exercise – to help them pursue particular ways of life or lifestyles. Here, the body becomes part of an ongoing 'identity project'. Our body is both something we are and something we have. It becomes the means of expressing our individuality and aspiration as well as our group affiliations. By focusing on our bodies and working on them for public displays, we turn ourselves into our own 'project' (Nettleton and Watson, 1998, p. 1).

An example of this process is the current Western preoccupation with constructing 'healthy bodies'. Westerners spend billions every year on gym or health club memberships, on over-the-counter medications, health supplements and on dieting manuals. Chris Shilling (1997) points out the contradictions here:

> At a time when our health is threatened increasingly by *global* dangers, we are exhorted to take *individual* responsibility for our bodies by engaging in self-care regimes. These regimes promote an image of the body as an island of security in a global system characterized by multiple risks. Furthermore, they are not simply about preventing disease, but are concerned with making us feel good about how our bodies appear to ourselves and to others.
>
> (Shilling, 1997, p. 70)

Body projects can be seen as a way for individuals to express themselves, to feel good and to gain some control over their lives. For instance, people may focus on their bodies in a more sustained way when they suddenly become ill or infirm. Body projects can also be a way to challenge accepted societal ideas about what 'normal' or 'natural' bodies should look like. In this respect, individuals celebrate their difference and create alternative identities through a range of body modification activities such as tattooing, piercing and body-building (Holland, 2004). As one woman body-builder puts it: 'When I look in the mirror I see somebody who's finding herself, who has said once and for all it doesn't really matter what role society said I should play' (Rosen, 1983, quoted in Shilling, 1997, p. 71).

The speaker in the quotation above seems to believe she is making a 'free choice' and can resist societal pressures to conform to certain norms. However, is this really the case? To what extent are body projects expressions of individual preference? What of the powerful cultural influences all around us: for example, the fashion presented to us on the high street or the messages we get from the media and advertising industries?

Although most social psychologists would probably agree that bodies, identity and the social world mutually shape each other, they disagree over the respective weight of these factors. Phenomenological psychologists place the emphasis on our lived experience of embodiment, arguing that because we have the capacity to reflect on our choices, we have some agency to make decisions about who we want to be. Discursive psychologists, however, argue that body projects reflect the pervasive influence of society. They are social practices constrained by the ideals, meanings and identities available in culture. Our bodies are discursive in the sense that they both reflect and express cultural ideals and ideologies. 'Free' choices are not as free as they may seem. For instance, in the 1950s, Marilyn Monroe's curvaceous figure was considered the embodiment of femininity in Western culture. Nowadays, women's bodies are subject to the 'tyranny of slenderness' (Chernin, 1983) in which a youthful, athletic and slender body is equated with beauty and happiness (Bordo, 1993).

Feminist philosophers have been particularly concerned with these issues and have made some of the most important contributions to these debates. This is because, at least in part, where bodies have appeared in psychological and socio-political analyses, these bodies have generally been male – invariably presented through the cover of some notion of universal humanity in which the feminine disappears. The aim for many feminist theorists is to focus on the female body, working with it centrally, in such a way that women's experiences, rather than those of men, are explored and realised.

Mind–body dualism, outlined above, crucially has also been associated with other binaries, such as reason and passion, self and other, psychology and physiology. And with all these binaries one element is always subordinate to the other (Grosz, 1994). One association critical to feminist thinking is the correlation of mind with man and body with woman, where man is associated with the rational and knowable intellect and woman the irrational and unknowable body. Feminist philosophers such as Elizabeth Grosz have, as a response, sought to articulate a *corporeal feminism*, where the female body is placed centre stage and recognised in all its difference as something both material and social. Grosz draws on a number of different philosophical influences to theorise a notion of sexed embodiment using as a model the Möbius strip – an inverted three-dimensional figure of eight (see Figure 7.1). With the Möbius strip, like the body, according to Grosz, there is no clear distinction between inside and outside and, instead, a unity in which there is an inflection of mind into body and body into mind.

> The body is a most peculiar 'thing', for it is never quite reducible to being merely a thing; nor does it ever quite manage to rise above the status of thing. Thus it is both a thing and a nonthing, an object, but an object which somehow contains or

coexists with an interiority, an object able to take itself and others as subjects, a unique kind of object not reducible to other objects. Human bodies, indeed all animate bodies, stretch and extend the notion of physicality that dominates the physical sciences, for animate bodies are objects necessarily different from other objects; they are materialities that are uncontainable in physicalist terms alone. If bodies are objects or things, they are like no others, for they are centers of perspective, insight, reflection, desire, agency.

(Grosz, 1994, p. xi)

Most social psychological theorists would probably agree with the need to resist the mind–body, individual–social and agency–structure dualisms discussed in this section. However, there are differences in the ways that various social psychological perspectives conceptualise the interpenetration of the body, psychology and the social world. Specifically, the views of discursive and phenomenological psychologists on the manner and mechanisms of this merging can be contrasted. This is the focus for the rest of this chapter.

Figure 7.1 The Möbius strip

2.3 Summary

Mind–body dualism has been a pervasive problem since the seventeenth century. One consequence of this dualism is the way in which bodies have been treated in psychology. They have generally either been ignored or reduced to biology. However, our bodies are much more than simply biology; at the very least, they are the interface between the individual and the social world or, more radically, they are inherently social objects. There is growing recognition of the interaction between our bodies, our psychology and the society in which we live. Here, structure and agency, the individual and society are seen to interpenetrate and, as a result, there is now recognition that embodiment is a social psychological issue and not something that should be left to biology alone.

3   Discursive psychology and the body

In Section 2 of this chapter you saw how society and culture are implicated in both the body and personal identity. The embodied self is 'a social body' in that it is an organic object of discourse. It mirrors, reflects, projects, and represents the language-based categories that society takes to be the '"natural" order of things' (Blake, 2000, quoted in Holland, 2004, p. 112). In other words, bodies are not simply 'natural', pre-given objects – that is, the biological substrate of human nature – but are also the site of psychological and social forces.

The ideas of the post-structuralist philosopher Michel Foucault (whom you first came across in Chapter 1) have influenced the ways in which discursive psychologists see and understand the body. Foucault's concept of discourse is all-inclusive: whereas some discourse analysts would make a distinction between what is material and what is discursive, Foucault (1972) argued that the material world is only made meaningful through discourse. The body and bodily practices are part of the material world, but the meaning of signs, symptoms, behaviours and practices is thoroughly discursive. Note that this section uses the term 'discursive psychology' throughout when referring to discursive research from a psychological perspective influenced by Foucault. It is important to recognise that there are different strands of discursive psychology, which are more or less influenced by this particular philosophy, but here we refer only to Foucauldian discursive psychology as it is the strand of discursive psychology which has most directly addressed issues of embodiment. The four features of discourses highlighted here are:

- discourses contain shared social meanings

- discourses are relative to historical context

- discourses entail power relations

- discourses have effects in constituting the body and body practices.

3.1   Discourses: shared social meanings

Discursive psychologists focus on the shared social meanings embedded in discourses. 'Language is regarded as providing shared cultural resources that are constitutive rather than reflective of meaning and that are involved in the shaping and regulating of subjectivities, experiences, practices and bodies' (Burns and Gavey, 2004, p. 553). Maree Burns (2006) elaborates on the discursive psychologist's concern with the social meanings that are attached to bodies:

> Bodily meanings do not originate from, nor are they fixed within, individual bodies. Rather, they are to be found within culturally and socio-politically meaningful and historically mutable discourses and discursive practices ... The body is ... taken to be representational, to be expressive of meanings and ideas.
>
> (Burns, 2006, p. 6)

The idea that the body can express cultural meanings and ideas is a compelling one. The example of 'Michael Jackson's Body Project', especially his unhappiness with his 'wide nose and dark skin' could be interpreted as an attempt to reinvent his ethnic identity (see Box 7.1). The important question is why? What cultural meanings and inequalities are being expressed through his body project? Consider the example below.

The bodily practices associated with anorexia and bulimia express cultural meanings and values and highlight inequalities. These apparently irrational practices can be interpreted against a backdrop of culturally accepted (patriarchal) standards of femininity (Bordo, 1988; Burns and Gavey, 2004). Following Foucault, Susan Bordo (1988) argues that eating disorders should be understood as women's 'collusion' with patriarchal standards of femininity and disciplinary technologies of the body. In particular, Bordo sees the anorexic woman as an extreme example of the way in which women 'voluntarily' subject themselves to self-surveillance in an effort to conform to feminine cultural norms. Disciplinary technologies are powerful, at least in part, because of the way in which they involve people's bodies and habits such that people are themselves the unwitting agents of their own control.

> And watching the commercials is the anorectic, who associates her relentless pursuit of thinness with power and control, but who in fact ... destroys her health and imprisons her imagination. She is surely the most startling and stark illustration of how cavalier power relations are with respect to the motivations and goals of individuals, yet how deeply they are etched on our bodies, and how well our bodies serve them.
>
> (Bordo, 1997, p. 444)

Bordo's argument – that anorectics' choice to exert control over their bodies by starving themselves is imbued with social power relations – is also relevant for understanding the body project of Michael Jackson, since his body project must also be understood as socially located.

3.2 The historical context of discourses

Discourses are not static: they change, and for that reason need to be seen in their historical context. Some examples from medical science can help to illustrate this point. Illness categories change over time as new terms emerge and others go out of favour. Kenneth Gergen (1999), a social psychologist, notes that it was only in the 1930s that the diagnosis of 'depression' was formally established. Today, however, depression is a significant entry in the *Diagnostic and Statistical Manual of Mental Disorders* of the American Psychiatric Association, and has several sub-types. It is also now widely treated – through antidepressant drugs – as if it can be explained solely in biological terms as a disorder of brain chemistry, in spite of strong evidence supporting psychological and social interventions (Butler and Beck, 2000). Although it is unlikely that the incidence of depression has actually increased dramatically, what is being highlighted is a significant change in the way society views mental health problems, their diagnosis and treatment.

_____ *Pause for reflection* _____

Can you think of any illnesses that have recently come into popular parlance? The relatively newly established diagnoses of Myalgic Encephalitis (ME)/Chronic Fatigue Syndrome (CFS) and Repetitive Strain Injury (RSI) are two possible examples. The question is, did they exist before they were 'invented'? Did they exist under a different label? Or have they either newly appeared or become more common in recent years? The diagnosis of ME/CFS entered medical discourse in the 1980s, but in the nineteenth century similar bodily symptoms and signs were classified as hysteria or neurasthenia (Horton-Salway, 1998).

_____

The thrust of Foucault's work was to plot the history (what he calls *genealogy*) of how particular discourses get taken up. He argued that, at the beginning of the eighteenth century, bodies were beginning to be understood as both useful and productive to the capitalist system, and attention was focused on ensuring their efficiency. This, according to Foucault, was achieved through subjugating discourses, which ensured 'docile bodies'. As he put it: 'the body is directly involved in a political field; power relations have an immediate hold upon it; they invest it, mark it, train it, torture it, force it to carry out tasks, to perform ceremonies, to emit signs' (Foucault, 1977, p. 25). Foucault referred to the control of the body through *disciplinary technologies*, designed to shape and train the 'docile body': the docile body is one that is 'subjected, used, transformed and improved' (1977, p. 136). Examples of this are body projects, health regimes and self-surveillance on slimming programmes.

3.3   Discourses and power relations

Foucault sees power relations as embedded in our social organisations and discourses. A particular issue he identifies is the way *power and knowledge* are intertwined. Specifically, he critiques the way modern societies control and discipline people through the language and practice of sciences (namely, measuring, examining and analysing). Foucault sees the sciences as establishing standards of 'normality' which become discourses people soak up unknowingly. This is why medical recognition and diagnostic testing is so important to people who suffer from controversial conditions such as ME/CFS or RSI. If the experience of illness is not legitimated and labelled through a medical diagnosis, it is difficult to explain to others and have the illness socially and medically accepted (Horton-Salway, 1998).

Disciplines such as psychology, medicine, psychiatry, sociology and education, among others (what Foucault calls 'disciplinary regimes'), generate languages of description and explanation where we learn to classify ourselves and view our bodies as normal/abnormal, healthy/unhealthy, sane/mad, thin/fat, and so on. Here again we can see the construction of 'binaries' and the potential for 'Othering' and marginalisation. A key question for discursive psychologists is: whose interests are best served by particular discourses? To develop the example from medicine, Foucault's answer is that professional experts benefit when people come to view their bodies in terms of the biomedical discourse. However, it is not that medical professionals (as a group) hold all the power, but rather that people are complicit in expert discourses and are persuaded to comply with them. In other words they participate in the power relationship. When we make statements like 'the doctor knows best', we passively hand over our bodies to the control of medical experts. We also monitor and control ourselves to achieve standards defined in dominant discourses. For example, ME/CFS sufferers are often keen to pursue a proper diagnostic test that will prove without doubt the existence of the illness. The ongoing pursuit of a positive test is linked to a need to fit the gold standard of proof as defined by dominant discourses of empirical science.

Foucault also recognised that it is possible (and desirable) to *resist* discourses. In keeping with Foucaultian ideas, in studies that are sharply critical of what they see as the medical establishment's monopolisation and sequestration of women's bodies in relation to reproduction, feminist writers such as Ann Oakley (1984) have urged women to take back control.

3.4 Discourses constituting the body and body practices

According to Foucault, discourses are 'productive'. They construct particular versions of how people should be – in terms of being 'real' or 'normal' – and they have certain effects. Applied to the body, discourses defining a 'normal body' get taken up as 'truths', which then invalidate other accounts. A discourse on able-bodied people being 'normal', for instance, has the effect of constituting disabled bodies as somehow abnormal, unattractive, to be pitied or avoided. A discourse on sexuality that presents heterosexuality as 'natural' by that very token presents homosexuality as deviant.

Box 7.2   Queer theory and transgenderism

One particularly important theoretical development that is starting to have a profound impact on the social sciences is *queer theory*. Queer theory is hard to define but is concerned with disrupting binary categories of identity (such as gay and straight, male and female) and, therefore, it provides a radical challenge to many of the assumptions underpinning common-sense understandings of self and identity, in the West at least (see Butler, 1990, and Seidman, 1996, for a good summary). It tends to assume a Foucaultian critique of identity categories as a means of exercising modern power (power of men over women, heterosexuals over homosexuals). It emerged out of academic work, principally in the humanities, alongside HIV (human immunodeficiency virus) activism and the politics of second-wave feminism. Since the 'crisis in social psychology' in the 1970s (see Chapter 1), psychology has had to engage with the many critical challenges that have come its way. This has most obviously included the challenge from feminist theory, which has led to a radical transformation of some, though by no means all, sections of the discipline and also now must include the challenge from queer theory. Transgenderism – a term for all who cross dress and/or change sex and/or blend genders – is a particularly important example of the potential of queer theory not only to disrupt conceptual binaries (such as gender) but also fundamental bodily binaries (such as sex itself). Loren Cameron is a trans person who 'queers' the male/female binary, blending sex and gender so neither is obviously fixed nor prioritised. His self-portrait (see Figure 7.2) is a celebration of the body and through its nakedness it reveals a sexual ambiguity that would not be apparent if clothed, when he could appear as a man or woman. Cameron does not claim to be anything other than himself and, in so doing, challenges ('queers') both the medicalisation of the trans-body and dualistic ways of thinking about identity and the body that form the foundations of modern thought in the West.

For Foucault, the medical encounter is a classic example of bio-power and surveillance. Through the 'clinical gaze', the body comes to be treated as 'an object to be reviewed, inspected, tested, penetrated, laid bare' (Twigg, 2002, p. 426). Medical technologies and practices allow the body to be presented and viewed in new ways.

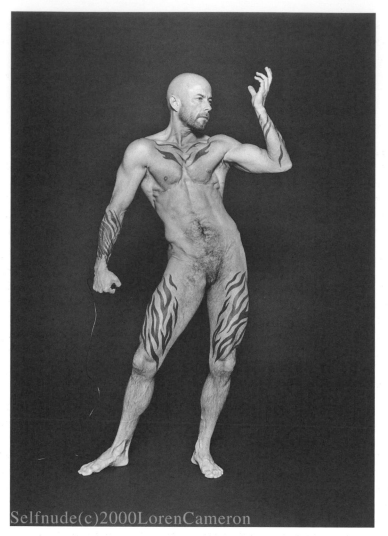

Figure 7.2   Self-portrait of Loren Cameron

_____ *Pause for reflection* _____

What implications might such objectifying practices have for patients receiving treatment, say, in hospital? If you have experience of being in hospital, think about how your body was treated and how this influenced your perception of your illness and the health-care system.

Julia Twigg (2002) observes how disciplinary practices result in destabilising experiences for patients in health-care systems:

> Hospital is an alienating experience in which the loss of sense of self that comes with the weakness of the body in illness is compounded by hospital practices that

render their bodies subject to discipline and control, confined to certain areas, subject to regulations concerning eating and excreting, attached to machinery, exposed to view.

(Twigg, 2002, p. 426)

Box 7.3   Evaluating the discursive approach

Research such as that described in the preceding section makes a powerful case for the view that our bodies and bodily practices are constituted by discourse. Discursive research highlights shared cultural meanings and locates these in a historical context. Its particular value lies in the critique it offers of what we perceive as the 'natural' order. It also demonstrates how discourses can have pernicious effects: for example, in relation to gender, illness and medical science.

However, some critics argue against the theoretical stance and methodology of discursive psychologists who subscribe to a Foucaultian position. Whereas discursive psychologists from this perspective might argue that there is nothing meaningful outside discourse – nothing that is extra-discursive – critics point to our everyday lived experience, such as the experience of playing sport, engaging in sex or practical forms of art like dance (Burr, 1999; Butt and Langdridge, 2003; Nightingale, 1999; Radley, 1995). That is, the body 'eludes discourse, not because of its physicality per se, but because it signifies in ways that discourse cannot adequately embrace' (Radley, 1995, p. 12).

Phenomenologists, in particular, while supporting the use of qualitative evidence, take issue with what they see as the sidelining of actual bodily experience. For them, meaning originates not in discourses but in lived experience: only through this is it possible to understand what it means to have and be a body, to be sick, in pain, oppressed, and so forth. They take particular issue with Foucault, noting that while he spent a great deal of time writing about the body, he largely ignored people's actual experience of, say, illness or their sexuality. In particular, phenomenologists disagree with Foucault's assertion that there is nothing meaningful outside discourse and that what passes for truth about the body is only the knowledge that has been accepted in society.

3.5   Summary

Discursive psychologists who follow Foucault emphasise the social nature of embodiment through their focus on discourse. For Foucaultian discursive psychologists, the body and bodily practices are part of the material world, but the meaning of signs, symptoms, behaviours and practices is thoroughly discursive. That is, there is nothing meaningful outside discourse and therefore all understanding of bodies and bodily practices must be through an analysis of discourses. Four features of discourse have been highlighted: the social nature of discourses; the historical nature of discourses; the relationship between discourses and power; and the way discourses constitute the body and body practices. Of particular importance for this form of discursive psychology is the relationship between discourse and power and how discourses can oppress but also be resisted.

4 Phenomenological accounts of 'lived experience'

Phenomenologists seek to describe people's lived experience, meanings and consciousness (i.e. the way we perceive, think and feel). They focus on how bodies are experienced at a subjective and intersubjective (relational) level. Friedrich Nietzsche (1844–1900), an early existential philosopher, insisted on the primacy of the body, and resisted mind–body dualism, arguing for the unity of mind (or soul) and body:

> I am body entirely, and nothing beside; and soul is only a word for something in the body. The body is a great intelligence, a multiplicity with one sense, a war and a peace, a herd and a herdsman. Your little intelligence, my brother, which you call 'spirit', is also an instrument of your body, a little instrument and toy of your great intelligence. You say 'I' and you are proud of this word. But greater than this – although you will not believe in it – is your body and its great intelligence, which does not say 'I' but performs 'I'.
>
> (Nietzsche, 1961 [1883], pp. 61–2)

There are many manifestations of the body and it is because of this that we often think dualistically – separating body and mind – when in reality all we have is an intelligent body: body and mind are one and the same, not simply biology; we are our body and, through this, perform selfhood. This bodily experience is often pre-reflective – we experience and use our bodies before we think. And it is through using our bodies in our everyday activities that we perceive the world, relate to others and, in the process, learn about ourselves.

'The body is the vehicle of being in the world', says the phenomenological philosopher Maurice Merleau-Ponty (1962 [1945], p. 82). It is integral to our perceptions and to any understanding of human experience. It is the 'horizon latent in all our experience ... and anterior to every determining thought' (p. 92). Our body connects us to the world and – if we tap into our bodily experience – offers us the way to understand that world (including ourselves and others).

Two key ideas are highlighted in phenomenological accounts of the body:

- bodily consciousness
- a body–world interconnection.

These are discussed below in turn before being considered in relation to some phenomenological research findings on the experience of living with multiple sclerosis (MS).

4.1   Consciousness of the body

Phenomenological theorists distinguish between the *subjective body* (as lived and experienced) and the *objective body* (as observed and scientifically investigated). These are not two different bodies as such (phenomenologists pride themselves on overcoming dualisms!); rather they are different facets of our experience and consciousness.

The *body-subject*, or subjective body, is the body-as-it-is-lived. I do not simply possess a body; I am my body (Merleau-Ponty, 1962 [1945]). My lived body is an embodied consciousness which fluidly and pre-reflectively engages the world. So it is that, before I can even think about it, I find myself in the world of my daily activities, projects and relationships: these are encountered as a context for the body's possible action. Food is to be eaten, a child is to be played with, a pen is to be applied to paper, and a lover is to be touched. As we engage in our daily activities, we tend not to be conscious of our bodies and we take them for granted. This is the body that is 'passed-by-in-silence' (Sartre, 1969 [1943]).

In contrast, the *body-object*, or objective body, is the body that is known by others. We observe and objectify others' bodies. 'We can peer at, leer at, admire, criticise, probe, investigate and dissect another's body' (Finlay, 2006a, p. 21). In so doing, we become aware of it as a contained, material, physical thing. We also do this to our own bodies. We do this when we become ill and can no longer take our bodies for granted, since they no longer do what we expect them to do. Then we might find ourselves focusing on specific parts of our body: an aching head, an itchy scar or a tiny cut on our writing finger. As S. Kay Toombs (1993, pp. 70–1) explains: 'Illness engenders a shift of attention. The disruption of lived body causes the patient explicitly to attend to his or her body as body ... The body is thus transformed from lived body to object-body.'

Having distinguished between the subject-body and object-body, Jean-Paul Sartre draws our attention to a third ontological (i.e. to do with our sense of being) dimension of the body: bodily self-consciousness. Here, the body is constituted through others. This body comes into being when the person becomes aware of the regard of another. 'I exist for myself as a body known by the Other', as Sartre puts it (1969 [1943], p. 351).

As we become aware of the regard of another we begin to exist in a new bodily self-conscious way:

> When the body is the object of someone else's gaze, it may lose its naturalness ... or instead it may happen that I grow enhanced in its modality of being. For example, under the critical gaze the body may turn awkward, the motions appear clumsy, while under the admiring gaze the body surpasses its usual grace and its normal abilities.
>
> (van Manen, 1990, p. 104)

Here, Max van Manen is explaining how the objectification of the body results in a disruption of the unity of the pre-reflectively lived body. Our body is experienced as an object somehow separate from the self. At the same time, we are living our body in a more self-conscious way. It is through this kind of interactive relational process, Sartre says, that we gain an awareness and understanding of both ourselves and others.

_____ *Pause for reflection* _____

Are you aware of times when you feel your body is 'objectified'? How does this happen and what is the effect? Think also of different ways the bodies of men and women might be objectified.

_____

4.2   A body–world interconnection

Our consciousness of our bodies remains fundamentally tied up with our everyday embodied activities and relationships. The body thus represents both our particular view of the world as well as our *Being-in-the-world* (Heidegger, 1962 [1927]). Martin Heidegger (2001) draws a distinction between *corporeal things* and the *body*, questioning whether the sense of embodied selfhood that we all possess needs to coincide with the limits of a corporeal body. The corporeal thing stops and is bounded by the skin whereas our sense of embodied selfhood – our *bodiliness* – may extend beyond this 'bodily limit'. Heidegger uses the example of pointing, where our sense of *bodiliness* does not stop at the fingertip but, instead, stretches out beyond the skin to the object captured in our gaze. Perception, action and interaction are interconnected as body and world merge, at least to a degree. Our bodies, phenomenologists argue, are not just contained by what is inside our skin; they reach out into the world.

Take, for instance, the experience of a footballer who has just kicked a long ball towards the net. As the ball swerves too far in one direction, the footballer leans in the other direction attempting to pull the ball back. The footballer's body and ball (world) are still in relationship. As another example, consider what happens when our arm ('body') reaches for a cup (the 'world') to have a drink: for a brief while we embrace the cup as part of our body. Or consider a young gang member getting the gang's symbol tattooed on his or her arm. Both the tattoo and the gang member's reason for getting tattooed tie their body to their social world. In these ways, through our actions, our bodies – our selves – are seen as being intertwined with the world: we are in the world and the world is in us. As mentioned earlier, Grosz (1994) – drawing on Merleau-Ponty – uses the concept of the Möbius strip to capture this interaction between body and world.

In his last incomplete and tantalisingly mysterious work *The Visible and the Invisible*, Merleau-Ponty (1968 [1964]) offers a radical reworking of the nature of embodiment. He shifted his focus from embodied consciousness to a notion of intercorporeal being – what he termed *flesh*. Here, he says, we are connected to others and the world in a *double belongingness*. The example used by Merleau-Ponty is touching – for instance, our right hand with our left – and the way in which this is always reversible: when one hand is touching

re 7.3   Tattooing: the intertwining of body and world

(that which is perceiving) then the other is touched (the object of perception) and vice versa. Neither is reducible to the other and both are of the same order of meaning. He draws on the metaphor of 'chiasm' – from chiasma, the crossing over of two structures – to show that the world and body are within one another, inextricably intertwined: 'the world is at the heart of our flesh ... once a body–world relationship is recognized, there is a ramification of my body and a ramification of the world and a correspondence between its inside and my outside and my inside and its outside' (1968 [1964], p. 136). Our embodied subjectivity is never located purely in either being touched or in the act of touching, but in the dynamic intertwining of these two aspects, or where the two lines of a chiasm intersect with one another. Grosz (1994) built on this idea – in her case using the Möbius strip as a visual analogue – to develop a corporeal feminism where the relationship between body and world (individual and social) is fully realised.

The idea of some kind of merging of body and world is counterintuitive and is not an easy one to grasp. The feminist-phenomenologist Iris Young offers the following account of the lived experience of being pregnant, which further elaborates this notion of an intertwining of body and world:

[Pregnancy] challenges the integration of my body experience by rendering fluid the boundary between what is within, myself, and what is outside, separate. I experience my insides as the space of another, yet my own body ... [But also] the boundaries of my body are in flux. In pregnancy, I lose the sense of where my body ends and the world begins. The style of bodily existence, such as gait, stance, sense of room I inhabit, which have formed in me as bodily habits, continue to define my body subjectivity. My body itself changes its shape and balance, however, coming into tension with those habits ... I move as though I can squeeze around chairs ... as I could have seven months before, only to find my way blocked by my own body sticking out in front of me, in a way not me ... As I lean over in my chair to tie my shoe, I am surprised by the graze of this hard belly on my thigh. I do not anticipate this touching of my body on itself, for my habits retain the old sense of my boundaries ... The belly is other, since I did not expect it there, but since I feel the touch upon it, it is me.

(Young, 1985, pp. 30–1)

4.3   Experiencing multiple sclerosis: a case illustration

The idea of a body–world interconnection and distinction between objective and subjective body is explored further in the following extract, drawn from some phenomenological research Linda Finlay conducted on one person's (Ann's) lived bodily experience of having MS (Finlay, 2003). In the extract, the focus is on the process by which Finlay came to analyse what Ann's body feels like subjectively. Her story – obtained via an in-depth interview (see Box 7.4) – emphasises the way her sense of embodied experience is both complex and ambivalent. Her body, experienced as both subject and object, is engaged in trying to operate in, and cope with, the world.

> ## Box 7.4   An existential phenomenological method
>
> In this research I used an *existential-phenomenological* method (Giorgi, 1985; Valle and Halling, 1989) aiming to describe the lifeworld. I assumed Ann's expressions reflected her perceptions of her lifeworld. Throughout both the interview and analysis I tried to set aside previous assumptions and understandings I had of both Ann and MS. I strove to adopt an attitude of openness to her story as it unfolded.
>
> I interviewed Ann, using an in-depth relatively non-directive approach, on two consecutive days. The interview began with a general question: 'What is living with multiple sclerosis like for you?'. Thereafter, I prompted her to offer concrete examples: 'Can you describe an example of an actual situation when that happened?'.
>
> To analyse the interview, I first created a narrative drawing extensively on her verbatim quotes. I then undertook repeated, systematic readings of the transcript using the analytical method suggested by Wertz (1983). I focused specifically on seven 'existential dimensions' of the lifeworld: Ann's sense of embodiment; selfhood; sociality; temporality; spatiality; project; and discourse. These interlinked 'fractions' (Ashworth, 2003) act like spectacles through which to view the data. Taking embodiment for example, I'd ask: 'What is Ann's subjective sense of her body? How does she experience and move in her body? Does she feel big, small, clumsy, happy tense, comfortable, disconnected, in pain? ...'
>
> (Finlay, 2006b, p. 190)

ACTIVITY 7.1

As you read the description of research findings in Extract 7.1 and the method used, note the way theoretical ideas about body–subject, body–object and the body–world 'intertwining' are applied. Reflect on the advantages of this method of researching the body, in terms of the findings as well as the theory and methodology. What do you think psychologists from other theoretical perspectives might say about the limitations of this type of research?

EXTRACT 7.1

In January 2000 – while Ann was recovering from a severe bout of flu – numbness in the fingertips of her right (dominant) hand spread up her arm. After a couple of weeks she lost control over her arm, leaving her unable to write or to use her hand for any fine movements. Although her symptoms were *relatively minor in medical terms*, Ann felt her life had been derailed [...]

Ann comes to see her right arm as an 'it', something *a-part* from herself, something out of control. 'It had a life of its own ... And it just used to fall off things ... it would just suddenly come up like this and it was very strange.' She now has to learn to do things in new and different ways, aware that she can no longer take her body for granted. She fatigues easily and certain tasks are no longer easy to do. Describing her difficulty with doing up the buttons on her children's clothes she explains her altered consciousness: 'I have to watch, visually do it ... it is much more difficult.' Ann notes with an embarrassed laugh, personal care also presents problems: 'I had to learn things like how to clean my "toilet" with just my other hand.' [...]

As she seeks to preserve her 'mummy role', she also sees it being threatened. Her worst nightmare is having her relationship with her children disrupted. 'Initially it was difficult giving the children a proper cuddle which was just so terrible!' She realises with horror that she may permanently lose her ability to touch and feel them: 'I then thought, "I won't be able to feel the softness of their skin properly"' [demonstrates by caressing her own cheek softly]. 'I mean that's sort of a mummy-thing. And that upset me.' [...]

With her fatigue and the loss of sensation/co-ordination problems in her arm, the unity between Ann's self–body–world is disrupted. Her on-going engagement with the world – her bodily intentionality – is thwarted, as she can no longer do things she had previously taken for granted. With her arm desensitised and spatially dislocated she has to learn how to carry out everyday living tasks (for herself and children) in new and unfamiliar ways. She must look at her arm, as she does up buttons or reaches into her handbag, to understand what 'it' is doing. Certain gestures are no longer within her bodily scope and her possibilities for action shrink. That her arm is out of her control and that she can no longer feel the connection between herself and the world adds to a profound sense of *bodily alienation*.

At the same time, Ann has an acute awareness of *inescapable embodiment*. She cannot, however much she wants to, disassociate herself from her malfunctioning body. She has to cope with her life despite her body feeling fatigued. She cannot separate her arm from herself. As she rails 'Why me?', she is confronted by the truth that the multiple sclerosis is in her, that it is her. She is forced to negotiate with her arm and gradually learn to incorporate it, in its altered state, back into herself. She learns a new way of Being-in-the-world where her eyes and arm work together engaged in daily living tasks. She must modify her actions to handle a new world of 'restrictive potentialities' (Merleau-Ponty, 1962 [1945], p. 143).

Ann experiences her body ambivalently. Her arm is something both a-part from and a-part of herself and the world [...] For Ann, her pre-reflectively lived *subjective body*, is disconnected. The comfortably familiar body [...] which represents her continuing perspective on the world, now contains both an absence and a new, unfamiliar aspect. Her old arm is no longer there and it is as if she has gained a new appendage: an 'it', an unseeable, unpredictable attacker, who does things without her volition. It feels out of her control, as if an alien infiltration has arbitrarily taken over and might suddenly turn round and 'kick [her] in the face again'. 'It' is the enemy, one called multiple sclerosis, who forced itself into her consciousness and took away her life as she knew it. But her task is to resist and subdue the enemy.

So, Ann scrutinises her body. Her arm is part of her *objective body* – one that she can observe, examine and be disconnected from. Each morning she runs through the different parts of her body, checking they are still there and functioning; evaluating her levels of fatigue and energy. She views her body with a medical gaze. With her professional understandings of multiple sclerosis she 'sees' the myelin sheaths of her peripheral nerves being eroded away. She assesses her own physical functioning as she has assessed others' and as others have assessed her. Sartre (1969 [1943]) refers to this process of disease as 'being-for-others'. The sick person understands and reflects upon their experience through concepts derived from, and defined by, others – in this case the medical profession.

Yet, even as she 'splits' her body she also seeks to re-connect with her body. Her morning ritual 'check' offers a way of simultaneously embracing both her subjective and objective body. As she runs through her body parts and assesses her functioning level for that day, she is affirming her body identity as a part of herself, apart from herself, as parts of a whole and as part of the world. 'The body, aware of itself in being aware of the world, stands in a relation "of embrace" with the world ... Each morning I awake to "that blending with the world that recommences for me ... as soon as I open my eyes"' (Merleau-Ponty, 1968 [1964], paraphrased by Wider, 1997, p. 138).

(Finlay, 2003, pp. 162–3, 166–8)

This brief extract from the analysis of Ann's story suggests that her sense of self-body unity, her daily life projects and her relationships with others (especially her children) are being threatened. Yet as her life is derailed, she is also seeking to reclaim it by attempting to connect with her alienated body. The split between the objective and subjective body is clear – though complicated through the way Ann seeks to reflexively reintegrate the subjective and objective in her morning rituals – and important here for Ann's own understanding of her illness and also the treatment of such conditions by health-care professionals. Importantly, Ann's illness is encountered in the context of her family and other relationships – that is, the intersubjective and social realms of her life. Her experience of having/being a body with MS cannot be separated from her world. 'Just as the multiple sclerosis is "in" her, it is "in" her embodied intersubjective relations with others' (Finlay, 2003, p. 172). As Merleau-Ponty has famously explained: 'There is no inner man [*sic*] ... Man is in the world, and only in the world does he know himself' (1962 [1945], p. xi).

Box 7.5   Evaluating the phenomenological perspective

The value of research findings such as the study of Ann is the way that lived experience and personal meanings are brought to the fore. When such research is done well, its findings will possess poignancy and even an element of poetry. Through its insights it should touch the reader and help them better understand the experience being discussed. It may also have implications for policy and practice: in this case, the treatment of MS.

Although discursive psychologists would applaud the use of qualitative, interpretative methods derived from a narrative approach, they would argue that the research is unduly descriptive and takes insufficient account of the influence of discourses on subjectivity. They would argue against a focus on personal, subjective meanings because they believe – following Foucault – that there is nothing meaningful outside discourse. Meanings, they would say are collective and arise from the wider social discourses. A broader canvas is needed which takes

> into account power relations. For instance, the way Ann objectifies her body is connected to prevailing biomedical discourses, which in turn operate through a system of self-surveillance.

Where phenomenological and discursive psychologists agree is that discourses impact on individual meaning-making. However, they disagree on the *extent* of influence exerted by discourses. The phenomenological focus on 'experience' is critiqued by discursive psychologists who argue that 'experience is *always* [our emphasis] constructed and mediated discursively' (Gillies et al., 2004, p. 100). Phenomenological psychologists, on the other hand, argue that the discursive approach leads to the loss of the body – and our lived experience of it – from the psychological project (Langdridge, 2007). Critical debates such as these have characterised the field of social psychology for several decades. Increasingly, however, social psychologists (coming from different perspectives) are seeking to span the divides by offering more synthesised – or if not synthetic, then at least multi-faceted – analyses which take into account both experience and discourse. Val Gillies and others recommend studying 'the socially constructed nature of bodily processes from an embodied standpoint – where embodiment is viewed as always a total expression of both the discursive and non-discursive' (Gillies et al., 2004, p. 100). Other contemporary theorists, such as Ian Burkitt (1999), seek to bridge the divide by offering a more synthesised account of the body as natural, relational and socially constructed.

Burkitt leads the way in formulating embodiment as experience intertwined with social, cultural and historical dimensions. In his critique of the discursive turn, which he believes leads to the loss of the body in its focus on discourse, he aims to rematerialise the body while also acknowledging its social construction. The body and its experience, he says, need to be understood as multidimensional: 'active, communicative bodies located in space and time are seen as the source of the symbolic understanding of the world, yet this is also influenced by already established ideologies which seek to define both symbolic and material existence' (Burkitt, 1999, p. 21).

Burkitt suggests a four-fold model of the person as being simultaneously:

- a productive body (capable of doing activities that can change his or her life)

- a communicative body (with the power to symbolise meanings through speech and gesture)

- a powerful body (capable of altering the conditions of life)

- a thinking body (as human agency and communication requires thinking).

Burkitt argues that thinking of the body in this way allows us to understand that we are not just trapped and constrained within social relations. Instead, we possess the capacities to change these relations as well as to transform some of our physical/natural world. This helps us to think about the role of the body in agency and not just as a biological structure, so helping to go beyond agency–structure dualism.

4.4   Summary

Phenomenologists focus on how bodies are experienced at a subjective and intersubjective (relational) level. Phenomenological psychologists seek to transcend the mind–body dualism, arguing that all we have is an intelligent body, with the body and mind one and the same: not simply biology; we are our body and, through this, perform selfhood. This bodily experience is also often pre-reflective and extra-discursive – we experience and use our body before we think about it. And it is through using our bodies in our everyday activities that we perceive the world, relate to others and, in the process, learn about ourselves. More radically still, some phenomenologists argue on an ontological level that there can be no distinction between minds and bodies or subjects and objects, since the two are one and the same thing – inextricably intertwined as the flesh of the world.

5   Conclusion

In this chapter we have examined different approaches to the topic of embodiment. Moving beyond biology, you have seen how personal and social dimensions intertwine and how something as apparently 'natural' and 'individual' as the body is, in fact, highly 'social'. We have examined psychological approaches to the body – both discursive and phenomenological – and how they conceptualise differently the interconnection of body and world. In some ways these perspectives can be seen as compatible or complementary as they each illuminate different dimensions of our bodily experience and practices. However, they also offer competing accounts: for instance, in the way they theorise the role of meanings and discourse, and in their methods.

Ultimately, though, perhaps we should simply celebrate the rich, multi-faceted nature of embodiment. Christopher Aanstoos (1991, p. 95) describes the body as an openness onto a world and says: 'The body forms our deepest relational intertwining with the flesh of that world ... The body–world boundary is a porous one, permitting of unceasing interpenetrability.' It is this complexity that makes the body such an elusive yet important phenomenon for social psychology.

References

Aanstoos, C.M. (1991) 'Embodiment as ecstatic intertwining' in Aanstoos, C.M. (ed.) *Studies in Humanistic Psychology*, Carrollton, GA, West Georgia College.

Ashworth, P. (2003) 'An approach to phenomenological psychology: the contingencies of the lifeworld', *Journal of Phenomenological Psychology*, vol. 34, no. 2, pp. 145–56.

Blake, C.F. (2000) 'Foot-binding in Neo-Confucian China and the appropriation of female labor' in Schiebinger, L. (ed.) *Feminism and the Body*, Oxford, Oxford University Press.

Bordo, S. (1988) 'Anorexia nervosa: psychopathology as the crystallization of culture' in Diamond, I. and Quinby, L. (eds) *Feminism and Foucault: Reflections on Resistance*, Boston, MA, Northeastern University Press.

Bordo, S. (1993) *Unbearable Weight: Feminism, Western Culture and the Body*, Berkeley, CA, University of California Press.

Bordo, S. (1997) 'Anorexia nervosa: psychopathology as the crystallization of culture' in Gergen, M.M. and Davis, S.N. (eds) *Toward a New Psychology of Gender: A Reader*, London, Routledge.

Burkitt, I. (1999) *Bodies of Thought: Embodiment, Identity and Modernity*, London, Sage Publications.

Burns, M. (2006) 'Bodies that speak: examining the dialogues in research interactions', *Qualitative Research in Psychology*, vol. 3, pp. 3–18.

Burns, M. and Gavey, N. (2004) 'Healthy weight at what cost? "Bulimia" and a discourse of weight control', *Journal of Health Psychology*, vol. 9, no. 4, pp. 549–65.

Burr, V. (1999) 'The extra-discursive in social constructionism' in Nightingale, D.J. and Cromby, J. (eds) *Social Constructionism, Discourse and Realism*, London, Sage.

Butler, A.C. and Beck, J.S. (2000) 'Cognitive therapy outcomes: a review of meta-analyses', *Journal of the Norwegian Psychological Association*, vol. 37, pp. 1–9.

Butler, J. (1990) *Gender Trouble: Feminism and the Subversion of Identity*, London, Routledge.

Butt, T. and Langdridge, D. (2003) 'The construction of self: the public reach into the private sphere', *Sociology*, vol. 37, no. 3, pp. 477–94.

Chernin, K. (1983) *Womansize: The Tyranny of Slenderness*, London, The Women's Press.

Connell, R.W. (1987) *Gender and Power: Society, the Person and Sexual Politics*, Cambridge, Polity Press in association with Blackwell.

Finlay, L. (2003) 'The intertwining of body, self and world: a phenomenological study of living with recently diagnosed multiple sclerosis', *Journal of Phenomenological Psychology*, vol. 34, no. 6, pp. 157–78.

Finlay, L. (2006a) 'The body's disclosure in phenomenological research', *Qualitative Research in Psychology*, vol. 3, pp. 19–30.

Finlay, L. (2006b) 'The embodied experience of multiple sclerosis: an existential-phenomenological analysis' in Finlay, L. and Ballinger, C. (eds) *Qualitative Research for Allied Health Professionals: Challenging Choices*, Chichester, John Wiley.

Foucault, M. (1972) *The Archaeology of Knowledge*, London, Tavistock.

Foucault, M. (1977) *Discipline and Punish: The Birth of the Prison*, (trans. A. Sheridan), Harmondsworth, Penguin.

Gergen, K.J. (1999) *An Invitation to Social Construction*, London, Sage.

Giddens, A. (1991) *Modernity and Self-identity: Self and Society in Late Modern Age*, London, Polity Press.

Gillies, V., Harden, A., Johnson, K., Reavey, P., Strange, V. and Willig, C. (2004) 'Women's collective constructions of embodied practices through memory work: Cartesian dualism in memories of sweating and pain', *British Journal of Social Psychology*, vol. 43, pp. 99–112.

Giorgi, A. (ed.) (1985) *Phenomenology and Psychological Research*, Pittsburgh, PA, Duquesne University Press.

Grosz, E. (1994) *Volatile Bodies: Toward a Corporeal Feminism*, Bloomington, IN, Indiana University Press.

Heidegger, M. (1962 [1927]) *Being and Time* (trans. J. Macquarrie and E. Robinson), New York, Harper and Row.

Heidegger, M. (2001) *Zollikon Seminars: Protocols, Conversations, Letters* (ed. M. Boss, trans. F. Mayr and R. Askay), Evanston, IL, Northwestern University Press.

Holland, S. (2004) *Alternative Feminities: Body, Age and Identity*, Oxford, Berg Publishers.

Horton-Salway, M. (1998) 'Mind and body in the discursive construction of ME: a struggle for authorship of an illness', PhD thesis, Loughborough University.

Jackson, M. (1988) *Moonwalk*, London, William Heinemann.

Langdridge, D. (2007) *Phenomenological Psychology: Theory, Research and Method*, Harlow, Pearson Education.

Merleau-Ponty, M. (1962 [1945]) *Phenomenology of Perception* (trans. C. Smith), London, Routledge and Kegan Paul.

Merleau-Ponty, M. (1968 [1964]) *The Visible and the Invisible* (trans. A. Lingis), Evanston, IL, Northwestern University Press.

Nettleton, S. and Watson, J. (eds) (1998) *The Body in Everyday Life*, London, Routledge.

Nietzsche, F. (1961 [1883]) *Thus Spoke Zarathustra* (trans. R.J. Hollindale), Harmondsworth, Penguin.

Nightingale, D.J. (1999) 'Bodies: reading the body' in Parker, I. and the Bolton Discourse Network, *Critical Textwork: An Introduction to Varieties of Discourse and Analysis*, Buckingham, The Open University Press.

Oakley, A. (1984) *The Captured Womb: A History of the Medical Care of Pregnant Women*, New York, Basil Blackwell.

Radley, A. (1995) 'The elusory body and social constructionist theory', *Body and Society*, vol. 1, no. 2, pp. 3–23.

Roseneil, S. and Seymour, J. (eds) (1999) *Practising Identities*, London, Macmillan.

Sartre, J-P. (1969 [1943]) *Being and Nothingness* (trans. H. Barnes), London, Routledge.

Schwartz, J. (1997) 'The soul of soulless conditions? Accounting for genetic fundamentalism', *Radical Philosophy*, vol. 86, pp. 2–5.

Seidman, S. (1996) *Queer Theory/Sociology*, Oxford, Blackwell.

Shilling, C. (1997) 'The body and difference' in Woodward, K. (ed.) *Identity and Difference*, London, Sage.

Toombs, S.K. (1993) *The Meaning of Illness: A Phenomenological Account of the Different Perspectives of Physician and Patient*, Dordrecht, Kluwer Academic Publishers.

Twigg, J. (2002) 'The body in social policy: mapping a territory', *Journal of Social Policy*, vol. 31, no. 3, pp. 421–39.

Valle, R.S. and Halling, S. (eds) (1989) *Existential Phenomenological Perspectives in Psychology: Exploring the Breadth of Human Experience*, New York, Plenum.

van Manen, M. (1990) *Researching Lived Experience: Human Science for an Action Sensitive Pedagogy*, Ontario, State University of New York Press.

Wertz, F. (1983) 'From everyday to psychological description: analysing the moments of a qualitative data analysis', *Journal of Phenomenological Psychology*, vol. 14, pp. 197–241.

Wider, K.V. (1997) *The Bodily Nature of Consciousness*, London, Cornell University Press.

Young, I.M. (1985) 'Pregnant subjectivity and the limits of existential phenomenology' in Ihde, D. and Silverman, H.J. (eds) *Descriptions*, Albany, NY, SUNY Press.

Chapter 8

Conclusion: social psychology matters

by Wendy Hollway, The Open University

Contents

1   Social psychology matters

Taken together, the chapters in this book have given a portrayal of contemporary social psychology, focusing mainly on the UK. The picture that has been presented is of social psychology as dynamic, provisional, multiple, conflictual and sometimes internally divided. This is not a typical picture presented in social psychology textbooks: there the material is often strictly divided into areas, in each of which findings are reported, questions answered and progress registered. In contrast, our conviction that historical understanding is important to understandings of the present, and our recognition of the many different perspectives that operate within social psychology, have led to a different emphasis. Understanding the history of social psychology leads to scepticism about facts and certainty and disrupts the notion that there has been smooth progress in the development of the discipline. It necessitates the recognition that today's knowledge, like yesterday's, is situated and provisional. In social psychology, this is particularly the case because the objects of our knowledge are constantly affected by historical changes, among which are the effects of social psychology itself. For example, common knowledge about obedience to authority has increased due to the popularisation of social psychological knowledge: only a few weeks before I wrote this, Derren Brown, a popular magician and hypnotist in the UK, staged in his TV show one of Stanley Milgram's (1974) experiments, reproducing a version of the social psychology of obedience to millions of viewers (see Chapter 2, Section 4).

Therefore, one of the tasks of this concluding chapter is to leave open, rather than close down or tidy up, the way that readers understand contemporary social psychology. None the less we have imposed several forms of organisation on the material presented in the earlier chapters: learning requires the organisation of material into categories, but the lines of questioning should be left open and links continually forged among the categories. The first two chapters were designed to help you understand social psychology historically in terms of where it started, how and why it changed (Chapter 1) and the different approaches and methods that characterise it (Chapter 2). These are not definitive histories (histories, too, are situated knowledges), but together they demonstrate how it is possible to step back from the content of social psychology to identify how it is part of various overarching patterns. We devised the four interrogative themes that run through the book (power relations, situated knowledges, individual–society and structure–agency) in order to assist in this process of stepping back.

Providing a further structure is the choice of topics, reflected in the chapter headings. We tried to represent topic categories that originate in different traditions of thought. For example, the study of prejudice and conflict derives classically from psychological social psychology (PSP), whereas the study of emotions is a newer concern in PSP, as well as an old philosophical psychology question. 'Self' has a more central place in the sociological social psychology (SSP) tradition. Two further topics are liable to be studied more outside than inside social psychology, one from each side of the individual–society dualistic divide: embodiment is often the province of biological psychology, and families the subject of sociological study (and, via children, as part of developmental psychology).

As explained in Chapter 1, the problem of binaries is widespread in Western thought and, therefore, also in Western social science and philosophy. However, the dualism of the terms *individual* and *society* (or 'the social') is of unique importance to social psychology because the discipline has come to be defined in terms of this dualism (the study of individuals in social contexts). This is why it has featured so saliently in this book and can even be found in the labels of three out of four of our approaches, where the couplet of terms refers to each side of the dualistic divide (cognitive social, discursive psychological and social psychoanalytic). We also saw this dualism played out historically in the separation of psychological and sociological social psychology, even when they were addressing the same topic, such as the self. Because agency is thought of as an individual property, and structure is usually thought about in terms of social structures that constrain agency, the two dualisms in our interrogative themes are closely coupled.

In the following section, I focus on our other two interrogative themes (situated knowledges and power relations), which are also closely coupled. They, too, involve stepping back from the content of social psychology in order to situate its knowledge, especially within power relations. In particular, I reflect on this pair of themes when applied to methodology and its connection with social psychology's various theories of the subject (ontologies). In Chapter 2, the same idea was summarised as 'methods produce knowledge'. I situate social psychological knowledge first in terms of the wider world – historical changes and geographical variations – and second in terms of what was happening in the discipline itself. Finally I raise some insistent questions that arise from the four interrogative themes.

ACTIVITY 8.1

Take a moment to note down any questions that have troubled or fascinated you in the course of reading this book, especially if they recurred in different chapters. If you have made notes of such issues as you have been reading, go back to them now to jog your memory.

1.1   Situating social psychology

The theme of situating social psychology overarches all the others. Time and again, we have seen how the knowledge produced was, and is, dependent on the setting, and understood at many levels. It makes sense to situate new knowledge in several ways at once, notably in relation to time and place, and in terms of social changes; all of which are inextricably linked in influencing how a topic of knowledge emerges or remains invisible. For example, the idea of personal identity, which surfaced in John Locke's philosophy in the late seventeenth century, would not have been possible in previous centuries when ideas of the person were bound up in two very different conceptualisations – the religious one of the soul and the community-based one of position in a kinship network.

A contemporary example can be found in Chapter 3, on families, by Helen Lucey. One effect of the rapid changes in the structure of contemporary families in the UK and elsewhere has been that research on families has questioned previously taken-for-granted assumptions about how a family is defined and what was assumed to be a 'stable' family. A topic like singleness has emerged from obscurity because it has become a statistically and ideologically more prominent way of living. Critical discursive research on the gendered division of domestic labour can likewise be situated in terms of how it was influenced by feminist politics and changes in gender relations which called into question working women's unequal domestic responsibilities. You can see here how social psychological knowledge often follows contemporary concerns. In these examples of new thinking and research on families, situated knowledge means situating research so that the knowledge produced avoids reproducing partial images or images that uncritically represent some groups in a more favourable light: for example, ideas of good mothering that assume a nuclear family when many families diverge from this white middle-class norm.

Similarly, Chapter 6 by John Dixon starts by situating the topics of prejudice and social conflict in the 'century of blood'. Dixon is geographically specific in pointing out that the Second World War was important in putting these topics on the political agenda in the USA, thus channelling resources that ensured the growth and prominence of these topics in social psychology. Examples such as the one from Andersonstown in Northern Ireland are also situated – historically, geographically and politically. We see how people select different accounts, depending on their religious affiliations, thus reproducing discourses in which they are invested by virtue of their identities.

Thus far my examples show how social psychological knowledge (like any other kind) is situated in wider contexts. The examples refer to settings external to social psychology (and external to its parent disciplines of psychology and sociology). However, the subject also needs to be located in relation to forces internal to existing knowledges. Our four approaches (cognitive social, social psychoanalytic, discursive psychological and phenomenological) inevitably privilege some features of the world at the expense of others. They also do so by using particular methodologies, whether these are philosophical or empirical.

For example, the early twentieth century was a time of success and dominance in biological science and so William James's (1884) emphasis on treating emotions as bodily is understandable. Since then, in psychology there have been challenges to this emphasis on bodies and embodiment as first a behaviourist and latterly a cognitive approach became dominant. More recently still there has been a recurrence of biological explanation with the new dominance of genetics and neuroscience. There has, therefore, been very little social psychological work on the body and embodiment over the last century – a gap that is addressed in Chapter 7 by Linda Finlay and Darren Langdridge. However, the dominance of an approach does not mean that no others can emerge. The 'turn to language' or 'discursive turn' in the second half of the twentieth century was influenced by the way that social sciences outside psychology were developing. It, too, enabled a new set of questions to be asked. In Chapter 4, Brian Parkinson shows how discursive psychology sets aside biological and cognitive accounts: for example, by focusing on emotion talk, not actual emotions. In the twenty years of its existence, discursive psychology has, arguably, been instrumental in shifting the power relations within social psychology.

Perhaps more surprising is the impact of methodology on social psychological knowledge. In Chapter 2, Milgram's experimental work was used as a detailed case study to situate the production of social psychological knowledge on obedience to authority. There it was argued that the power relations associated with the experimental – scientific – method and the setting of this research were central in producing the findings. In this example, you can see that it is impossible to separate the two interrogative themes 'situated knowledges' and 'power relations'. By situating knowledges, it is possible to analyse the power relations that come to affect the knowledge that emerges, when it does so, and how dominant it becomes. Michel Foucault's (1997) (poststructuralist) account of power–knowledge relations is invaluable to the understanding of the workings and effects of power relations in social psychology. Throughout most of the twentieth century, students of psychology were educated under the dominance of the scientific-quantitative method. By presenting several different approaches in this book, and by including more qualitative than quantitative approaches, we have aimed to contribute to the proliferation of diverse social psychological knowledges and the contestation of the power relations perpetuated when any one paradigm is dominant.

As this book shows, methodologies and perspectives are closely linked. Probably all social psychology explanations that limit themselves to a single exclusive perspective will have their dominance challenged. For example, the discursive challenge to biological and cognitive accounts of emotion helped social psychologists to recognise the influential role of language and meaning in interaction and experience. However, the failure to take account of bodily experience or individual agency in discursive psychological accounts has occasioned further challenges. These come from both phenomenological and social psychoanalytic directions. In Chapter 7, Finlay and Langdridge argue that bodies are the core site of psychological and social meaning; that experience is not only constructed and mediated discursively but also extra-discursively through embodiment. Similarly, in Chapter 5 on 'self', Simon Charlesworth's (2000) phenomenological approach to working-class experience illustrates the extent to which something such as social class is embodied. Wendy Hollway's and Tony Jefferson's (2005) example of Vince (also Chapter 5) shows the way that in experience and social meaning conflicts can be unconsciously transformed into physical illness. By highlighting unconscious processes, this example extends a cognitive social account of how agency is understood; an account that emphasises agency as a product of conscious intentional choice.

Every social psychological perspective, accompanied by its closely linked methodology, relies on a particular ontology, either implicitly or explicitly. For example, Chapter 4 on emotion shows how, when self-report was uncritically used as a method of researching people's emotional states (methodology), researchers were assuming that the nature of individual being (ontology) was such that their words simply and faithfully represented enduring internal processes. Now, thanks to the discursive psychological critique, cognitive social research is likely to problematise the relation between emotions and their (verbal) representations. Research methodology and design should then take this into account.

Chapter 3 on families and Chapter 5 on self show how a chosen (social psychoanalytic) ontology should be followed through in the methodological approach (how do you explore unconscious processes in qualitative research?), and that the consequent methods then affect the image of people that the research produces.

Methodology can produce a new ontological emphasis too. Chapter 6 on prejudice and conflict reduction explains that research into prejudice largely used to be based on forms of self-report. This method was informed by the ontology (identified above) that was previously common in experimental social psychology. The chapter illustrates how the subsequent application of reaction time in experimental methodology produced results suggesting that implicit or hidden prejudice was more widespread than people's overt claims would suggest. The accompanying change in how the individual was theorised necessarily included ideas about parts of the self of which people were less aware, less in control of, or less willing to disclose. The emphasis on cognitive categorisation was given a slightly new turn, away from conscious thought expressed in words and towards less explicit, more emotional internal processes. This occurred at a time when emotional processes had been long out of favour in social psychology.

1.2   Insistent questions

Of the many possibilities, I have chosen three insistent questions: one that focuses on ontology, one that focuses on epistemology and one about the link between social psychological knowledge and application.

Are there any enduring truths about the nature of the individual subject that is the focus of social psychological enquiry?

In the current climate of emphasis on situated knowledges and postmodern scepticism about 'grand narratives', the idea of anything universal or enduring is not popular. However, I would like to suggest that the individuality and the relationality or sociality of the self are both essential if we are to see the complexity and richness of humanity. This is an example of using 'both/and thinking' (see Chapter 1) to go beyond individual–society and agency–structure dualism. How social psychologists understand the individual and social aspects as working together within and between people in particular settings depends on the approaches that we use. In different ways, the range of approaches presented in this book attempts to employ 'both/and' approaches. I hope the chapters above have given you an idea of the different strengths and weaknesses of each.

If methods produce knowledge, how do we judge what are better, more adequate kinds of social psychology for understanding its subject matter?

This question arises when one takes a critical perspective, as we have done in this book, on how social psychological knowledge is produced. If power relations are implicated in all knowledge production, and if methods influence what we can find out, does it not follow that we should be equally sceptical about all knowledge production? This position is often referred to as relativism, and it has become more common in the wake of several decades of questioning established knowledge, fact and truth. However, I don't think that it does follow that we should be equally sceptical about all knowledge production. Foucault (1997) made clear that power relations were not the same as states of domination, where power is absolute. Importantly, he also theorised power as both positive and negative (it does not always conceal or distort, but can also reveal and liberate). The reality of how individuals act and relate in the specific contexts and histories of their lives is open to, and requires, research investigation. None the less, it is impossible to apprehend reality directly, unmediated through the concepts, meanings and discourses that social psychology and commonsense make available to us. These can be more or less distorting. Think of how one tradition in the social psychology of emotion (see the discussion of Paul Ekman's research in Chapter 4) takes six ordinary English language emotion words to generate visual stimuli, and then mediates knowledge about 'universal' emotions through this lens. This tradition of emotion research apparently does not recognise that it is mediating emotional reality through its chosen categories. The link to power (perhaps not obvious) is as follows: if a Western, English-language, set of emotion words is used to categorise emotions which are more culturally specific to other parts of the world, this has the effect of rendering the latter invisible and certain kinds of knowledge consequently lost, perhaps with effects on the people living within those subordinated cultures.

Methodologies vary in how complex, nuanced, rich and faithful they can be to aspects of the reality they are addressing. The difficulty of conducting research stems from the fact that social psychological (like all other) phenomena do not reveal themselves directly to us. Everything, starting with the questions we ask (and therefore the questions we don't ask) affects what we produce. The theoretical and methodological resources that attend research are designed to produce better, if inevitably partial and provisional, knowledge.

Finally, there is one more question that is never far from social psychological debate: *What should be the relationship between social psychological knowledge and the effects it has in the wider world?*

If social psychology is regarded as producing dependable and enduring facts, it can be applied quite unproblematically, with the challenges perceived as being more technical than political or epistemological. This position has been widely challenged. Applications of social psychological knowledge are still important, but a critical perspective suggests that we need to bear in mind the partiality and provisionality of knowledge and also acknowledge the unintentional as well as the planned effects. In particular, the principle of situating our findings is crucial politically. As we have seen, social psychology proceeded for decades as if its laboratory findings on student populations could be automatically generalised beyond this setting. In applied social psychology it is always important to ask, who does this apply to? To answer this, we have to understand why our findings apply in the group and in the situation they do, otherwise we cannot work out the limits of their applicability. This is a further example of leaving knowledge open, because another way of putting this answer is to say that it depends on each specific case and those can only be worked out in situ.

Additionally, our appreciation of social psychology's effects must recognise the provisionality of its knowledge over time. People and their social worlds are changing all the time. What applied in the 1950s will not work in the same way in the 1990s. Ironically, part (even if a small part) of what changes is a consequence of social psychological knowledge itself. It permeates commonsense knowledge. And the traffic is two-way. In one sense, there is more social psychological knowledge outside the discipline – in everyday conversation, in communal life and in literature and the media – than there is in social psychology. It is just not formalised. All of us social psychologists are, first and foremost, members of our particular ordinary worlds, like everyone else. Our common knowledge is inseparable from our professional knowledge and provides a rich resource in understanding those around us. We can draw on this and at the same time use the methodological rigour that, at its best, the discipline of social psychology offers to question, test, refine and formalise that knowledge.

References

Charlesworth, S. (2000) *A Phenomenology of Working Class Experience*, Cambridge, Cambridge University Press.

Foucault, M. (1997) *Ethics: Essential Works of Foucault 1954–1984*, Harmondsworth, Penguin.

Hollway, W. and Jefferson, T. (2005) 'Panic and perjury: a psycho-social exploration of agency', *British Journal of Social Psychology*, vol. 44, pp. 1–18.

James, W. (1884) 'What is an emotion?', *Mind*, vol. 9, pp. 188–205.

Milgram, S. (1974) *Obedience to Authority: An Experimental View*, London, Tavistock.

Acknowledgements

Grateful acknowledgement is made to the following sources:

Text

Chapter 1: Spears, R., Hollway, W. and Edwards, D. (2005) 'Three views on hate', *The Psychologist*, vol. 18, no. 9, September 2005, The British Psychological Society.

Chapter 5: Poem: Pastoral Angst Words & Music by John Cale & Bob Neuwith © 1994 John Cale Music Incorporated, USA (50%)/Dry Clam Music (50%). Universal/Island Music Limited (50%)/Bug Music Limited (50%) Used by Permission of Music Sales Limited. All Rights Reserved. International Copyright. Secured.

Chapter 7: Extract 7.1: Finlay, L. (2003) 'The intertwining of body, self and world: a phenomenological study of living with recently-diagnosed multiple sclerosis', *Journal of Phenomemological Psychology*, vol. 34, no. 2, Brill NV.

Figures

Figure 3.1: Copyright © John Birdsall, www.JohnBirdsall.co.uk; *Figure 3.2*: Copyright © Gareth Fuller/PA/Empics; *Figure 4.4*: Fridlund, A.J. (1994) *Human Facial Expression*, Academic Press; *Figure 4.5*: Copyright © Paul Ekman; *Figure 4.7*: Copyright © Clement Cooper; *Figure 4.8*: Reddy, V. (2000) 'Coyness in early infancy', *Developmental Science*, vol. 3, no. 2, Blackwell Publishing Ltd. *Chapter 5:* Cartoon: Copyright © Steven Appleby; *Figure 6.2*: Hugenberg, K. and Bodenhausen, G.V. (2003) 'Facing prejudice: implicit prejudice and the perception of facial threat', *Psychological Science*, vol. 14, no 6, November 2003, Blackwell Publishing Ltd; *Figure 6.3*: Copyright © Owen Humphreys/PA/Empics; *Figure 7.1*: Copyright © Charly Franklin/ Taxi/Getty Images; *Figure 7.3*: Copyright © Hulton Archive/Getty Images.

Index